# THE GUILD®

A Sourcebook of
American Craft Artists

KRAUS SIKES INC.
NEW YORK, NEW YORK

PUBLISHER:

**William M. Kraus**
Chairman of the Board

**Toni Fountain Sikes**
President

**Donald Traynor**
Vice President

**G. Stanley Patey**
Treasurer

**Bonnie L. Burke**
Business Manager

**Vicki Finke**
Production Coordinator

**Rose Noone**
Office Manager

SALES REPRESENTATIVES:

**Claudia Bloom**
**Susan Fee**
**Liz Fisher**
**Ellen Schiffman**
**Cynthia Snook**
**Lyn Waring**

PRODUCTION AND DESIGN:

**The Sarabande Press**
New York, NY

**Toppan Printing Co.**
Color Separations, Printing, Binding

PUBLISHED BY:

**Kraus Sikes Inc.**
1232 Madison Avenue
New York, NY 10128
212-410-4110

DISTRIBUTED BY:

**U.S. Book Trade Publication:**
North Light, an imprint of
Writer's Digest Books
1507 Dana Avenue
Cincinnati, OH 45207
513-531-2222

**Distributed outside of the U.S.A. and Canada by:**
Hearst Books International
105 Madison Avenue
New York, NY 10016

THE GUILD:

ISBN (softback) 0-935603-45-X
ISBN (hardback) 0-935603-43-3
ISSN 0885-3975

Elizabeth MacDonald (see pages 332 & 435) created the painted ceramic tiles that are used as the background for the book jacket.

Cover artists (left to right): Top Row: Mesolini Glass Studio, p. 99; Bracci & James, p. 165; Michael Rocco Pinciotti, p. 315. Middle Row: Bobby J. Medford, p. 18; Ned James, p. 379; Martha Cropper, p. 168. Bottom Row: Ira A. Keer, p. 130; Hall/Zeitlin, p. 404.

Photographers: Jerry Davis, p. 99; Erin Kelly, p. 315; Will Carson, p. 168; Steven Greenway, p. 130.

Printed in Japan

# Table of Contents

## COMMENTARIES

# Introduction

Five years ago we introduced THE GUILD as a new concept—a publication that marketed the work of American crafts artists to interior designers and architects.

Little did we know that we would be witnessing a new era for contemporary American crafts in the years that followed. The response has been more than gratifying; designers and architects across the country have enthusiastically embraced THE GUILD as a means of finding beautiful and functional solutions to their design problems.

But the movement didn't stop there. The crafts field is suddenly dealing with a whole new group of people, a visually literate public that appreciates original work, individuals who are secure enough to venture into the world of unique, one-of-a-kind pieces. These people shop for innovative home furnishings at the new breed of retail stores springing up across the country, they work with professionals in designing their homes and offices, and, yes, they use THE GUILD to find exactly the right artists for what they have in mind.

All of this is convincing proof that American crafts have a significant and still-growing audience. This audience has great respect for quality craftsmanship and a passion for good design. And they are hungry for accessibility to the best work available today.

It is exciting to play a role in the evolution of the crafts field as these talented artists make further inroads into America's head and heart. In the past five years THE GUILD has presented the work of thousands of craft artists—a veritable who's who in the field. To date, nearly 100,000 copies have been distributed in this country, the Far East, Europe, and South America. The five volumes have represented the energy and excitement of American handcrafted work in the forum of international design.

This book, THE GUILD 5, pays tribute to a significant design movement and to the craft artists whose work is feeding that movement. A look through these pages will show you what these remarkable people are doing. Enjoy!

**William M. Kraus**
**Toni Fountain Sikes**

# Vessels and Baskets

# Ruth E. Allan

**R.E.A. Studio**
**P.O. Box 2111**
**Wenatchee, WA 98807**
**(509) 662-6991**

Ruth Allan's one of a kind decorative porcelain vessels are wheel thrown, hand carved, and carefully polished so the surface has a compelling tactile quality. The unglazed work is salt saggerfired to create the unique color effects. Forms include a variety of sizes and profiles. Tall pieces are also available in "Burning Mountain Series" (black tops). All vessels are waterproofed. Prices start at $100 retail. Price list available on request.

Work shown is saggerfired porcelain.

(Right) "Satin Blush Series" 12"h × 7"w, 9"h × 4"w
(Far Right) "Vortex Series" 19"h × 9"w
(Bottom, L to R) "Vortex Series" 10"h × 15"w, 5"h × 10"w, 4"h × 7"w

Photos by Eggers Photographic Design

# Patricia Barrett

P.O. Box 7148
Marietta, GA 30065
(404) 973-2398

Patricia Barrett creates unique basketry constructed of hand-dyed, fade-resistant rattan, embellished with a wide variety of unusual materials including silk and metallic thread, wire, and lacquer.

Prices range from $300-800. Please contact the artist for information regarding designs and commissions.

# Steven Branfman

**The Potters Shop**
**31 Thorpe Road**
**Needham Heights, MA 02194**
**(617) 449-7687**

Steven Branfman works in the Raku pottery technique producing vessels that range in size from 12" high to those over 36" tall and 24" in diameter. Pictured is typical of Branfman's designs. Retail prices range from $200–$800. More of his work appears in the previous editions of the Guild.

Since receiving his Masters with honors from the Rhode Island School Of Design 15 years ago, Branfman has had over 60 solo and group shows, and has appeared in numerous publications including *American Craft, The Crafts Report,* and *Ceramics Monthly.* He has completed many commissions both individual and corporate and his work appears in collections in the U.S. and Europe.

Slides of available work are sent on request. In addition, the artist will work with clients in developing vessels to their design specifications. Custom work takes 8–12 weeks.

Vase, 22"h.

Vase, 24"h.

Vase, 26"h.

# Linda Brendler Studios

P.O. Box 4615
Modesto, CA 95352
(209) 522-3534

Working in the area of crystalline glazed porcelain for 18 years Linda Brendler has focused on the challenge of developing rare, unusual colors. The process is difficult, requiring a delicate balance of time and temperature with results varying. Crystals are actually grown in the glaze at high temperatures held for an extended period of time.

Possessing a timeless quality her one-of-a-kind work is unique in its beauty and intensity. Pieces are exhibited and sold in selected galleries and museums nationally and are also in many collections. They vary in height from 8 to 18 inches.

Linda Brendler holds an M.F.A. degree in Ceramics, having studied with Carlton Ball and Dr. Herbert Sanders.

Slides and resumé are available upon request.

Photos by Charles Frizzell.

# Joyce Clark-Binen

19200 Shubert Dr.
Saratoga, CA 95070
(408) 973-0492

Joyce Clark-Binen received her M.A. in sculpture from San Jose State University in 1983. She has been involved in ceramics professionally for 15 years and her work is shown in galleries and corporate collections throughout the United States.

Each piece is first formed on a potter's wheel and then altered to the desired form by paddling, stretching and tearing. After the first firing, slips and oxides are airbrushed onto the bisqueware. The pieces are then stacked in a sagger with table salt and glossy magazine pages and fired again to a temperature of approximately 1800°.

All work is one-of-a-kind and can not be exactly reproduced. Each piece comes secured to a clear acrylic base.

Prices range from $150-$1,000.

(Below) Salt Fumed Vessel 20″ × 22″

# Jan Daniels

**410 Hacienda Court**
**Los Altos, CA 94022**
**(415) 941-2083**

Saggar-fired, hand-built stoneware by Jan Daniels is almost sculptural in its ability to conjure up images. Organic materials are used to create a palette of rich color. Some pieces are burnished and fired in sawdust to a sleek black lustre. The forms have a primitive, bare-bones look, yet are equally at home in southwest, contemporary or classic environments.

The artist's work has been widely exhibited in museums and galleries in California, Oregon and Washington and is in private collections in the United States and Japan. Sizes vary from 10" to 26". Resume available upon request.

(Top) "Spirits Gathering" 15" × 18"
(Bottom) "Adagio" 14" × 8½"

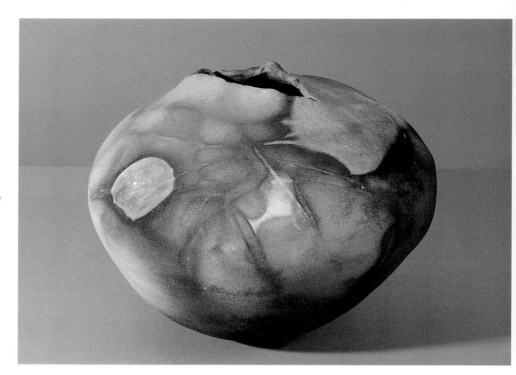

# Allester Dillon, Clay and Fiber

1565 Vendola Drive # 11
San Rafael, CA 94903
(415) 491-4037

Using coils of clay, Allester Dillon produces a variety of objects from woven baskets, seven inches high, to sculptures as tall as seven feet. Her forms are loosely tied to basic geometric shapes: triangles, pyramids, squares, rectangles, ovals and circles. She uses a rough sculptural clay and her methods of construction are always visible in the finished piece. Her most recent work involves cutting openings into the clay to show the inside structure, while adding tied and twined reeds. The work is not functional. The clay is low fired and washed with ceramic stains in soft colors. The reeds may be dyed or left natural. The height of these objects varies from 15" to 44". Prices range from $500 to $2500 retail.

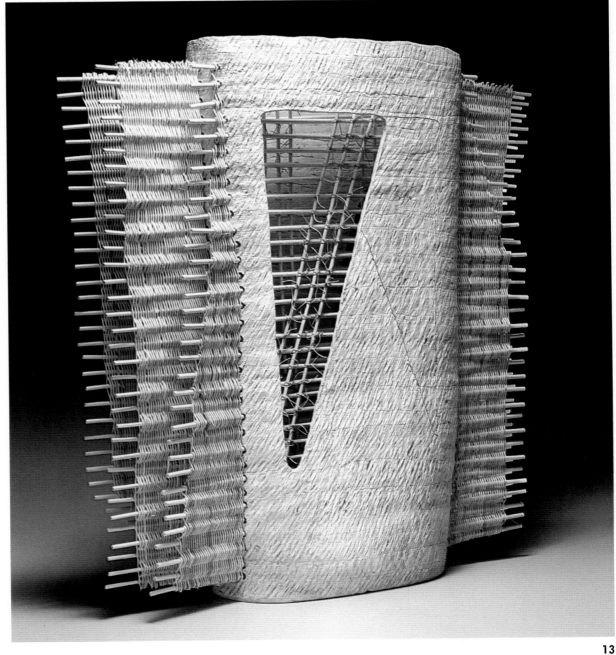

# Ron Fleming

**Hearthstone Studios**
4731 N. Evanston
Tulsa, Oklahoma 74130
(918) 425-9873

Ron Fleming's wooden vessels are distinctive for their flowing form and sensual hand-carved designs.

Fleming's pieces have exhibited internationally and are represented in galleries and private collections throughout the United States.

A portfolio is available upon request.
(Top Left) "Temple Jar," redwood burl, 10″ × 12″
(Top Right) "Reeds in the Wind," boxelder burl, 13″ × 8½″
(Bottom) Detail of "Temple Jar"

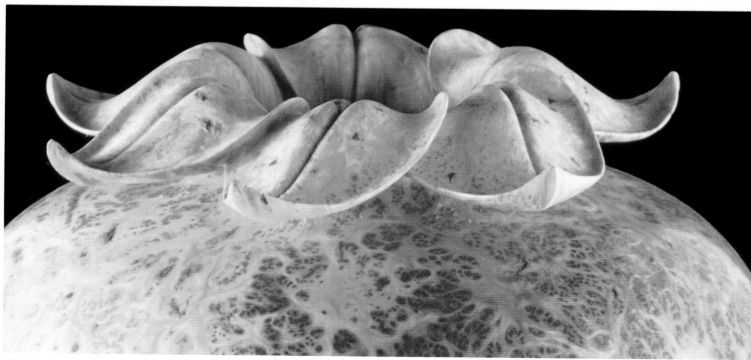

# Rosette Gault

**Rosette Gault Studio**
**619 Western Avenue**
**Seattle, WA 98104**
**(206) 682-2325**

Magnificent in an alcove, on a special shelf, or in pairs at an entry way, these elegant ceremonial vases are a distinctive highlight in your home or office.

Each will be individually made for you. You may specify sizes and colors. The examples shown here retail at approximately $800 and are 23″–29″ tall and less than 4″ in side view. Custom wood display shelves are also available which bolt the pot securely to the wall. Simpler and/or smaller designs begin at $385. Average lead time is 3–8 weeks.

Rosette Gault, M.F.A., began her study of ceramic arts nineteen years ago with Betty Woodman and Larry Clark. Her work has been internationally recognized for its originality and uniqueness. Each piece is designed to provide years of viewing pleasure and fascination.

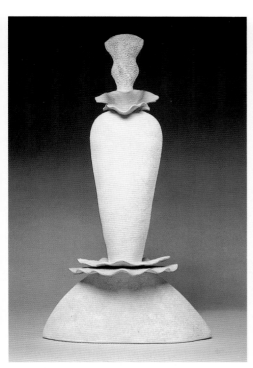

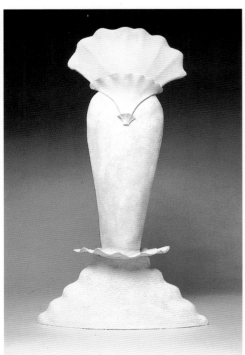

# Sandy Hastings

**Sandy Hastings Ceramics**
**4438 S.W. 74th Avenue**
**Miami, FL 33155**
**(305) 264-5657**

Sandy Hastings creates distinctive, large scale sculptural ceramic vessels and wall forms. Shapes are derived from nature and geometric forms. Works range from one-of-a-kind to limited editions. Each piece is individually hand-built using a low-fire clay body and airbrushed in a wide array of colors.

Close collaboration with architect and designer has resulted in the creation of special objects for specific spaces.

Hastings' work is well represented in many private and corporate collections throughout the United States, Canada and Europe.

Standard sizes range from 5" to 48" high. Production time varies from 2 to 12 weeks, depending upon the project. Retail prices range from $200.00 to $2,000.00. All work is signed and dated.

(Right) Draped Deco approx. 44" h.
(Left top) Georgia's Flower approx. 33" h. × 25" w.
(Left bottom) Brazilia approx. 36"h. × 24" w.

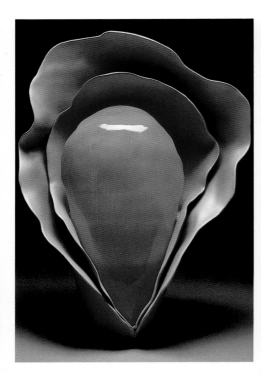

# Kari G. Lønning

36 Mulberry Street
Ridgefield, CT 06877
(203) 431-0617

Kari G. Lønning incorporates an extensive education in ceramics and textiles in her one of a kind baskets. Fifteen years of experience gives her the ability to design and create classic vessel forms with contemporary applications.

In 1985 she received the American Craft Museum Design Award.

Lønning uses waterfast and fade-resistant fiber-reactive dyes on rattan reed. Her palette is one of muted peach, lavender, teal, blue, greys, and taupes. Custom color work is available.

Since all work is executed by the artist, availability of finished work and delivery time on commissioned work will vary. All work is signed and dated. Prices start at $600. and will vary due to size and complexity of pattern.
(Top left) "Ocean" 14½" × 18"
(Top right) "Garden Feathers" 15" × 21"
(Bottom) "Windows" 13" × 16", "Clouds" 12" × 17"

# Bobby J. Medford

7066 W. Bopp Road
Tucson, AZ 85746
(602) 883-7453

Bobby Medford makes ceramic vessels and wall pieces utilizing both sculptural techniques and throwing. He is known for his use of color, creating designs of pastel Southwestern urbanity as well as vibrant African and Picassoesque images. His work is in major retail, corporate and resort collections. Medford is represented by galleries in 13 states and in Canada.

Wall plates range in size from 16" to 36" in diameter. Height of thrown or manipulated vessels ranges from 20" to 60".

Commissions may specify color, size, and type of design. Six to eight weeks are required for completion of most orders. Retail prices range from $300 to $3,000.

Slides and a resume are available upon request.

# Anne Mayer Meier

**Creative Textures**
169 Sandalwood Way
Longwood, FL 32750
(407) 332-6713

Anne Meier has been producing a broad range of contemporary baskets to complement residential and corporate settings since 1979.

Her sculptural forms and decorative vessels incorporate original design concepts, aesthetic excellence, and superior craftsmanship.

Meier's limited production pieces derive from classical forms and are embellished with unique juxtapositions of line and color. Her recent one-of-a-kind work, the story baskets, continues to explore the non-functional vessel in ribbon weave technique. Then, each piece is painstakingly painted with hundreds of tiny patterns, all part of Meier's personal symbol system.

Meier's work is shown nationally and is included in many collections. Prices range from $80–$1500. Meier invites inquiries.

(Top left) Symbol Series: Wall Platter
(Lower left) Symbol Series: Tapestry
(Top right) Symbol Series: Totem
(Lower right) Limited production work: New Quilt; Windwalker

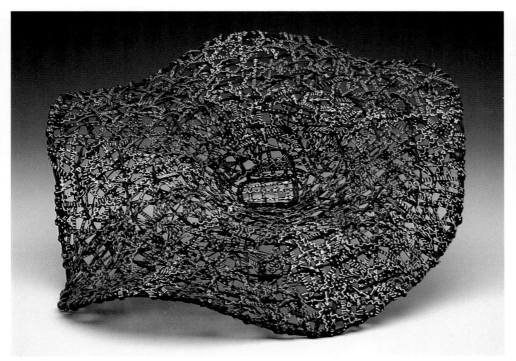

# Charles Pearson
# Timothy Roeder

Whitehead Street Pottery
1011 Whitehead Street
Key West, FL 33040
(305) 294-5067

Represented by:
The Signature Shop and Gallery
3267 Rosewell Rd., N.W.
Atlanta, GA 30305
(404) 237-4426

Kahale Kai Trading Co.
Kong Lung Center
Lighthouse Rd.
Kilauea, Hauai, HI 96754

These sculptural hand-built slab constructions represent yet another collaboration by Artist Charles Pearson and Timothy Roeder.

These raku fired pieces are first glazed with metallic oxides, fired individually to 1900° F, removed from the kiln and buried in seaweed, giving them their primitive surface characteristics.

These one of a kind pieces are priced starting at $425.

Information on commissioned work for specific environments i.e.: office, lobbies etc. can be obtained by writing directly to their studio.

Resume and slides are available upon request.

(Top) "Monolith No. Three" Raku Fired
9" × 13" × 20"
(Bottom) "Monolith No. Seven" Raku Fired
13" × 13" × 9"

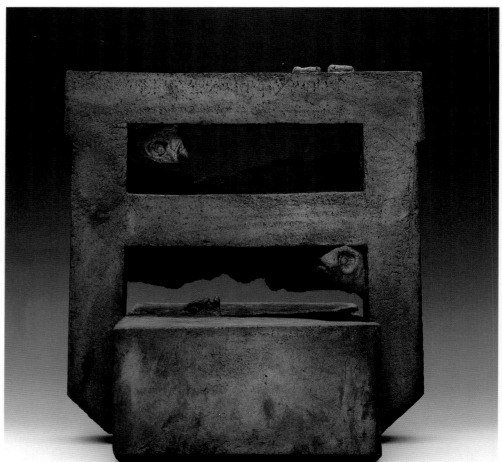

# Beverly Plummer

**2720 White Oak, Left**
**Burnsville, NC 28714**
**(704) 675-5208**

Beverly Plummer's handmade paper bowls add a touch of warm color and texture to any office or home environment.

Built up from multiple layers of cotton and abaca fibers, they are sturdy and require no special care. Colored with light-fast pigments, they are also treated to be dust and moisture-resistant.

Colors and sizes can be customized for any environment. Available vessels are shipped within two weeks. Custom designs require 4–6 weeks. Prices begin at $85.00

Large, wall-mounted plates are also available.

Corporate Collections include: Wachovia and Continental Banks: Cellular One: Burroughs-Wellcome Corporation and Eastman Pharmaceuticals.

Pictured bowls range in size from 15" to 24" in diameter and are 9" to 12" high.

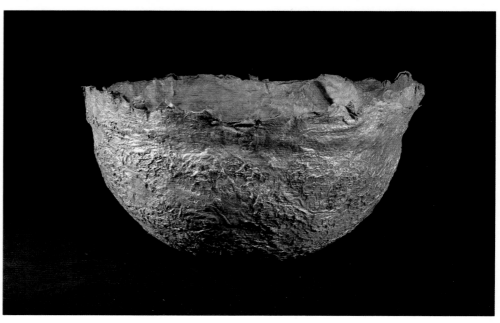

# Mollie Poupeney

**21 Francisca Drive**
**Moraga, CA 94556**
**(415) 376-3401**

After firing her traditionally burnished coiled pots, Mollie Poupeney deliberately breaks them with a hammer and fires each piece individually in an open fire before she reconstructs. Her recent work has expanded to include design elements inspired by thousand-year-old Anasazi pottery shards which she translates into the vibrant acrylic colors shown here. Other one-of-a-kind pieces are more subdued, rendered in greys, off-whites and subtle silver and copper metal flake "glazes" that reflect her 33 years experience as potter and painter.

Poupeney's articles have appeared several times in *Ceramics Monthly*. Her work is included in many private and corporate collections in the United States, Canada, and Near East. She is a member of the Baulinas Crafts Guild and the Association of California Clay Artists.

# Betsy Ross

1160 Fifth Avenue
New York, NY 10029
(212) 722-5535

Betsy Ross's Vessels are an amalgam of wheel-thrown and hand built components. Each piece is hand painted and embellished with lusters creating metallic-like qualities, and are signed numbered and catalogued by the artist.

Her works are exhibited in galleries, represented in private collections, selective publications, and international competitions.

Ms. Ross enjoys collaborating with architects and designers. Commissions accepted. Prices from $200 to $700 retail.

The Vessels featured on this page range from 12" to 23".

# Laura Ross

311 Tucker Station Rd.
Louisville, KY 40243
Studio: #502-244-6892

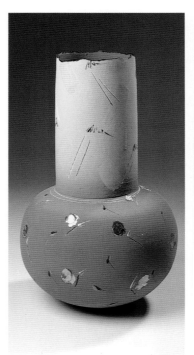
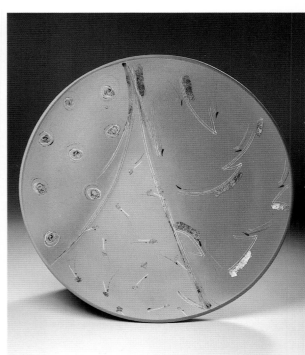

The "Painted Series" is a contemporary treatment to traditional forms in clay through the use of paint and reed design. Concerned with simplicity of form and fine craftsmanship, Laura Ross produces this decorative line of low-fired vessels which are air-brushed with stains rich in color, individually painted with contemporary designs, and enhanced with bronze-leaf.

Laura Ross exhibits at major craft shows, contemporary galleries, and design showrooms throughout the United States.

Wholesale prices range from $36–$300. Information is available upon request.

# Claire Sanford

**124 Hamilton St**
**Cambridge, MA 02139**
**(617) 576-4615**

Claire Sanford creates decorative metal vessels with strong graphic silhouettes and subtle details and surfaces. Fabricated primarily out of copper and brass, the pieces are textured and patinated to render a rich weathered and worn complexion. The repetition of lines or overlapped surfaces adds a rhythmic movement to the simple forms. The vessels can be free standing or placed on pedestals as seen below.

Prices range between $500 - $900.

(Left) Commission total height 70″ each vessel 30″ × 6½″ × 6½″. Patinated copper, painted steel pedestals. 1988.
(Top right) "Deep/Dark" 20″ × 5½″ × 5½″. Patinated copper. 1986.
(Bottom right) "Round Container w/Vessels" 12″ × 8″ × 8″. Patinated copper and brass. 1989.

# Robert C. Shenfeld

1421 Stolp Avenue
Syracuse, NY 13207
(315) 479-5991

Robert Shenfeld's large ceramic wheel-thrown vessels with slab-built lids make a bold statement in both corporate and residential environments. The dry matte-glazed surface is composed of slips and engobes over a stoneware clay body. Subtle variations of underglazes are then airbrushed onto the surface.

Shenfeld's works range in size from 36" to 72" tall, including the slab-built lids. Each piece is one-of-a-kind and signed by the artist. Contact the artist for more information on sizes and prices. Commissions are welcome.

(Below) 18"w × 50"h.
(Right) Left: 24"w × 72"h; Center: 18"w × 50"h.; Right: 18"w × 54"h.

Photos by Anthony Potter.

26

# Robert A. St. Pierre

P.O. Box 2654
224 St. George Street
Duxbury, MA 02331
(617) 934-0046

Robert St. Pierre's wooden vessels are made from laminated rings of exotic and domestic woods. These unique pieces appear to be turned on a lathe but St. Pierre uses only saws and sanders to create works of unequaled craftsmanship.

St. Pierre's award winning vessels are found in numerous private and corporate collections and have been featured in the store windows of Tiffany's, Copley Place, Boston.

Vessels vary in size, design and wood. Commissions are accepted.

Prices according to size and wood used.

Mahogany, 20"H × 23"W

Zebra Wood, 36"H × 20"W

Padouk, 40"H × 18"W

# Eva S. Walsh

**The Basketmaker**
**P.O. Box 2266**
**Winter Park, FL 32790**
**(407) 628-0422**

The ability to blend the inherent characteristics of fibers with her vision is what makes Eva Walsh an award-winning artist. She creates finely crafted decorative and functional pieces. She gathers her own natural materials and dyes the reed herself.

TOP—Baskets tightly woven in harmonious color combinations enhance contemporary and traditional settings ($50.00–$300.00 RETAIL).
BOTTOM—Unique sculptured pieces twined in subtle colors invite interesting groupings. ($200.00 Up—RETAIL)
Three-dimensional woven wall-units are priced per square foot upon request. Private and corporate commissions welcome.

# Stephen Zeh ◆ Basketmaker

P.O. Box 381G
Temple, ME 04984
(207) 778-2351

Baskets by Stephen Zeh are handcrafted of carefully selected brown ash from the wilderness of Maine. Elemental materials, tools and methods weave a rich historical past into these highly-refined vessels. Each is designed to be durable, pleasing to the senses and functional in today's living environment.

Zeh's baskets are included in private and museum collections. His work, advertised in *The New Yorker* and shown in *Vogue Knitting,* is widely known for quality craftsmanship and integrity of design.

Ordering time ranges from two months to one year. Complete information is available for $3.

(Top and bottom left) #185, Nest of Seven, 3"-14" in diameter, $3,450.
(Center right) #178, #177, swing handle egg baskets, 10" and 8" in diameter, $575 and $450, respectively.
(Bottom right) #180 swing handle apple basket, 14" diameter, 10" high, 18" overall height, $775.

# Lee Zimmerman

4186 Towanda Trail
Knoxville, TN 37919
(615) 522-8458

Lee Zimmerman's baskets reflect twenty years of experience in fine arts and interior design. She has worked in basketry since 1978 and has exhibited in the Southeast and nationally since 1983.

Rattan is custom colored using permanent, natural fiber-reactive dyes. Limited production requires one to three months' preparation. Prices range from $200 to $1000, depending on intricacy of design.

Lee works closely with designers and clients for corporate and private commissions.

(Right) "Victoriana," 12"×16". Hand-dyed rattan. $750.
(Below, left to right) Oval, 8"×12"×18". Barrel, 12"×16". Round, 10"×16". All featuring "Tennessee Thistle" pattern.

# Sculptural
# Objects

# Shawn Athari

Shawn Athari's, Inc.
13450 Cantara Street
Van Nuys, CA 91402
(818) 988-3105

Shawn Athari has been working in the glass field since 1975, with her sole focus on glass fusing since 1984. The last several years have been dedicated to creating glass sculptures inspired by cultural artifacts.

Ms. Athari has exhibited her work throughout the United States and has received many prestigious awards. She has traveled extensively, teaching various aspects of her glass art.

Galleries: Elaine Horwitch, Santa Fe.
Sans Soucie, Palm Springs.

Collaborative work is welcome.

(Bottom left) Inspired by Totem of Skidegate, from Queen Charlotte Islands. Original in the Provincial Museum. 21″×43″.
(Bottom middle) Eagle Pole with Raven and Beaver, from the Queen Charlotte Islands 21″×43″. Original in the Provincial Museum.
(Top right) American Indian Mask with authentic Indian Headdress. 30″×48″.
(Bottom right) Fish Dance Mask, Balsas River, Mexico. Blue eyes represent rain or water. 14″×21″.

Photos: Kevin Hass

33

# Christopher Belleau

**69 Tingley Street**
**Providence, RI 02903**
**(401) 351-6770**

Christopher Belleau's unique glass creations are the result of years of dialogue between the artist and the material. The artist has a bachelors degree in art from the University of Wisconsin and studied glass at Penland School for crafts, Penland, North Carolina. He has exhibited nationally and his work is in collections around the world. Pictured at the top is a group titled "Peter and the Dachshund" made from blown glass that was acid etched. Belleau has broken with traditional glass techniques to create the colorful heads pictured on the bottom.

Blown and acid etched, they were then painted with auto enamels that were baked on.

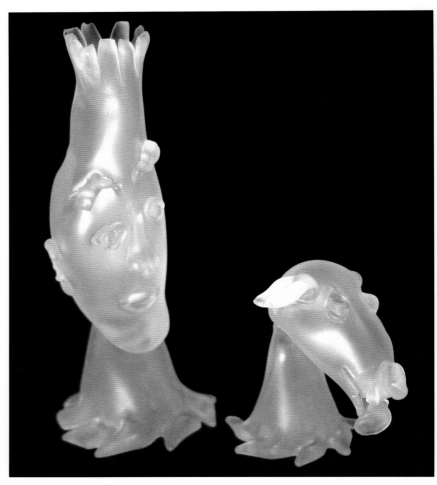

# Jody Bone

**12001 Des Moines Way S
Seattle, WA 98168
(206) 248-3563**

Jody Bone creates cast glass pieces, many are of primitive head or mask shapes. The pieces are usually one of a kind, occasionally some are a limited edition. They are set in a variety of bases, ranging from carved wood to stone. The wood can be treated in a variety of styless, fauve finishes are especially good with the glass. Some pieces are available in colored glass, depending upon availability. The pieces can also be translated into wall, window, or screen treatments to fit an architectural design.

Jody Bone has shown in a number of gallery and museum shows nationally and internationally.

Prices range from $500- $3000, commissions priced individually.

Slides available upon request, commissions are accepted.

"Spaceman with Tux" right 23″ × 8W × 2½″D

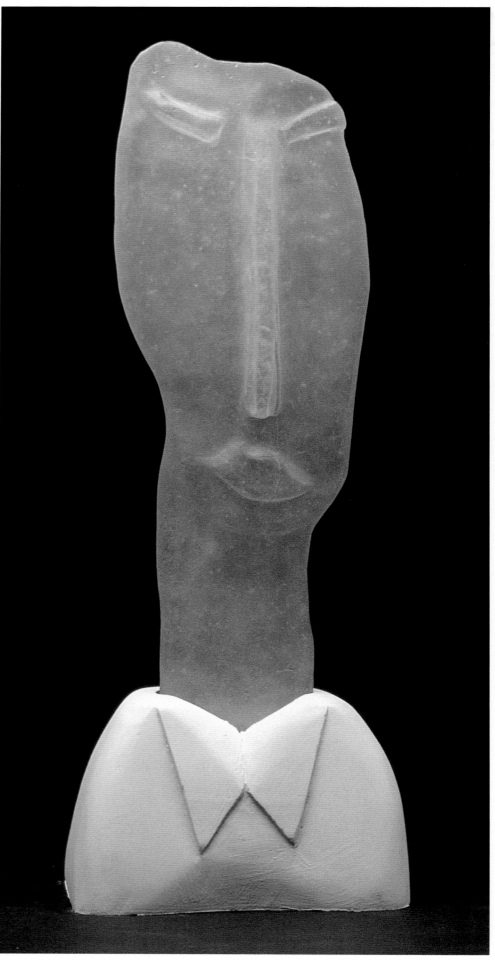

# Nancy Moore Bess

5 East 17th Street
6th floor
New York, NY 10003
(212) 691-2821

Utilizing traditional techniques associated with basket weaving, fencing and thatching, Nancy Bess combines raffia, cords and linen with accent elements to create a selection of basket forms and fiber constructions. Some pieces are mounted in custom lucite boxes, others rest on Japanese river stones. A wide range of related wall pieces are available and are mounted in lucite boxes to ensure easy maintenance and installations.

Wholesale prices for these one-of-a-kind and limited edition basket forms start at $90; prices for related fiber constructions begin at $160. Special orders for larger works and multiples are welcome. Additional information is available upon request.

(Top left) "Black/Gold" series with gold, silver and copper leaf, 4½"h.
(Top right) Grouping from current series reflecting Japanese folk art influence, 4½"h.
(Bottom center) "Broken Armor" one panel of two, 11"h.

# Barbara Davis

**179 Scituate Street**
**Arlington, MA 02174**
**(617) 643-9040**

Barbara Davis' fiber designs are noted for their sophisticated sculptural and textured qualities. Her work is created from natural materials, overlaid and intertwined—reed, hand-pressed paper, and mixed media. The pieces blend subtle, iridescent colors. Light plays on the surfaces creating shadows and reflections.

Davis crafts her objects in a variety of shapes and sizes. The pieces are versatile, suited for both contemporary and traditional settings, and can be shown free-standing, in custom-made lucite displays, or wall-mounted. The award-winning work is displayed in corporate collections, residences, and museum galleries.

Sizes range from miniature (several inches) to large scale (4—6 feet). Costs are $150 to $3000. Commissions are accepted.

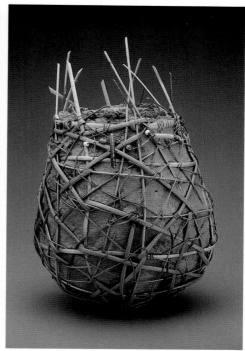

# The Secondary Market for Contemporary Crafts

The explosion of interest in craft has set off a couple of complementary rumbles. The craft field has attracted avid collectors who are putting together substantial collections. The inevitable next step is the development of a secondary market for collectors who wish to part with their collections.

Less than ten years ago the British auction houses began sales of contemporary decorative arts. And in the spring of 1989, this event crossed the Atlantic when Christie's auctioned off the ceramics collection of Earl Millard of St. Louis and the glass collection of Ted and Kay Evans of Cleveland. This was the first time any significant American collections had been made available for sale. This highly publicized and controversial auction proved there is a secondary market, broke price barriers, and verified a place for craft collectors and collections.

Terms such as "investment" and "blue chip" are now part of the buying and selling vocabulary in the contemporary craft field. Contemporary craft is still relatively less expensive than two-dimensional art, but the price range for both primary and secondary sales has climbed to $100,000 for key pieces of the highest quality.

Where contemporary ends and "collectible" begins will remain subjective until market experience develops a standard. Price range and marketing methods are still growing. Galleries are still developing collectors and collectors are still developing their collections. Museums have been and remain hesitant to acquire objects until the field is more proven; many have only begun to make acquisitions. However, there are several curators and institutions active in showing and acquiring contemporary craft objects. These exhibition and acquisition programs are acting to document and chronicle this movement and thus have an active effect on the secondary markets.

If the collector is emerging the museum cannot be far behind. The collector is traditionally the gatherer and repository of contemporary objects who holds them until time proves their value. Then the donation or loan to museums expands the field, increases the value of the work, and keeps the cycle created by that sale into a secondary market.

What these phenomena mean to the collector is a slight change in the way he regards his purchases and a major change in the way he catalogues them. Documentation or "provenance" which tells whether the work came from the artist or an intermediary, how much it cost, if it was a published piece, etc. can influence the value of the work or collection on resale into the secondary market. Documentation becomes important.

Artists should be documenting the growth and change in their careers as well. They should record evidence of spreading fame in the media. They should note when objects are made, when and where publicized, when sold, to whom, for how much.

The interrelationships of the players in the field—artists, collectors, museums, dealers, media, and now auction houses—is becoming quite apparent as their actions begin to contribute to the future value of contemporary craft.

**Leslie Ferrin**
**Director, Ferrin Gallery**
**Northampton, Massachusetts**

# Don Drumm

**Don Drumm Studios and Gallery**
**437 Crouse Street**
**Akron, OH 44311**
**(216) 253-6268**

Don Drumm is a pioneer in the use of cast aluminum as a sculptural media. During his thirty years of doing commissions, he has produced work ranging from ten story murals in sand blasted concrete, to monumental free standing steel structures, wall reliefs in applied cement or cast aluminum for corporations and private homes. In addition the small sculptures have been used by executives, government officials, and individuals as gifts, awards and honorariums world wide.

Also available, are studio produced aluminum sculpture and crafts. Retail pricing for limited edition sculpture begins at approximately $200.00. Catalogs and slides of architectural work or crafts are available. Please indicate your interest. Call to discuss projects.

(Top) *Man and Horses*, 42″ × 16″, anodized aluminum. Variations available.
(Bottom left) *Horse and Warrior*, 18″ tall, cast aluminum. An award sculpture commission.
(Bottom right) *Eagle*, 4′ × 5′ cast aluminum. Commissioned for a private home.

# Glenn Elvig

**7716 Lakeview Lane N.E.**
**Minneapolis, MN 55432**
**(612) 780-2028**

Glenn Elvig's award-winning work has been enthusiastically received in galleries and showrooms in England and the United States. *Fine Woodworking* magazine and network television stations have featured his work.

Elvig's free standing & wall hung sculptures range from smaller residential to large site-specific public, corporate and church installations. Clay, metal or glass are often combined with the wood to create these truly unique pieces. Prices range from $500–30,000.

The artist is available to supervise installation.

A portfolio of slides and information is available upon request.

"Legends VI"—Maple Burl/Mahogany 8"w. × 10½"h. × 7"d.

Printed in Japan   © 1990 The Guild: A Sourcebook of American Craft Artists

"Legends VII' — Western Boxelder Burl 9½"w. × 15"h. × 10"d.

# Michael K. Hansen & Nina Paladino

California Glass Studio
1815 Silica Avenue Unit D
Sacramento, CA 95815
(916) 925-9322

Michael and Nina have been working together for 13 years. Their glass is represented in galleries and private collections throughout the United States and Canada.

Pictured are handblown vessels from the Layers II series, and a plate. The vessels are finished by polishing the openings, giving the work a contemporary look.

A complete catalog is available upon request.

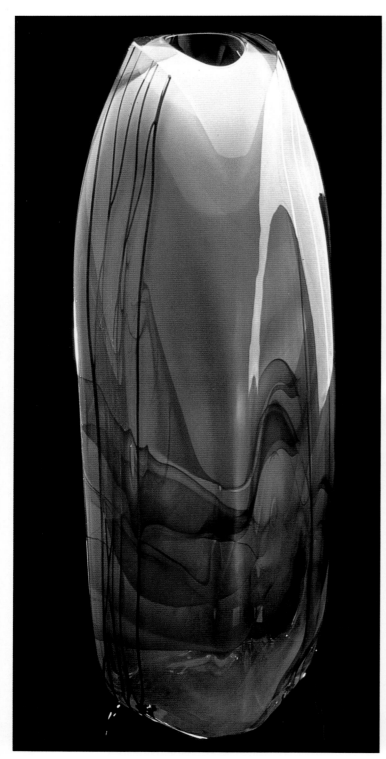

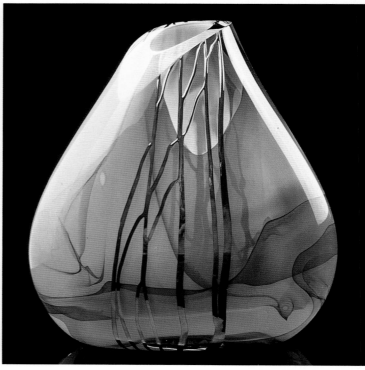

# Marialyce R. Hawke

**3 Marvin Circle**
**Chico, California 95926**
**(916) 343-6512 or (916) 342-7290**

Marialyce Hawke earned an MFA in sculpture and painting and has been creating art for thirty years with a concentration in glass for the last twelve years. Her art glass can be found in museums, galleries, private collections, nationally and internationally. Personal vision forms the one-of-a-kind and limited editions of dimensional glass sculptures. Hawke employs techniques such as sandblasting, laminating, fusing, slumping and painting to create each unique piece. The sculptures also incorporate complimentary materials such as marble, wood, handmade paper, and found objects. Slides, resume, price list, gallery listings, available upon request. 8 wks to 16wks delivery. Sizes maximum 24"h × 24"w × 24"l. Commissions welcome. Retail for $1,100 to $10,000.

(Top left) "Dragon of the Id"
15"l × 10"w × 17"h.
(Top right) "Contemplation" 11"l × 9"w × 14"h.
(Bottom left) "Atlantis Visitation"
16"l × 7"w × 14"h.
(Bottom right) "Animal Mind"
10"l × 8"w × 10"h.

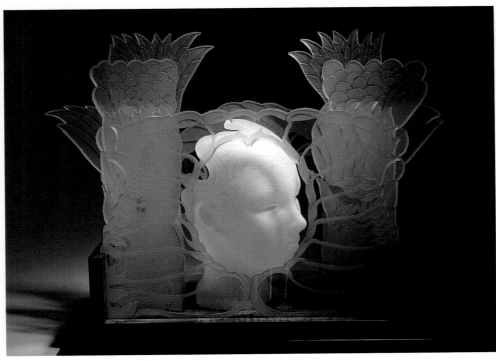

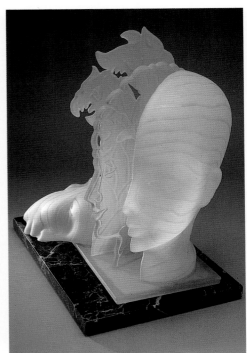

# Christian Heckscher

**Sphinx Design Inc.**
**811 Galloway St.**
**Pacific Palisades, CA 90272**
**(213) 459-5438**

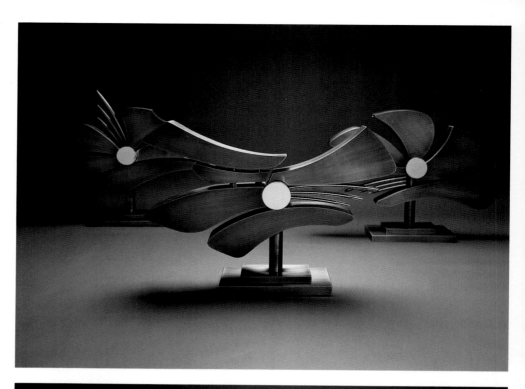

Since 1971, Christian Heckscher has skillfully created and produced a unique range of etched metal artwork (Brass, chrome, copper), combining artistic expression with functional forms. He has specialized in one-of-the-kind pieces or limited series of elevator doors, murals, residence doors, fireplaces and sculptures.

Embracing a variety of styles—traditional, art deco and contemporary—Heckscher's craftsmanship can be adapted to client's budget and specification.

He also welcomes a collaboration with architects or interior designers.

His work has been commissioned by major hotels, restaurants, casinos, office buildings and private homes.

All surfaces are protected by a coat of clear metal lacquer.

Installation available nationwide.

Price and fabrication time is estimate by the project.

(Bottom) Etched brass elevator doors commissioned by "The Mirage" Hotel/casino, Las Vegas 1989

Printed in Japan   © 1990 The Guild: A Sourcebook of American Craft Artists

# I'Lee Hooker

**Ceramic Fountains**
**55 Spring Lane**
**Tiburon, CA 94920**
**(415) 435-3276**

These sculptural stoneware fountains are a refreshing and innovative addition to your garden or patio. Each fountain contains about 1 to 2 gallons of water and a small electric pump. They range in size from 12″ to 30″ in height and 12″ to 21″ in width. The water re-circulates back into the ceramic vessel and is completely self contained. Besides the visual pleasure of water, you have the added element of the sound of mountain streams, as the water drops back into the vessel. Each fountain has its own unique sound, depending on the amount of water and the individual course the water takes. They range in price from $600 to $900.

# Sidney R. Hutter

**Hutter Glass & Light**
P.O. Box 3067
Jamaica Plain, MA 02130
(617) 524-0478

Sidney Hutter's work covers a wide range of sculptural glass techniques and images. Hutter works mainly with commercially available plate glass, which he alters through traditional techniques of cutting, grinding, polishing, drilling, laminating and sandblasting. The sculpture also incorporates complementary materials such as metal and wood.

His sculptural glass works vary in scale from tabletop to floor and wall constructions. Design capabilities also include functional objects such as tables and lamps.

Prices for works begin at $3,000.00 depending on scale, complexity and materials used. Hutter is willing to collaborate with architects and designers. Commissions require two to six months and prices do not include delivery or installation.

Hutter's work has been exhibited internationally and is in both public and private collections.

Slides and resume are available upon request.

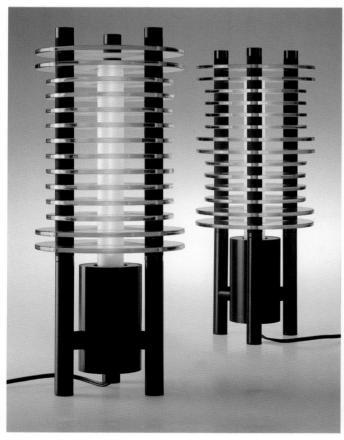

Tricirc Lamp #11 & #12, 16" × 6.5" × 6.5" each

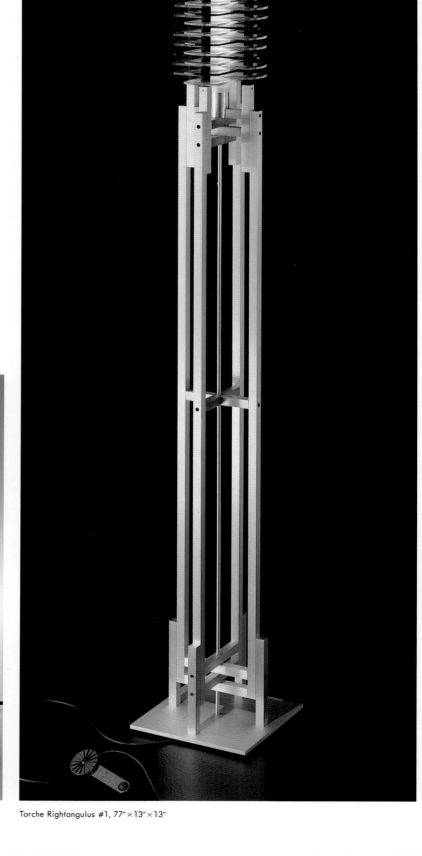

Torche Rightangulus #1, 77" × 13" × 13"

46

# David Jaworski

**11 Clerbrook Lane**
**Ladue, MO 63124**
**(314) 994-7771**

David Jaworski's works are a unique marriage of innovative metalsmithing in bronze or sterling and blown glass elements producing objects distinctive for their fluid, lyrical line and fine craftsmanship. These works have been shown internationally and are included in corporate collections such as AT&T, Monsanto, and Washington University. They are available as one-of-a-kind commissions or limited editions for both public and residential spaces.

Price range from $2,500–$15,000.

(Top right) bowl, sterling and glass, limited editions, 9"h × 12"d.
(Bottom) Dancer series, 16"h × 23"w × 12"d.

Rudie Ershen

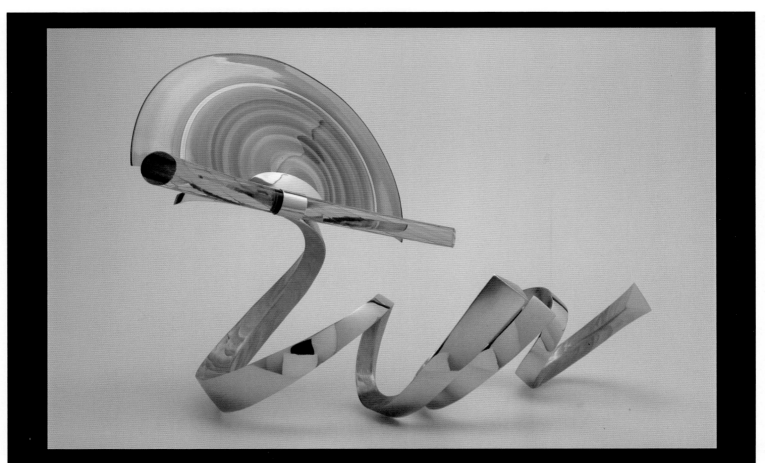

Rudie Ershen

47

# Carol Kropnick

**135 Eastern Parkway**
**Brooklyn, NY 11238**
**(718) 638-4909**

Carol Kropnick creates unique and provocative fantasy creatures with richly detailed surfaces. Her unique materials include antique textiles, leather, feathers, bone, and vintage beads. The finished works are surprisingly durable.

Nationally exhibited, Kropnick has created commissioned works for theater, display design, interior design, publishing and private collectors for 11 years.

Prices range from $750-2,000.

(Below) "Picesaurus", chamois, leather, paint, feathers, and jasper beads.
11"w. × 11"h. × 12"d.

# Carol Kropnick

135 Eastern Parkway
Brooklyn, NY 11238
(718) 638-4909

(Top left) "Mask for George", leather, feathers, paint, and antique beads,
12"w. × 15"h. × 6"d.
(Top center) "Mysticasauria", leather, bone, and paint, 10"w. × 10"h. × 11"d.
(Top right) "Tortolan Cove Grouper", lace, leather, silk, dye, and paint,
13"w. × 19"h. × 8"d.
(Bottom left) "Lounge Lizard V", lace, leather, paint, dye, and antique beads,
12"w. × 10"h. × 9"d.
(Bottom right) "Hawkatoo", feathers, chamois, paint, and dye, 8"w. × "h. × 13"d.

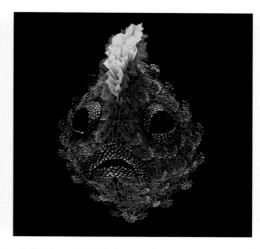

# Joan Long

152 East 94th Street
New York, NY 10128
(212) 860-2668

Joan Long is an artist, who has been working in ceramics for the last ten years. Her interest in mythological images and ancient cities are incorporated as sculptural details in her work.

The objects are hand built and are designed to be used indoors as well as in an outdoor setting. These pieces are high fired and employ exides producing unglazed glased finishes.

"In the fountain" 3'h (picutred below) a plexiglass dish filled with Japanese stones contains the source of water. (Above) "What Are those Spirits of Good and Evil Doing Around My Birdbath?" 3-1.2'h show the effect of oxides on the outside of the form, while the inside of the bowls are covered in a glossy blue glaze.

Completed pieces are available, and commissions for individual designs are accepted. Pieces vary in price starting at $500.

# Andrew B. Moritz

**Special Creations in Metal**
P.O. Box 7126
Bend, OR 97708
(503) 389-1107

Andrew B. Moritz designs and creates site-specific original sculptures in steel and bronze. His pieces are distinctive for their attention to light, texture and life, and he will work with clients to achieve desired effects. Moritz has been sculpting in metal professionally since 1971 and is represented in both private and corporate collections internationally.

Prices begin at $1,000.

Please call or write for further information.

(Right) "Fertility Vase", welded bronze, 18″×10″×18″
(Below) "of Serengeti", welded bronze and steel, 40″×20″×6″

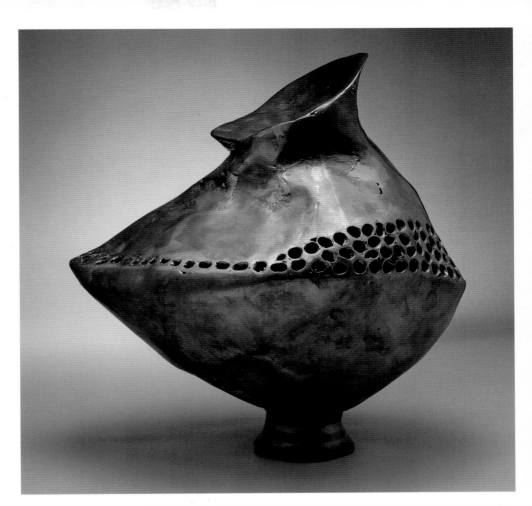

# Rick and Janet Nicholson

**Nicholson Blown Glass**
**5555 Bell Road**
**Auburn, CA 95603**
**(916) 823-1631**

Nicholson Blown Glass is a two person studio where the emphasis is on creativity and innovation over production.

Each piece is a freehand expression of the excitement and risk taking only found in the small, experimental glassblowing studio.

The piece shown on the right is attached hot to a cast foot and finished as one. Other work involves flat vase forms and limited edition, constructed sculptural pieces.

A slide portfolio and price list are available upon request. Commissions are accepted.

(Right) Form on cast foot 12"h. × 10"w. $450 retail
(Below) Bowl 8"h. × 14"w. $500 retail

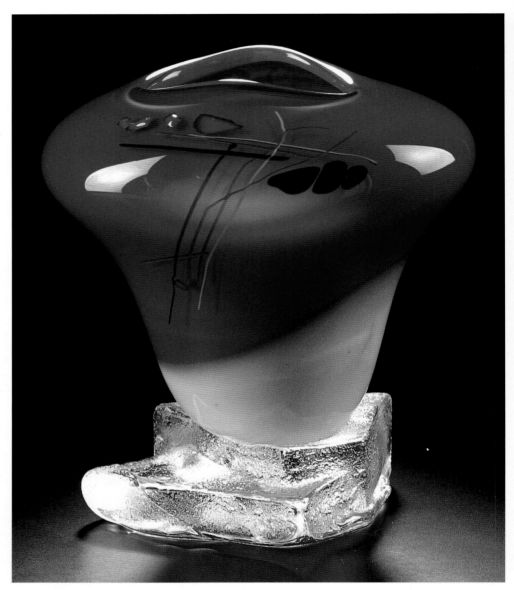

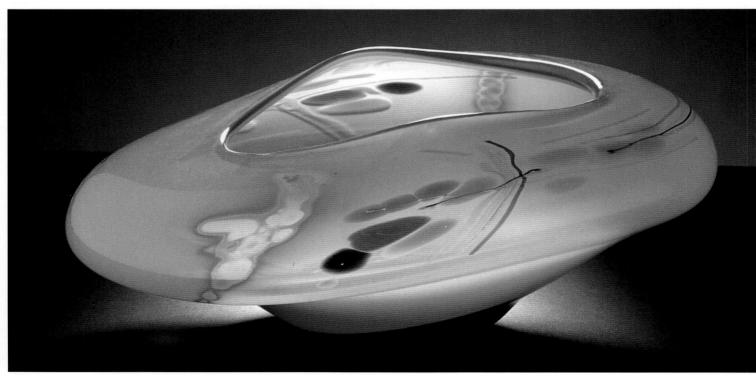

# Leroy Wheeler Parker

40 Meek Place
Lafayette, CA 94549
(415) 937-7336

Multi-media artist Leroy W. Parker is very productive. He creates hundreds of large watercolors, ceramic vases and columns, permanent installations in concrete and ceramics, large colorful handmade paper pieces (8′×4′ and larger) and marbleized fabrics.

Parker received an M.F.A. from the California College of Arts and Crafts in Oakland. He has been creating an extensive assortment of art forms for 20 years, continually producing new and exciting work which is exhibited nationally. Parker is currently a professor of fine art at San Jose State University.

Collumns from the collumn series.
Paintings from geometric research series.
Approx 5′×48″.

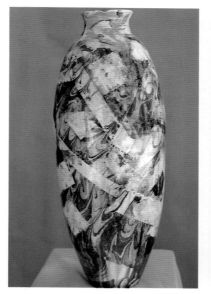

# Laura Peery

2509 N. Quantico Street
Arlington, VA 22207
(703) 533-7556

Laura Peery creates one-of-a-kind porcelain and mixed media figures that are toylike in scale, but convey the impact of mythic characters. She textures the clay with various fabrics, handbuilds and fires the numerous parts, then assembles each work, adding bits of fiber, metal, plastic and clay. Attention to detail and juxtaposition of materials draw in and surprise the viewer.

Prices range from $900–1300.00 Plexiglas cases are available for wall or table display.

Peery has a MFA in ceramics and has worked in her field for twelve years. She has exhibited nationally and internationally in numerous solo and group exhibitions. Permanent collections include the Smithsonian Institution, Washington, D.C.

(Left) "Man on Hold" 22"h. × 10"w. × 3"d.
(Top right) "Opportunity Girl"
18"h. × 9"w. × 2½"d.
(Bottom right) "Making Choices"
20"h. × 11"w. × 3½"d.

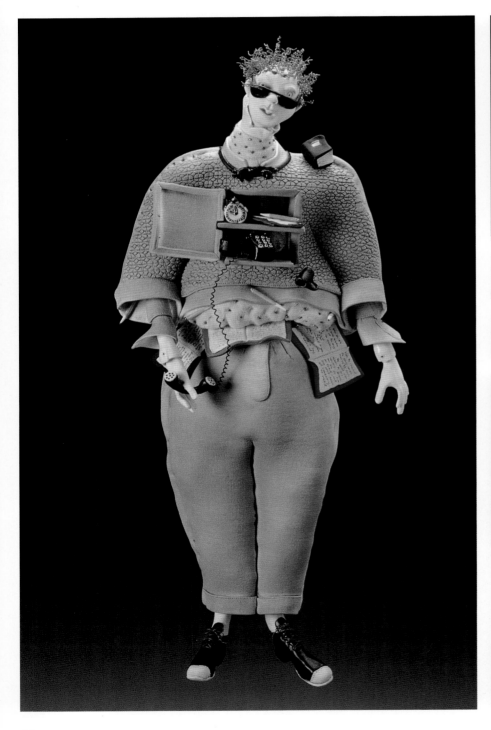

Photos: Richard Rodriguez, Arlington, Virginia (703) 276-0150

# Ralph Prata

Concrete Abstracts
Box 317, West Main Street
Bloomingdale, NY 12913
(518) 891-2417

Ralph Prata who resides in the Adirondacks, creates sculptural concrete carvings. His abstract carvings, both wall reliefs and freestanding forms, have drawn the attention of architects and designers.

Pratas works are created by making blocks of concrete; a mixed formula of cement, sand and aggregates. After casting a solid block of concrete of any desired size, Prata directly hand carves the concrete when it has set.

Most of the work is left in its natural concrete color. The freestanding piece shown here, 24″ × 8″ × 4″ and wall relief, 36″ × 24″ × 2″, are typical of the symbolic and abstract compositions Prata usually carves.

Prata accepts commissions for permanent indoor and outdoor use in private corporate environments. Work is priced by job, with prices ranging from $500 to $10,000, and usually includes installation.

# Marlena River

**California Medicine Icons**
**Box 918**
**Willits, CA 95490**
**(707) 459-5427**

Marlena River's work is inspired by Mayan, Aztec and African civilizations and incorporates her own mythology and symbols. Her sculpture is created in white clay, fired and painted with full spectrum colors. Pieces are available from 16" to 6', single or in collections. Marlena River is well known for her elaborate mask collections and tile murals.

Her work is shown in the Craft and Folk Art Museum Los Angeles, the Tesoro Collection Los Angeles and private collections throughout the USA.

Prices range from $500–$5,000. Please contact Marlena River for further information and slides.

Polychrome Ceramics 16" high: (Top Right) "Joy', (Bottom Right) "Self Portrait", (Left) Adventure unto myself

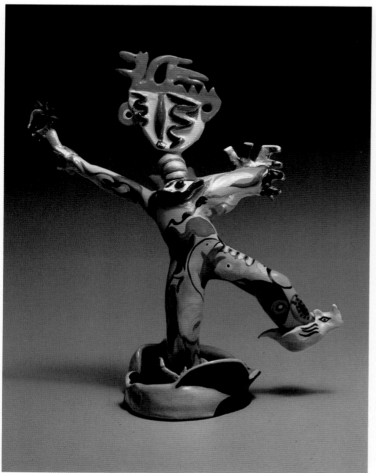

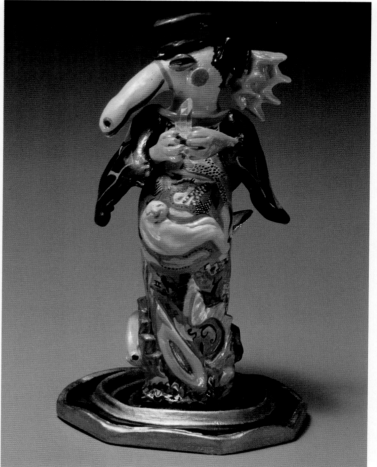

56

# Kurt & Marsha Runstadler

Runstadler Studios, Inc.
6549 Stanley Avenue
Carmichael, CA 95608
(916) 489-4460

Kurt and Marsha Runstadler specialize in three-dimensional glass and metal sculptures. These pieces range from pedestal and tabletop sizes to large scale free-standing or wall mounted major architectural installations.

Using primarily laminated plate glass and combinations of brass, copper or stainless steel, they offer a wide array of designs for the home, office or corporate environment. The Runstadlers offer a series of limited edition sculptures and accept public and private commissions as well.

The artists currently exhibit in museums and galleries in both the United States and Europe. Collections include Corning Museum, Saks Fifth Avenue and the Hilton and Sheraton Hotels.

Slides are available at a nominal charge upon request.

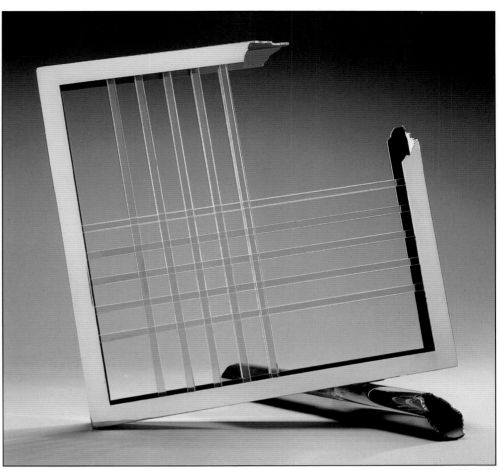

"Square Matrix" 19"w. × 19"h. × 18"d.

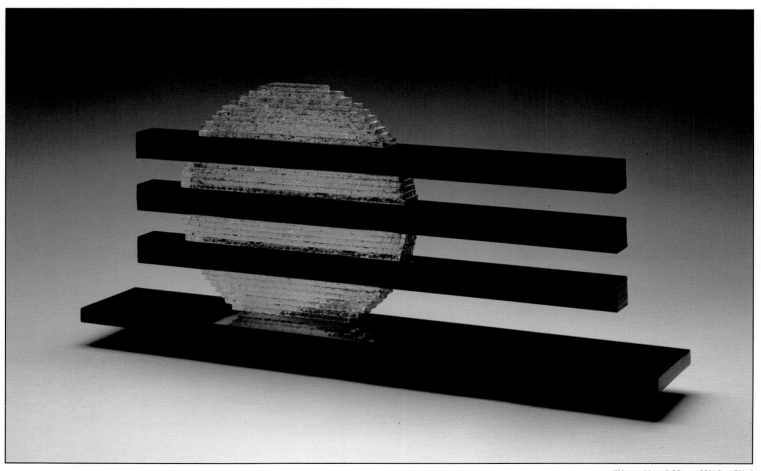

"Linear Moon" 25"w. × 11½"h. × 3½"d.

# Richard Silver

1708 Berkeley St.
Santa Monica, CA 90404
213-453-9673

Richard Silver creates unique sculptural vessels and non-functional sculptural forms in blown forms and laminated plate glass. Sizes range from 12" to the Architectural.

Silver is represented by many leading galleries in the U.S. and Canada. Commissions for work of any size are accepted on a limited basis.

Also available in blown glass and cast glass are wall sconces, tiles, Architectural elements, lighting and furniture.

Photographs and prices are available upon request.

Top lt. "Eclipse" 18 × 12" × 6" blown/laminated glass
Top rt. "Luna" 24" × 24" × 6" blown/laminated glass
bottom "Callisto" 32" × 18" × 6" blown/laminated glass

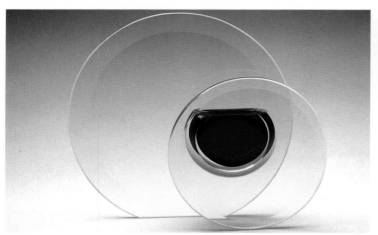

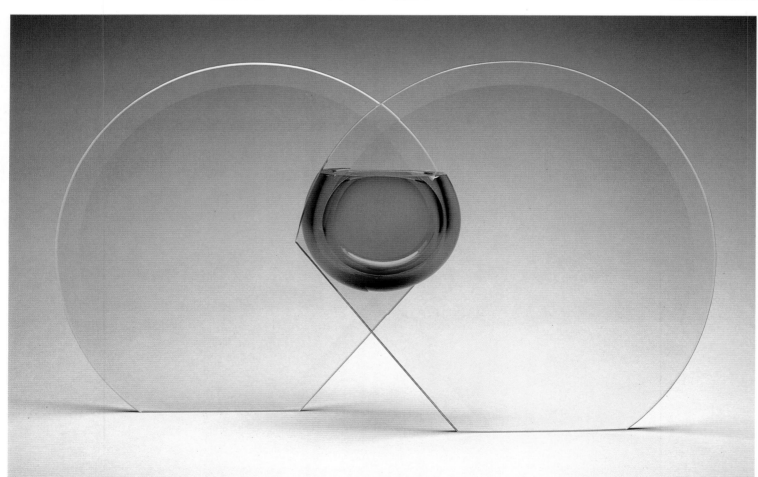

# Sculpture

# Pam Castaño

**Fabriquē, Inc.**
**1900 East McDowell Road**
**Phoenix, AZ 85006**
**(602) 252-9880**

Having worked in the areas of sculpture and furniture, Pam Castaño's experience is appreciated by architects and designers with her designs reflecting her sensitivity to sites as well as client's special needs.

With bold and colorful movement of form in space, she creates sculptural statements from the intimate to the monumental. Forms that seem to breathe and dance, Castaño's kinetic mobiles are suitable for indoor and outdoor settings. Entertaining, transparent and airy, these three dimensional creations add whimsey to any location. Constructed of perforated metal and steel tubing, they are finished with automotive paint in bright colors. Precision spinners and pinwheels bring the mobiles into graceful motion in response to the slightest air current.

A brochure and slide portfolio are available upon request.

Sculpmobile #1, painted steel, 8'h.

Kinetikos #5, painted steel, 10'w. × 16'l. × 11'h., 110 pounds.

# Mark Chatterley

231 Turner Road
Williamston, MI 48895
(517) 655-3686

Mark Chatterley deals with large scale sculptural ceramic pieces. He focuses primarily on the figure in an abstract, impressionistic manner. The works, with heights ranging from 12"–14', can be placed indoors or outdoors, and can withstand the extremes of the elements. Surfaces range from shiny metallic to a crusty, volcanic-like texture, giving the appearance of weathered stone or rusted metal. Site specific work is welcomed by the artist.

Work is priced by height, with prices of approximately $400 per foot.

(Left) "Sisters," stoneware, 6½'.

(Top right) "Wood Muses," stoneware, 6½'. (Bottom right) "Imaginary Landscape," stoneware, 6½'.

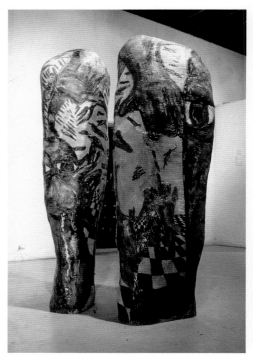

# Jonathan J. Clowes

P.O. Box 610
Walpole, NH 03608
(603) 756-3220

"A Small Still Voice"

Silhouetted against the soaring atrium ceiling this mobile reflects the moods and spirit of the Library at the Landmark College in Putney, Vt. "A Small Still Voice" (8'h. × 10'w.) is carved from laminated ash with forged spring steel fittings.

Jonathan Clowes' sculptures express a sense of peace, serenity, excitement, motion and elegance. The fluid lines and shapes reflect his training as a boat builder. His mobiles enhance commercial and residential spaces: atriums, stairwells, cathedral ceilings, conference or dining rooms, courtyards and gardens.

Inquiries, creative dialogue, collaborative and commissioned works in accordance with space and budget are invited. For slides, resume, and further information, please contact the artist.

"A Small Still Voice" (viewed from below)
"A Small Still Voice" (front view)

George Leisey, Bellows Falls, VT

# Mitzi Cunliffe

**Mitzi Cunliffe, Sculptor for Architecture**
200 Central Park South, Apt. 31-B
New York, NY 10019 October through May
(212) 246-3777

**IN FRANCE from June through September**
**Le MAS du Vieux Moulin, Route de Mons**
**83440 SEILLANS (Fayence) FRANCE**
(011-33) 94.76.97.77

Mitzi Cunliffe was born in New York City in 1918. B.Sc. and M.A. in Fine Arts from Columbia University. Lived in England from 1949-1976. 20 monumental sculptures installed throughout England and in South Bend, IN. During the 1960s, Cunliffe developed modular "Sculpture By The Yard," cast in concrete, fiberglass, anodized aluminum and fire clay, used for interior and exterior of public buildings. "Sculpture By The Yard" was exhibited at The American Embassy, London, and in 20 cities throughout Great Britain and Belgium from 1967-1971.

She is particularly interested in designing sculptural logos in every scale.

(Top right) "Cosmos" Wall of black fibreglass University of Manchester, England.
(Top left) Silver "Tribute Award" for "British Academy of Film and Television Arts" London.
(Bottom left) One-ton Crest in Portland Stone for Scottish Life House, London, England.

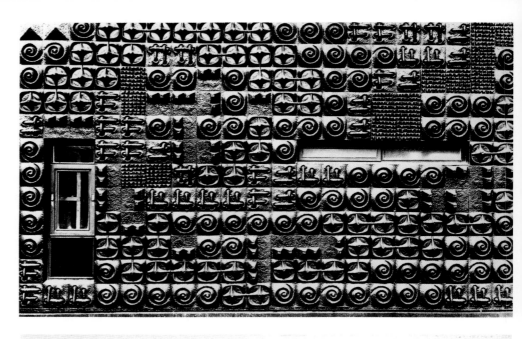

## Weaving 8 tons of Portland Stone . . .

When Mrs. Mitzi Cunliffe was commissioned to carve a sculpture for the new building of the Department of Textile Industries at Leeds University her design was a pair of hands with a texture of filaments woven round and between the fingers. Abrasive stones made by CARBORUNDUM were among the modern tools Mrs. Cunliffe used to carve this symbol of man-made fibres from an 8-ton block of Portland stone.

Products by CARBORUNDUM find interesting uses in the arts and crafts, as well as in almost every field of human industry.

Mrs. Cunliffe's sculpture in position on the new Department of Textile Industries building, which was opened by H.R.H. the Duke of Edinburgh last June.

"Man-made Fibres" Portland Stone weighing 6 tons on "Man-made Fibres" Building. University of Leeds, England.

# Timothy Flanigan

P.O. Box 187
Folsom, LA 70437
(504) 796-3672

Artist Timothy Flanigan works with copper, brass and stainless to create one-of-a-kind sculptures. Flanigan's fountains and wall sculptures reflect the woodland flora and fauna but, he does not merely copy the specimens he collects, he re-creates them in a manner that emphasizes the unique beauty of each bird, plant or flower.

Prices start at $400, excluding installation and transportation, All sculptures are suitable for indoor and outdoor use.

Collaboration on residential and corporate commissions are welcome. The time from initial contact to delivery can be 3-12 weeks, depending upon size and detail of commission.

For additional information, please contact Flanigan at above address.

# Jean Juhlin

Juhlin Studio
764 North 400 East
Valparaiso, IN 46383
(219) 464-0167

Bronze or stoneware.

Single figures or groups can be sized for the home environment or corporate space. Large architectural pieces are available which incorporate inter-related groups of stoneware figures mounted on pedestals. Several pedestals mechanically combine for the site specific commission.

Educated at the Art Institute of Chicago and exhibited internationally, Jean presently maintains a studio in the wooded dunes of Northwest Indiana.

Price range: Single stoneware 750–1500
Single bronze 1500–2000

Top Right: Bronze "Yearning"
Bottom: Stoneware "Pueblo Pomona"

# Tom Kloss

**321 Keneagy Hill Rd.**
**Paradise, PA 17562**
**(717) 687-8137**

Tom Kloss blends wry wit, sophisticated whimsy and fanciful imagination in the creation of his bird, fish, human and abstract sculptural forms. Kloss sculptures are exaggerated in size and scale and all one-of-a-kind.

Kloss creates with wood and metals. Sculptures are suitable for indoor and outdoor applications. Kloss favors bright colors and rich, detailed painted decoration on the super smooth surfaces of his sculptures.

Pictured are avian icons typical of the scale, feeling and finish of Kloss works. Sculptures are priced from $200–$6,000 depending on size and detail. Most works are completed within 90 days.

Kloss has been active as a sculptor and artist since 1965 and has exhibited widely. His work is in national and international collections.

Sculptures from 2 ft. to 16 ft. tall.

# Jeff Lederman

PO Box 3816
Santa Fe, NM 87501
(505) 753-4183

These sculptures, fabricated for indoor or out-door installation, are just one facet of the art of Jeff Lederman.

Whether the medium is sculpture, abstract painting, or furniture design, the impact of Lederman's work is created by its extreme thoroughness. They are whole statements which demand a response. In that sense, they bring you out of yourself; they need your participation. They are alive and memorable.

Commissions are welcome, and will result in a truly captivating work of art.

# James Mellick

**Department of Art**
**Calvin College**
**Grand Rapids, MI 49546**
**(616) 957-6326**

". . . the brilliance that made marble take on an almost liquid-like fluidity in the hands of the Italian Baroque sculptor Bernini, lives and breathes again in the exquisitely crafted wood sculptures and installations of James Mellick . . ." —Sara Albert, Grand Rapids Press, January, 1989. Mellick's narrative content and beautiful form provide layered meaning which digs deeper than the skillful surface. His free standing sculpture, wall reliefs and installations are enjoyed in private and public spaces and have earned him numerous exhibitions, awards and placement in many collections. Prices range from $3,000 to $25,000 for most work depending upon size, significance and complexity of form. Please write for further information and resume. Slides are available for a refundable $25 deposit.

(Clockwise from top) "Peace Burden," 38″×36″×11″, collection of Charles Penzone, Inc., Columbus, OH
"Savior," 66″×48″×31″, collection of John and Ginny Elam, Columbus, OH
"Burning of Ol' Yeller," 34″×40″×14″, collection of Ann and Tim Bieber, Chicago, Il

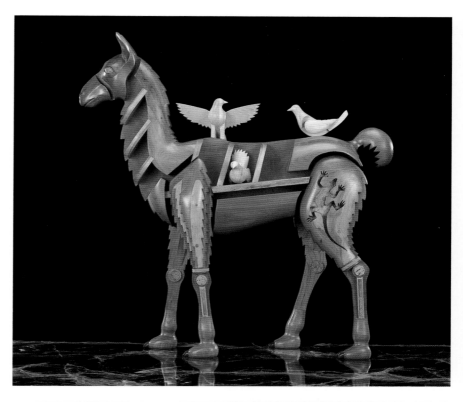

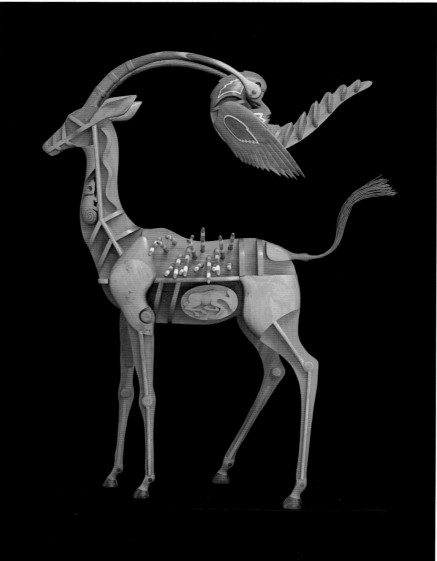

# Todd Miner

**435 South Fifth Street**
**Brooklyn, NY 11211**
**(718) 387–3699**

From a permanent installation at the Palladium with the company of artists, Jean Michel Basquiat, Kenny Scharf, Keith Harring, and Francesco Clemente; to the private collections of Joe D'Urso and Edward Albee; Miner is well represented in the downtown New York art scene. These Neo-Futuristic wall mounted sculptures range from $3,000 and up and are in additions of up to five. They are plated in nickle, copper which oxidizes, chrome, and in some cases gold leaf or silver. Miner has been critically acclaimed in the New York Times, The Washington Post, Artforum, the Village Voice, Art in America,

Arts Magazine, New York Magazine, and Details.

Miner's work has also been seen as a set design for the dance company of Elisa Monte in the 1984 Next Wave Production at the Brooklyn Academy of Music.

(Left) "Spiral Square, & Circles #1" ground steel with lacquer, 46"×32"×22"
(Right) "Cubist Figure #1" rusted steel & wood, 59"×29"×19"

# Abby Morrison

**Ace Woodwork**
**RR 1 Box 1125**
**West Rockport, ME 04865**
**(207) 594-0694**

Abby has worked in local burlwood for ten years producing one-of-a-kind vessels and furniture by accentuating the natural beauty of these organic forms. Her work is very tactile and the chairs (stools, etc.) amazingly comfortable.

With her strong background in traditional joinery, Abby is eager to work with other designers incorporating unusual and burled woods into larger projects on walls, in structural ways, or as whole burls. Although currently intended for indoor display, with care, pieces can be maintained outdoors.

Delivery is dependent on size of burl. Slides available for $15 refundable deposit. Vessels start at $400. Chairs start at $6500.

(Top right) *In Her Hand,* spalted rock maple burl 30" high.
(Bottom right) *Cornucopia,* ash burl 36" long.
(Bottom left) *Belly Bowl,* box elder burl 15" long.

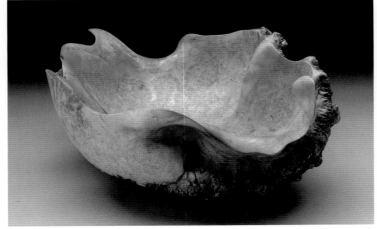

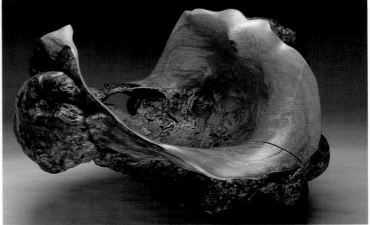

Photos by William Thuss

# Tom Neugebauer

RD 2 Box 8990 Sawkill Rd.
Milford, PA 18337
717-296-6901

"Forms that breathe, stretch, expand and dance."

Tom Neugebauer's work is widely exhibited and collected in both private and corporate settings. He produces one-of-a-kind and limited-edition sculpture and invites cooperative efforts with clients/consultants for site-specific commissions (indoor or outdoor).

While producing sculptures in both clay and in steel, he is known for his unique combinations of the two materials, often emphasizing dynamic, dance-like motion.

Tom is also recognized for his Pit-smoked and Raku vessels and wall forms.

Sculpture prices range from $900–$10,000.

Additional information and brochure available upon request.
[Right] "In the Beginning . . ." Textured, ground steel and pit-smoked clay. 7'4"H × 4'"W × 2'D.
[Top Left] "Dancers." Textured, ground steel and pit-smoked clay. 42"H × 26"Diam.
[Bottom Left] "Torso." Textured, ground steel and pit-smoked clay. 36"H × 17"W × 13"D.

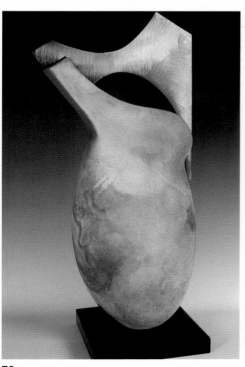

# Haywood Nichols

2904 Tremont Road
Savannah, GA 31405
(912) 233-9532

Haywood Nichols has worked as a professional sculptor for 15 years since receiving his B.F.A. in sculpture from the Atlanta College of Art. His works are in private collections on the East Coast. Nichols' commissioned sculptures cover a wide range of subject matter.

He welcomes collaboration on projects and is available for installation. A typical commission is completed six months after the design is approved. Prices start at $6,000, excluding installation and transportation. All wooden pieces are recommended for interior use.

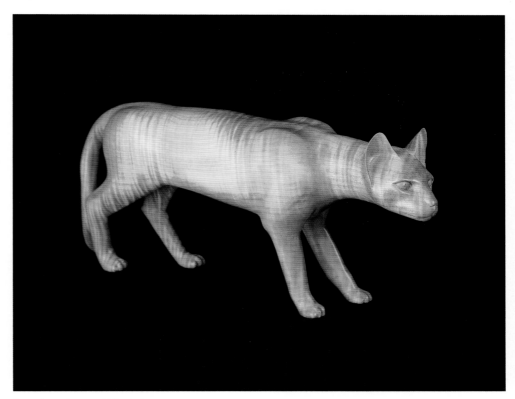

Cat, curly maple; 4"w. × 10"h. × 24"l.

Reclining Woman; 8"w. × 8"h. × 24"l.

# Gene Olson

**The Mettle Works**
**8600 North East Odean**
**Elk River, MN 55330**
**Phone |FAX (612) 441-1563**

Gene Olson's cast/welded/woven sculptures are durable pieces made of richly patinaed copper, brass, and bronze; or stainless and aluminum. They can be finished for either interior or exterior applications.

Olson has produced work ranging from $100,000 building fascades down to table top pieces. His work starts at about $900. On major pieces, he will produce models, drawings, budgets, and schedules for a design retainer, usually 10% of proposed budget.

Current Projects include: A 22' × 110' wall relief in anodized aluminum for the University of Wisconsin—River Falls and an 8' free standing bronze and stone piece for Pacific Gas and Electric, San Francisco.

(Below) "Shadows on the Moon" 4' × 3'h copper, brass, brone 1988

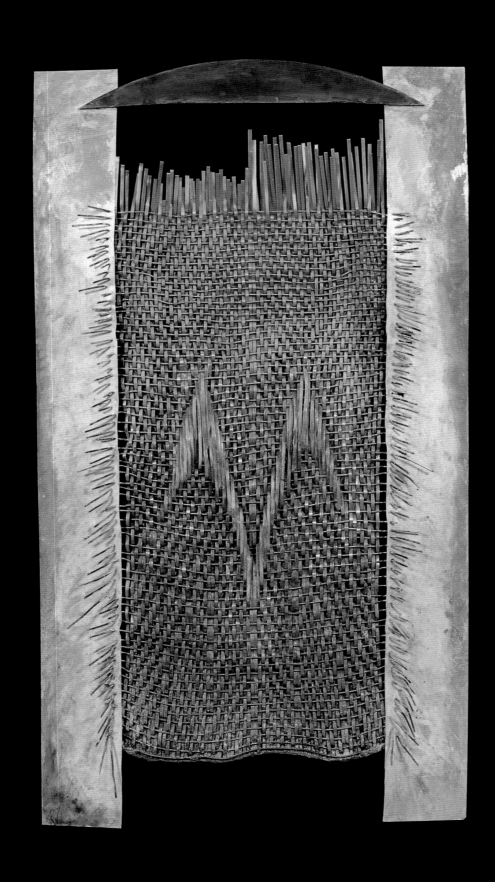

"Torii" 3' × 5'h woven copper, brass, bronze by Gene Olson (612) 441-1563

# Leo E. Osborne
# Lee Osborne

P.O. Box 342-Rt. 131
Warren, ME 04864
(207) 273-3208

Working together for 16 years, the Osbornes' diverse approach to fine art has won them awards of merit with organizations such as The Society of Animal Artists and recently the 1989 World Championship Award for Interpretive Wood Sculpture from the Ward Foundation. For six years they have been honored by being juried into the prestigious Birds In Art Exhibition at the Leigh Yawkey Woodson Art Museum.

These wooden wall sculptures are in private, corporate and museum collections. Commissions and collaborations are welcomed.

Limited edition reproductions of smaller wall sculptures are being marketed in the U. S. and Europe, and range in price from $500–1,000. Originals, as shown here, are priced from $5,000 upwards.

title: "Awakening", Least Tern and stones, 9"h. × 30"w.

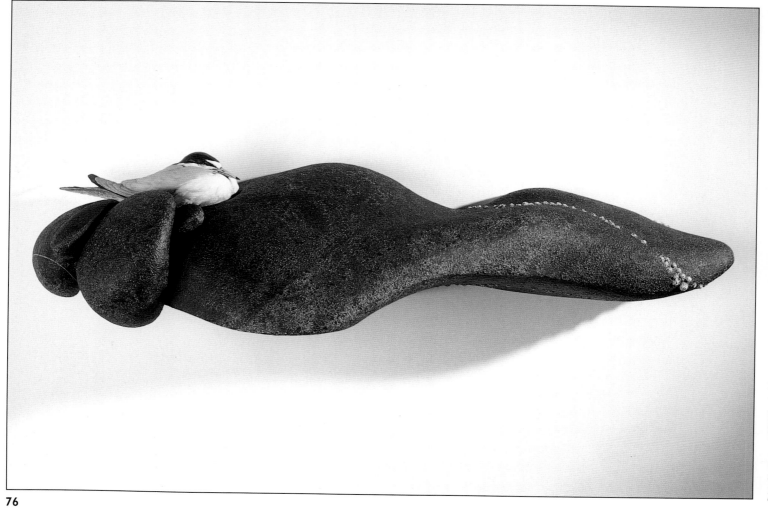

Printed in Japan   © 1990 The Guild: A Sourcebook of American Craft Artists

# Robert Pfitzenmeier

**Pleasant Valley Road**
**Mendham, NJ 07945**
**(201) 543-7830**

Pfitzenmeier's light reactive sculptural installations bring an exciting uplifting spirit to any space. The anodized niobium constructions gently rotate with minimal air movement. In direct sunlight they shower the area with a moving myriad of vibrantly colored reflections. The color is a result of light refracted on the metals surface. The colors are absolutely permanent.

Commission and collaborations welcome.

Installation by the artist is essential.

Pricing and portfolio available on request.

(Top) Anodized Niobium constructions, stainless steel frames, approx. 24" each.
(Bottom) "Microcosm" anodized niobium and stainless steel, Sand Lake School, Anchorage, Alaska

# Timothy Rose

**Timothy Rose Mobiles**
**340 Industrial Center Building**
**Sausalito, CA 94965**
**(415) 332-9604**

Timothy Rose has been creating and realizing mobile sculptures for more than 20 years. He has a degree in anthropology and has lived and exhibited in Europe. He presently works in Marin County, California.

The pieces shown here are from his current "Surprise" series of mobiles. They are highly colored, asymetrically balanced, and evocative of a 'surprise' in the viewer. All are constructed of wire, wood, metal and paint and can be replicated on various scales to suit the location.

Brochure and resume available upon request.

(Middle) "Flying Ladder" mobile, approximately 48"w.
(Top Right) detail of "Flying Ladder"
(Bottom) "Spring Garden Carousel" Surprise Mobile, approx. 42" diam.

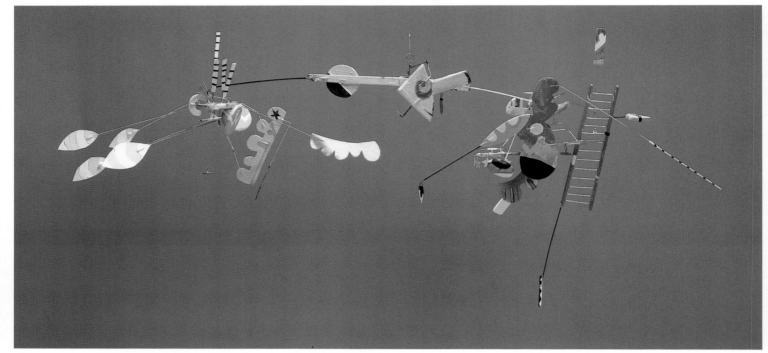

# Susan Ferrari Rowley

**3892 North Road**
**Churchville, NY 14428**
**(716) 768-7286**

Susan Ferrari Rowley designs and constructs site specific sculptures by commission for corporate spaces and private interiors. The sculptures are characterized by permanent, contemporary materials used in conjunction with concepts of transparency, space and light. Applications include suspended/aerial forms, wall hung reliefs, and floor pieces in the round.

The artist will collaborate with architects/designers clients, offering several design solutions prior to final selection. Pricing, creation and installation adhere to a predetermined schedule. Works are priced by the job, from small to monumental, starting at $1,000.00 and are negotiable.

Ferrari Rowley is widely exhibited both nationally and internationally with numerous awards, reviews and public commissions to her name. A portfolio and resume are available upon request.

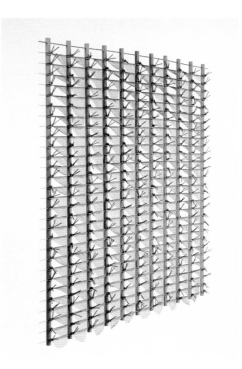

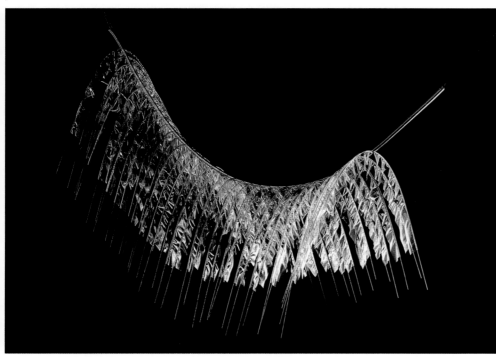

# Maureen A. Seamonds

**The Produce Station Pottery**
**723 Seneca Street**
**Webster City, IA 50595**
**(515) 832-5120**

Maureen Seamonds creates one-of-a-kind clay sculptures for both indoor and outdoor spaces. The flowing, sensuous forms work especially well in reflecting pools or used as fountains. The patterns of nature; drifting sands and snow, the endlessly changing cloud formations provide inspiration for these forms and encourage viewers to project their own experience into the fired clay.

Seamonds works with architects and designers to create site specific works. Prices range from $500.00 to $5000.00 and require two to three months for completion.

(right) "Echoes from the Canyon Deep"
w28" x h46" x d15"

# Anne Shutan

RR1 Box 991
Newfane, VT 05345
(802) 365-7118

Anne Shutan creates one of a kind pieces of furniture and sculpture. Through her work, she has discovered that art has as much to do with finesse and taking chances as with intelligence and craft. Shutan travels all over the country to discuss projects with her clients. She then returns to her studio to design and create the piece. The process from conception to delivery can take anywhere from one to six months. Prices start at $1000.

Please contact the artist for information regarding commissions.

A portfolio is available upon request.
(Below) Walnut table 30"w × 40"l × 30"h
(Right) Rosewood Sculpture 24" × 30"h

# Mavis Somers

P.O. Box 3986
Chico, CA 95927
(916) 342-0765

Mavis Somers lives and works in the northern California foothills. Utilizing native oak and black walnut, she captures the powerful beauty that has made the horse a timeless figure.

Mavis has been creating sculpture professionally for 20 years. The horse pictured below is set on 8 foot rockers and stands 5½ feet tall. Retail prices for rocking horses start at $8,000.00 and vary according to size and choice of wood. Additional information is available from the artist.

# David Stromeyer

**Cold Hollow Iron Works**
**R.D. #2**
**Enosburg Falls, VT 05450**
**(802) 933-2518**

David Stromeyer brings twenty years' experience to his environmental sculpture. Large selection of unique works for indoors and out available immediately. Site specific commissions accepted. Artist handles all aspects of design, fabrication, transport, and installation.

Price range: $18,000–$100,000.

"Yellow Stars in the Magenta Skies" 8′ × 10′ × 8′ painted steel.

"Turn for the Better" MA Percent for Arts Comm. for Worcester County Jail 19′ × 28′ × 37′ painted steel.

# Tom Torrens

**Sculpture Design**
**P.O. Box 1876**
**Gig Harbor, WA 98335**
**206-857-5831**

Using strong, simple forms and durable materials the Torrens's Sculptures are a delight to the senses. Their wistful, expressive tones pay homage to some distant land. Tom fashions works of uncommon strength and character. His bells and gongs are constructed of welded and formed corten steel. All metal elementsd have a natural weather surface with a polyurethane coating. His works are suitable for interior or exterior installations. Copper plated and painted surfaces are available. Tom has a master's degree in sculpture from Washington University in St. Louis. For the past fifteen years Tom has lived in the Pacific Northwest where he maintains his studio and is the Artist-in-Residence at Pacific Lutheran University. The quality of his works speaks for itself.

(Left) — Pyramid Gong, 8'ht, Corten Steel
(Top Right) — Hoop Bell & Frame Bell, 7'ht. × 3'w., Cedar and Steel
(Lower Right) — Big Ball Gong, 6'ht. × 5'w × 2', Copper Plated Corten
Brochure available upon request. Prices starting at $800.00.

# Lighting and Accessories

# Curtis and Suzan Benzle

Benzle Porcelain Co.
6100 Hayden Run Road
Hilliard, OH 43026
(614) 876-5237

Wall lighting Benzle features an arresting display of color and light. These translucent porcelain pieces capture light and shadow and are ideal for conference areas, offices, homes and any interior environment where ambbient lighting supports or replaces natural light. All pieces are fashioned of durable, translucent porcelain.

The Benzle's works are represented in such distinctive collections as The Smithsonian Institution, Italy's Museo Internationale Delle Ceramiche, the Cleveland Museum of Art, the Illinois State Museum and the Los Angeles County Museum of Art. Their work has been featured in more than 20 national and international publications including "American Craft," "Metropolitan Home," "CraftArts" (Australia) and "Geijutsu-Shinchi" (Japan).

Prices range from $20.00 (night lights)-$2000.00 (commissioned sconces). Photographs and resumes are available upon request.

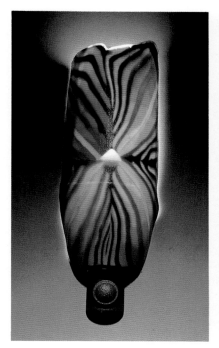 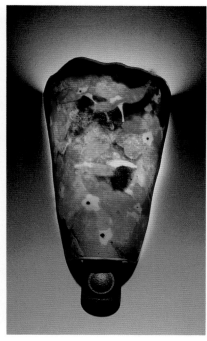

Night Light 5"h × 2½"w          Night Light 5"h × 2½"w

Sconce 3'h × 1½'w × 1'd

# Mark Bleshenski

**Markroy Studio**
**P.O. Box 63**
**429 Warren St.**
**Pinconning, MI 48650**
**(517) 879-5720**

Take a step forward in time with these beautifully handcrafted glass clocks from Markroy Studio. Available in a variety of colors and styles, these freestanding and wall clocks start at $175 retail plus shipping and handling. Custom designs and colors are available at extra cost. All pieces are copyrighted, signed and numbered.

Allow two weeks for delivery. Color samples and price list available on request. Quartz movements include batteries.

Nationally recognized artist Mark Bleshenski's other glass work can be seen on page 60 of "The Guild 4."

(Top) Delta 14 × 14 × 3" aqua/blue © 1989 Bleshenski
(Bottom) Salon 8.25 × 11.25 × 3" lilac/peach; Luna 7.25 × 18 × 3" lavender/lilac © 1989 Bleshenski

# Bradley R. Cross

**Harmony Hollow Bell Works**
P. O. Box 1303
Ann Arbor, MI 48106
(313) 668-8522   1 (800) 468-2355

Over the last 22 years, Bradley R. Cross' Harmony Hollow Bell Works has created a selection of over 300 designs encompassing bronze bells (windbells, door bells, dinner bells), windchimes (tubular and rodular), exterior mobiles (with bells and without), low-voltage landscape lights. All Harmony Hollow designs are constructed of high quality bronze, brass and copper. The windbells and landscape lights are sandcast bronze with a durable verdi gris patina. The windbells may be hung on the patio or deck, off the eaves of a house, or in a tree—anywhere they will catch a breeze. Low-voltage landscape lights are highly suitable for atriums or exterior corporate space, as well as domestic gardens. Prices range from $30 to $350. The single bell retails for $45; the contemporary bell mobile is $190, and the landscape lights are $200-$300. Color brochure available.

# Pat Hannigan

**Hannigan Porcelain**
**Dodge Road**
**N. Edgecomb, ME 04556**
**(207) 882-6430**

Pat Hannigan designs and creates contemporary porcelain pieces, inspired by Japanese Oribe ware of the 17th century. Since 1976 Pat has been working exclusively in porcelain, producing elegant and colorful tableware with a definite contemporary style.

Exhibited nationally her work includes both wheel-thrown and slabware pieces. A complete line of both functional and decorative one-of-a-kind objects is available including a variety of platters, tea- and coffeepots, vases and lamps. The rich high-fire glazes range from deep blues and greens to iridescent pur-ples and striking copper reds, complimenting the crisp whiteness of the porcelain itself.

Slides and brochure available upon request. Retail prices: $50–500.

(Left) Turquoise Coffee Pot with Pinks, 12"h. × 8"w.
(Top right) Copper Red Dinner Square with Pinks & Greens, 10" × 10".(Middle right) Turquoise "Pocketbook" Vase with Pink Plaid, 14"h. × 8"w.(Bottom right) Copper Red Platter with Pinks & Greens, 16"diam. × 4"h.

# House Jewelry

Kevin Loughran
P.O. Box 24152
Santa Barbara, CA 93121
(805) 962-9970

Kevin Loughran has pursued art all of his life, incorporating his experience with design, sculpture, jewelry and intaglio printmaking into his work.

His handcrafted switch plates are made of etched nickel on copper or brass. The light dimmers and switch covers fit standard American sizes and are easy to install and maintain. Prices range from $20 for a single switch plate to $300 and above for a four-switch "Ultimate Turn On" (see bottom left).

Loughran is available for commissioned works.

(Top) Single- and double-light switch covers.
(Bottom right) Light dimmer switches with knobs and back plates.
(Bottom left) "Ultimate Turn On" light dimmer switches and four-switch plate with custom switches.

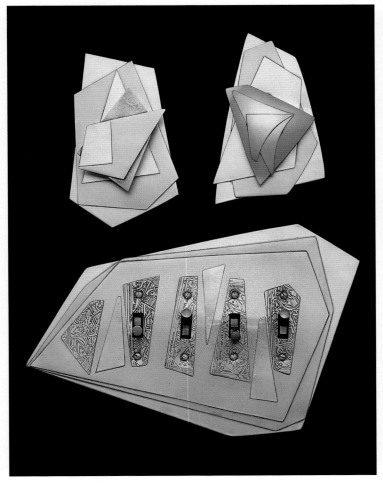

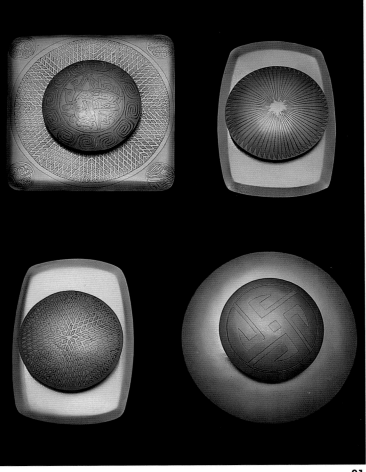

# JEJ

36 East 10 Street
New York, NY 10003
(212) 674-6113

The utilitarian and decorative work produced by the JEJ studio combines classical and contemporary enamel-styles. Each of these one-of-a-kind and limited edition pieces receives multiple firings to enhance the surface with a richness and depth of color.

J.EJ's enamels can fill a small niche or an entire room. JEJ's work compliments both the residential and/or corporate environment and is designed to enhance the space it will inhabit.

Bowls and plates range in size up to 12 inches diameter and are available in a wide variety of lead-free and acid-resistant colors which are permanent and will not fade. Prices range from $100-$475.

The artist is willing to collaborate with architects and designers on specific projects for their clients from inception of design through final installation. Commissions for large scale murals are also available.

More information is available upon request.

# Eric L. Jensen

**Lill Street Studios**
**1021 W. Lill Street**
**Chicago, IL 60614**
**(312) 477-1256**

Eric Jensen produces hand-made porcelain dinnerware. His work has a delicate elegance which belies its durability. A selection of shapes, colors and patterns is offered. Dinnerware may be complimented with any combination of tea set, pitcher, platter, serving bowls and cream and sugar sets.

Eric Jensen received his M.F.A. from the Cranbrook Academy of Art and has fifteen years experience as a ceramic artist. His work is collected and exhibited nationally and he has worked extensively with Chicago-area interior designers. The Chicago Tribune recently featured Jensen's dinnerware.

Prices range from $70-85 per place setting.

# Elizabeth Lamont Johnson

P.O. Box 1656
Morro Bay, CA 93442
(212) 868-1121

Elizabeth Lamont Johnson has been creating decorative mirrors for three years, and has denoted the long rectangle format as the "Cenotaph Series." The mirrors are intended to lean against a wall so as to reflect image and light patterns in a textural manner. They are particularly effective with a natural light source that changes throughout the day.

Johnson is interested in expanding the technique to architectural formats such as murals—interior/exterior, bathroom walls, wall niches, trim strips or other applications—as well as continuing the style shown here. She's willing to collaborate with designers on architectural formats.

Prices vary with size and format.

(Right) "Age of Youth", 18"w. × 72"h.
(Bottom) "Age of Youth", detail.

# LaChaussée Blown Glass Studio

**Dan & Joi LaChaussée**
**1959 E. Brainer Rd.**
**Freeland WA 98249**
**(206) 321-1232**

Joi and Dan make glass come alive. The depth of detail, clarity of color, and free formed gracefullness, are both physically and emotionally moving. Both the fish and lampshades are created to be unique, and each piece is individually signed by the artist. The glasswork comes in a choice of colors and varying styles.

The fish come in either a transparent, or opaque body with multiple scale colors, and eye colors which enhance their tropical nature.

There are four basic styles of lampshades: single optic, double optic, ribboned earth tones, and ribboned earth tones with full body transparent color.

Table model: 17"-18" × 22" high
Floor model: 22"-24" × 57" high
Swag model: 20"-24" diameter
All lamp bases are solid hand cast brass.
Inquiries welcome!

# Isaac Maxwell Metalworks

P.O. Box 830545
San Antonio, TX 78283-0545
(512) 227-4752

Architect Isaac Maxwell designs and directs his workshop in making entirely by hand metal objects including pendant and bracket lights, doors, planters, wastebaskets, chandeliers, torchieres, mirrors, paravents, firescreens and architectural accessories of punched copper, brass or plated copper sheet.

The workshop produces custom work for residences, churches, universities, stores, banks and restaurants.

Pieces may be commissioned or a selection may be made from a brochure. More information is available.

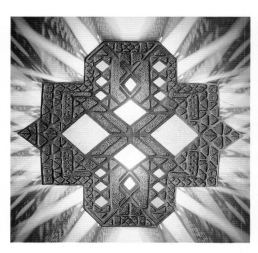

# Kathy McClelland-Cowan

**McClelland Art Glass**
**P.O. Box 627**
**Kapaa, HI 96746**
**(808) 822-3278**

Kathy McClelland-Cowan's works are a unique culmination of various art glass techniques. Her designs include painted, etched, fused and enameled glass, as well as architectural stained glass.

Her fused, slumped, and enameled glass is one-of-a-kind, with sizes varying from 1" pieces to 24" tiles. This glass can then be incorporated into architectural stained glass panels, tiles, and furniture inlay. As well as, framed wall art, bowls, dishes, and jewelry.

Commissions accepted. Bowls, sculptures, and framed works range in price from $200-2000.

(Top) "Cupid's Arrow and a Heartbeat", 12"×14" fused, slumped, and enameled glass. Photo: Dane Warner.
(Bottom) Cobalt bowl, 11½" dia.×4" d., fused, slumped, and enameled glass. Photo: K. McClelland-Cowan.

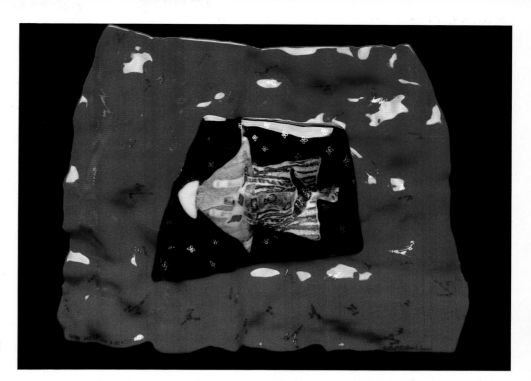

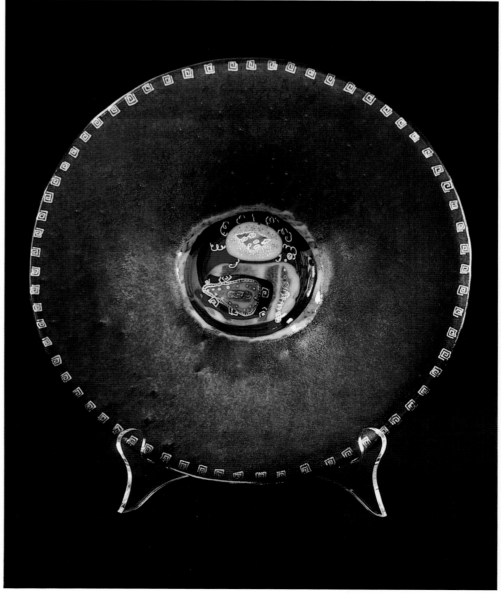

# Craft Media
# In My Marketplace

I have been interested in crafts ever since I was a young boy living in South Alabama. I remember sitting at my grandfather Lonnie Morris' feet surrounded by wood shavings that were flying away from his pen knife as he whittled and carved all sorts of wondrous things—wooden toys and "little devils" to guard the bird houses out in the back yard at Biggity Hall. This early love of things "crafted" has advanced in giant steps since 1948. I now use crafts as often as I can, because I feel that this art has a special place in my professional work.

As a restaurant designer, I am well aware that public spaces offer a great opportunity to give expression to interiors through the use of special commissioned art. In this context we, as designers and molders of the public's taste, are able to expose greater numbers of people to craft and to begin to generate a meaningful dialogue between the craft artist, his art, and the general public. We can do more to further advance the craft movement by selecting appropriate, fine craft works for our installations.

A commissioned, unique piece of craft media for my restaurant clients is one of the best opportunities to give both the craftsman and the restaurateur exposure. Good design sells. With advertising costs soaring, the restaurateur must look at every possibility for promotion. For example, by using newsworthy interior fittings such as craft works as focal points or for utilitarian purposes, he can open the door to editorial coverage by the press, which will benefit the restaurant and the artist. In addition, the interior design and its related accoutrements help my client promote and reinforce his concept of the restaurant for the general public.

As a specifier and collector of American craft media, I believe that the creative output of American craft artists deserves our attention not only for its monetary potential as an investment but as an investment in a developing American art form.

**Charles Morris Mount**
**Interior Designer**
**New York, New York**

# Mesolini Glass Studio

**Gregg S. Mesmer**
**Diane A. Bonciolini**
**13291 Madison Avenue NE**
**Bainbridge Island, WA 98110**
**(206) 842-7133**

Mesmer and Bonciolini bring together extensive backgrounds in art glass production to create award-winning dishware that is both practical and aesthetically pleasing. Mesolini dishware is created from handmade iridescent, transparent, or opalescent glass that is "slumped" into molds during a kiln firing. The distinctive "cut-off" edge, a Mesolini hallmark, results from incorporating the inherent unevenness of the raw glass.

An intrigue with color, iridescence, and the malleability of heated glass inspires their work. The brilliance, elegance, and durability of their dishware fulfills their goal of placing original, collectible artwork within the reach of those who appreciate functional beauty.

Each piece in this collection is signed and dated. Production pieces (see top right and bottom photo) range from $8.50 to $116.00 Limited production pieces (see top left photo) start at $150.00

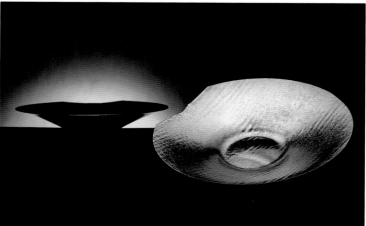

# Julie Munafo

**AGED METALS**
**copper · lead · brass**
**30 Narragansett Ave.**
**Jamestown, RI 02835**
**(401) 423-3318**

Julie Munafo uses traditional metal working
and casting techniques to compose household
and garden objects from copper, steel, brass,
and lead. The body of work consists of a full
range of candle accessories, including chandeliers and wall sconces, as well as
decorative trays, vessals, fountains, and
mirrors.

The Patination on each piece is unique and is
offered with gold leaf detail.

Price points are between $75 and $750.

# Robert Purvis

**Robert Purvis Metal**
**2447 Peshawbestown Road**
**Suttons Bay, MI 49682**
**(616) 271-6229**

Design embodies a powerful means to communication, so I regard it a privilege to manifest fantasy into reality.

(Below) Floor lamp
(Top right) Cocktail table
(Bottom right) Hall tree

# Society of American Silversmiths

P.O. Box 3599
Cranston, RI 02910
(401) 461-3156

The Society of American Silversmiths is an organization comprised of America's finest professional silversmiths who handcraft one-of-a-kind and limited production holloware and flatware. To receive a complete list of names, addresses, and phone numbers of those silversmiths whose work is pictured here, contact the Society.

WENDY YOTHERS, RI, 12" sterling salad bowl with servers.

SUSAN EWING, OH, 12" sterling and vermeil "Bullseye Teapot".

ROBERT A. BUTLER, NY, Sterling coffee set, 12" coffee pot.

# Society of American Silversmiths

**P.O. Box 3599**
**Cranston, RI 02910**
**(401) 461-3156**

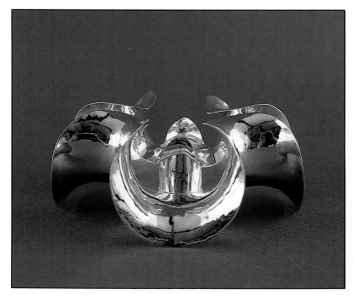

WILLIAM IVES, FL, 5½"h. × 2"w. sterling candlestick.

HAROLD ROGOVIN, NJ, Sterling coffee set, 12" coffee pot.

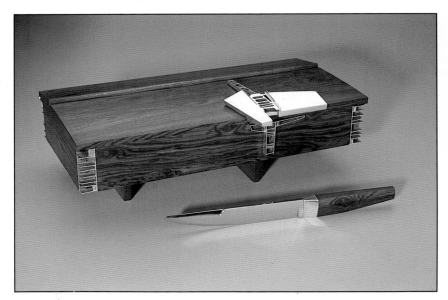

HAROLD SCHREMMER, RI, Executive letter box with letter opener.

# Wolf

**Wolf Wares**
**1511 Guilford Avenue**
**Baltimore, MD 21202**
**301-752-0925**

WOLF WARES is fabulous objects rendered with raised contemporary graphics, Byzantine to 21st c. motifs and brilliant colours that function in your home, office and gallery space. WOLF WARES is mirrors, frames, clocks, room dividers, screens, modular wall panels and moulding strips made of light-weight materials and coated with durable polymer resins.

WOLF WARES executes commissions and collaborates with architects, interior designers and creative homeowners. Custom designs, firm price estimates and completion schedules provided on request.

Prices retail $100.00 and up. Allow 6–8 week delivery. Send SASE for catalogue/price list. Slides available $2.00 per. Also See pg. 25-Guild 4.

Top right—"Strawberry Shortcake"—polymer resin, plastic beads, mica dust strawberries. 18"×12"×3"
Bottom—"Installation: Wolf Wares"—Mirrors, clocks, screen. Various sizes

# Furniture

# James A. Bacigalupi

**Bacigalupi Studios**
**529 McGlincey Unit E**
**Campbell, CA 95008**
**(408) 377-5802**

Bacigalupi Studios design and manufacture limited production and one-of-a-kind furniture and accessories for Residential, Commercial, and Liturgical purposes.

James Bacigalupi has performed a wide variety of commissions ranging from Bar Room interiors to furniture for Pope John Paul II.

All manner of materials are used including glass, metal and wood.

Prices available on request.

Roger Heitzman

# Peter Barrett

**Peter Barrett-Furniture Design**
**317 Cumberland Ave.**
**Portland, ME 04101**
**(207) 774-0981**

Peter Barrett designs and builds one-of-a-kind and limited production furniture for the home and office. His furniture is of simple line, built to the highest standards, and displays a timeless elegance. Woods are selected for color, texture, and graining, often combining contrasting woods to accentuate the lines of a piece and to punctuate details. Commissions and collaborations are welcome.

Portfolio and pricelist available upon request.

(Left) Display cabinet, pearwood, rosewood, holly, 20½ × 15½ × 73.

(Top right) Console table, quilted maple, rosewood, pearwood, 38½ × 17 × 30. Mirror, pearwood, rosewood, 38 × 18.
(Bottom right) Console table detail

# Christian H. Becksvoort

P.O. Box 12
New Gloucester, ME 04260
(207) 926-4608

Christian Becksvoort handworks his wood one piece at a time, following exacting standards for meeting human needs. His solid cherry furniture and accessories are highly innovative, durable and aesthetic designs that will give joy for generations.

Commissions and small productions. Prices from $300 to $10,000. Delivery time is 3 to 6 months.

Brochure available.

(Left) Northern Light, cherry frame with pine veneer panels $1/150$" thick.

(Top right) Cherry music stand & bow back chair.
(Bottom right) Cherry work counter

# Beeken/Parsons

**Bruce Beeken & Jeff Parsons**
**Shelburne Farms**
**Shelburne, VT 05482**
**(802) 985-2913**

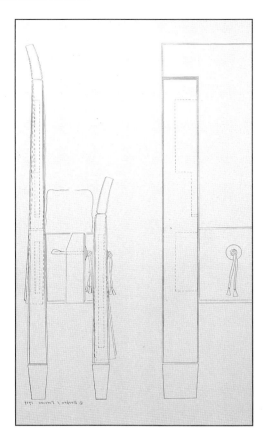

"Bruce Beeken and Jeff Parsons comprise a partnership that brings together the technical sophistication and efficiency of a production shop and the expressive qualities of one-off studio work. Seeking the flexibility to undertake production jobs, exhibition work, or, ideally, a combination of both, they have achieved a rare balance of productivity, personal involvement, and experimentation that integrates technical and esthetic concerns in an economically viable fashion. Their constant interplay between stripped down form and production methods such as shaping and bending enable them to develop subtle designs the simplicity of which belies considerable conceptual depth."

Edward S. Cooke/Assistant Curator of American Decorative Arts and Sculpture/Museum of Fine Arts Boston

Child's Bed/Sycamore, Maple, Chromed Brass, Silk Cording, Acrylic Sailcloth, Cotton and Silk Futon

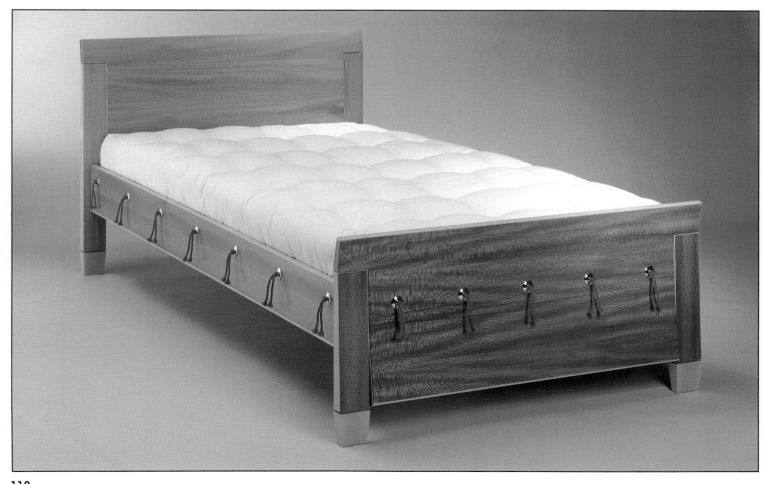

# James M. Camp

**J. Camp Designs**
**11 Longford Street**
**Philadelphia, PA 19136**
**(215) 333-2899**

J. Camp designs and executes functional sculptured wood pieces for home and business. The unique works are primarily done in walnut with hand-rubbed linseed oil finish to highlight the natural beauty of the wood. Other woods made available upon request. Camp specializes in cocktail and game tables. In addition music stands, stools, and other one-of-a-kind pieces may be commissioned. J. Camp is well known in the Philadelphia area with 25 years of experience in the field. The artist is available for consultation. There is a design fee. Prices range from $1,500–$10,000.

(Top) Spine Back Rocker
(Lower) Chess Age II

# John Clark

**John Clark Furniture**
**One Cottage Street**
**Easthampton, MA 01027**
**(413) 527–3038**

New departures from traditional forms and imaginative use of innovative materials characterize John Clark's furniture. He combines precise joinery with a variety of uncommon materials to produce distinctive pieces for homes and offices.

His proficiency in computer-aided design and a complete modern shop allow him to respond quickly and thoroughly to client-needs. Budget and delivery considerations are consistently honored.

John earned his MFA in furniture design from the Program in Artisanry at Boston University.

His work has appeared in several national publications and can be found in principal galleries and collections throughout the country.

Commissioned works vary appropriately in price, but most pieces are $1500-4000 retail. Detailed portfolio information and specific responses to inquiries are promptly provided.

Conference table, desk, bookcase, and moldings for a private office

End tables for an executive office reception area: bleached cherry, granite, ebony

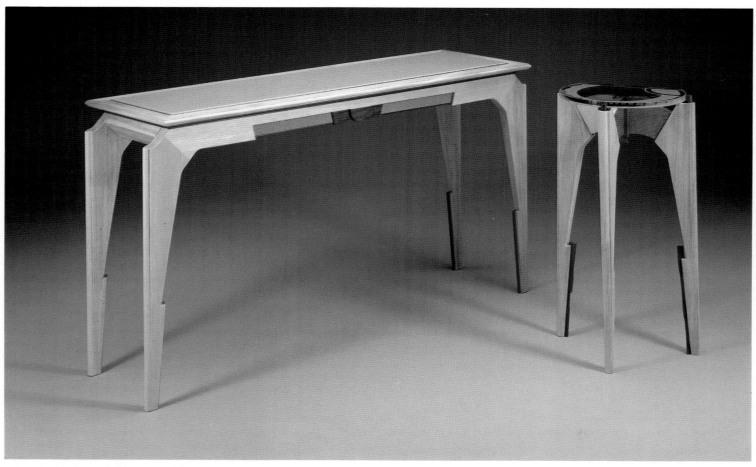

(left) "Tall Table": bleached mahogany, purpleheart, nevamar surface     (right) "Orbit Table": bleached mahogany, purpleheart, anodized aluminum, sandblasted glass

# Rich Clawson

**Grafix**
**504 North 20th Street**
**Billings, MT 59101**
**(406) 245-2995**

Using the cornerstone elements of utility design and craftsmanship, Rich Clawson has transformed architecture to objects in product groups that challenge the norm of the retail spectrum.

These groups include Hand Made Ables (geared toward lifestyle gifts and accessories), Wildthings (original print fabric and paper goods), and I X C L M (signature lighting and furniture in editions of one, ten, fifty, one hundred, and one thousand).

Pictured above—Grafix Studio interior view of signature works and found objects. Pictured below—the box joint table (in erratic set plywood design). This table is available in various sizes, designs, and wood options.

Prices range from less than $100 for standard products to $1,000-$4,000 for signature works. Product and price information available upon request.

# Randy Cochran

**Wood Studio**
Rt. 3 Box 427
Decatur, AL 35603
(205) 350-5270

A woodworker for 15 years, Randy Cochran builds custom cabinets and furniture from his own original designs and collaborative designs.

Working in solid hardwood, fine veneers, plastic laminates, metals, leather, glass, marble and synthetic stone, Cochran produces desks, tables, chairs, case goods, office furniture and cabinets.

The collaborative designs pictured are made of mahogany with surfaces of green marble and burgundy leather, custom matched to the client's office space. Credenza, 3½' × 7' oval; desk, 2½' × 10'. Cabinet in background, mahogany and glass.

A brochure, photos, slides and references are available upon request. Collaborative work is welcome. See also page 114 in THE GUILD 4.

# Michael Colca &
# Michael O'Neal

**SummerTree**
**711 Turtle Hill**
**Driftwood, TX 78619**
**(512) 847-5238, Austin (512) 282-0493**

SummerTree Partners, Michael Colca and Michael O'Neal, bring 25 years of experience to designing and crafting furniture of exceptional quality. The confluence of their ideas has brought forth "Medina", a selection with a uniquely Texas flair.

They work closely with interior designers, architectural firms and individuals. SummerTree welcomes residential and commercial projects in traditional and contemporary styling.

"Medina" Queen Size Bed in white oak; wenge accents. Full—$2,450., Queen—2,495., King—$2,769.
"Medina" Side Table in white oak—725., with shelf $825. Bed and Side Table available in other woods.
"Wishbone" Chair shown in walnut—$850. each (in sets of 4 or more).
Bench—Birdseye and hard rock maple; ebony accents. A custom design for bay window seating.
Showroom in Austin with Whit Hanks at Treaty Oak, 1009 W. 6th.

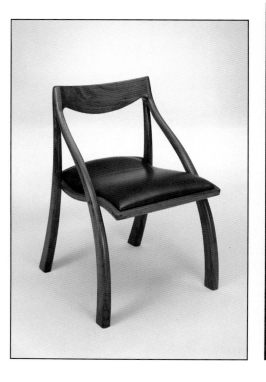

# Jeffrey Cooper

**Designer of Sculptural Furnishings in Wood**
**135 McDonough Street**
**Portsmouth, NH 03801**
**(603) 436-7945**

Kids pet these chairs!

They are lifetime treasures, handcarved to the right level of detail. You can order them in sets with a table or individually. Any animal can be the model, even your own puppy, kitty or pony. You may prefer the contemporary chair and table set shown.

Your child cannot break this chair—it is too sturdy and it will not fall over.

Jeffrey Cooper is a designer/craftsman working in Portsmouth, NH. He has studied at the University of Pennsylvania, Peter's Valley Craft Center, the League of New Hampshire Craftsmen and the University of New Hampshire.

Call or write for prices, current delivery schedule and information about the other wonderful, collectable things Mr. Cooper makes.

Pictured are a table 28 × 28 × 21H, a chair 14 × 14 × 28H, Bambi, Traveller, Jumbo and Nicole.
Winner of the 1989 Public Choice Award "Living With Craft" Exhibit at the 56th Annual League of New Hampshire Craftsmen's Fair.

# Jeremiah de Rham

de Rham Custom Furniture
43 Bradford Street
Concord, MA 01742
(508) 371-0353

Jeremiah de Rham draws upon his training in traditional furniture joinery and his interest in modern aesthetics to produce original designs of a singularly classic look. Designing and building custom commission pieces since 1981, de Rham works closely with the client to generate a design befitting the intended space and the client's practical requirements. A graduate of the North Bennet Street School's highly respected Furniture program, de Rham's craftsmanship is of the highest order. A loyal client following testifies to de Rham's pursuit of perfection in the execution of his work.

Design fees start at $100. Recent commissions priced from $5,000–$22,000. Collaboration invited. Call for scheduling information.

(Top) End tables. Cherry.
17½"h. × 15"w. × 22"l. (nesting tables available).
(Middle) Desk. Cherry, rosewood.
37"h. × 57½"w. × 33½"d.
(Bottom) Sheet Music case. Mahogany.
Gilded cast brasses. 34"h. × 45½"w. × 19½"d.
(Detail) Music case

# Peter S. Dean

465-D Medford Street
Charlestown, MA 02129
(617) 242-2536

Peter Dean designs and builds one-of-a-kind and limited edition fine furniture for the residential and corporate market. His designs are characterized by historic and contemporary architectural and cultural motifs that have been adapted, modified and reapplied to contemporary furniture designs. The designs range from conference tables and corporate offices to individual pieces designed specifically for client's homes.

Direct contact with clients and collaboration with architects, designers and other artists are welcome.

Existing designs can be adapted in terms of size, materials and function, or entirely new designs may be commissioned.

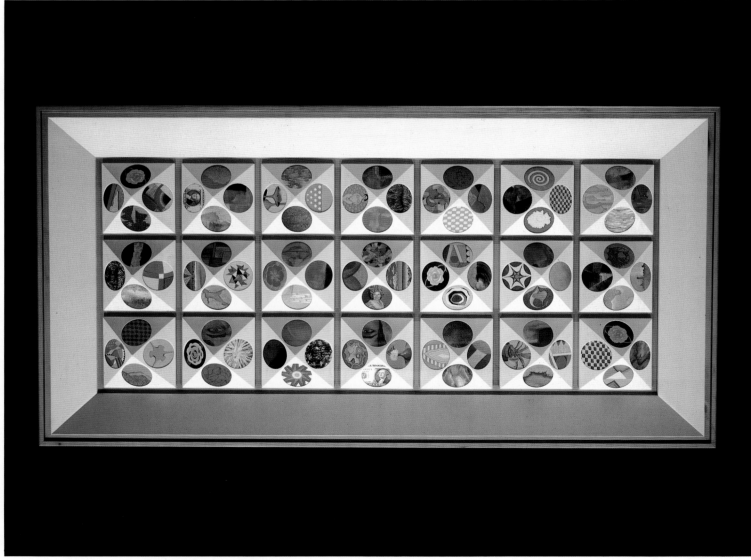

Coffee Table: 26" × 50" × 17" Pearwood, Holly, Glass, Paintings: Artist Oils

# Ron Diefenbacher

**Ron Diefenbacher Designs**
**12132 Big Bend**
**St. Louis, MO 63122**
**(314) 966-4829**

From design to delivery, Ron Diefenbacher uses a professional approach in assessing clients' needs and developing creative solutions. Combining artistic skill and an ability to work well with architects, interior designers, and private parties, Diefenbacher creates signature pieces which stress the individuality of each new project. These unique designs are placed in many private collections, executive offices, and fine galleries across the country.

In addition to custom work, Diefenbacher designs for the furniture industry. He has a Master of Arts in Furniture Design and teaches Woodworking and Furniture Design at Washington University in St. Louis.

Design fees, slide portfolio, references and prices available upon request.

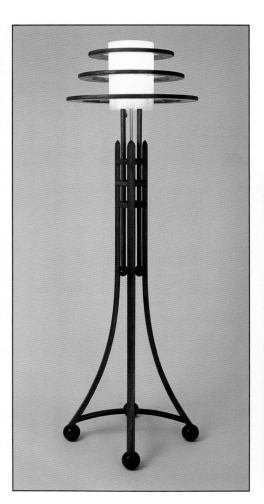

# John Dodd Studio

**1237 East Main Street**
**Rochester, NY 14609**
**(716) 482-7233**

John Dodd has maintained a successful furniture studio for the past twelve years. A graduate of the School for American Craftsmen, he has won numerous awards including artists' fellowships from the New York Foundation for the Arts in 1985 & 1989. His work has been exhibited in the American Craft Museum and other museums and galleries throughout the United States.

The current series of screens is designed to complement residential or commercial interiors with potential as room dividers, foyer or lobby pieces. Custom design makes possible the inclusion of elements such as display cabinets, shelves or table surfaces.

A rendering or model with firm price and completion date are provided upon receipt of a 10% design fee. Average time from design to installation is four months. Slides and pricing information available upon request.

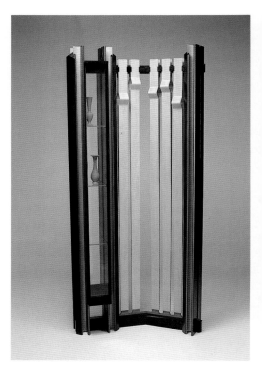

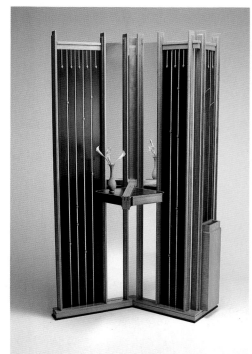

# Robert H. Effinger

**Newport Reproductions**
**59 Main Street**
**Fryeburg, ME 04037**
**(207) 935-3288**

Robert Effinger is acclaimed for 18th century reproduction furniture.

Goddard-Townsend pieces are one of his specialties. His award winning Goddard clock led to being published in *Fine Woodworking*. Commissioned pieces are treasured by clients from California to Florida. Many major pieces are created in mahogany, curly maple, cherry, and walnut.

The majority of work is done by commission. The artistry becomes evident in his ability to research and create a major piece from a client's single picture and few dimensions. He welcomes the challenge of recreating a masterpiece, to be treasured for many generations.

Mahogany Massachusetts bonnet top secretary 89"h. × 39"w. × 23"d., $14000.

Mahogany Goddard clock, 5"h. with hand painted dial, $4500.

# Michael Elkan

**Michael Elkan Studio**
22364 N. Fork Road
Silverton, OR 97381
(503) 873-3241

Michael Elkan lives in the foothills of Oregon's Cascade Mountains. Surrounded by the trees from which he draws his inspiration. Each sculpted object is made from a single piece of wood. Slowly air dried, much like musical instrument wood—whole dining sets can be made from a single tree.

Elkan's designs harmonize with the natural structure of the tree and show a deep understanding of human form as well; dining and rocking chair spindles canted at a variety of compound angles to fit the back, chair seats deeply contoured for extra comfort. Highly figured, collectable quality, native and exotic woods are his specialty.

(Above) "Slat work desk" Highly figured curly maple, 5 drawers
(Below) "Accordian base table" 84" × 42"— spring quilted Oregon maple burl, with 8 matching chairs

# Joel W. Evett
# Roberta L. Boylen

Studio Classico
226 Beech Street
Belmont, MA 02178
(617) 484-2539

Evett and Boylen create classic contemporary furniture. Their style unites cabinetry of fine design and construction with narrative imagery; panel paintings, relief sculpture and shadowboxes. While employing the finest traditional and modern techniques great attention is payed to all aspects of their work. From the designing of a cornice molding, the turning of a foot, the gilding of a detail to the final egg tempera glaze of an image, quality and longevity is the artists' goal.

The artists create one of a kind pieces and limited editions. In their commission work participation of designers and clients is encouraged.

(Left) Pompeii Cabinet: 5'3"×34"×22", aphromosia, wenge, maple, egg tempera.
(Right bottom) Pompeii Cabinet; interior.
(Right top) Mackerel Cabinet; 7'2"×28"×22", maple, birdseye maple, egg tempera, gold leaf.

# Gold Leaf Studios

443 I Street, NW
Washington, D C 20001
(202) 638-4660

Specializing in the conservation of gilded antiques, Gold Leaf Studios offers a full complement of guilding and frame-related services to museums, collectors and designers.

The Studio is equipped to handle frame fabrication, specialty matting and frame reproductions of carved wood and composition. Time honored traditional techniques are used by the Studio's craftsmen to conserve delicate patinas on valuable gilded antiques such as furniture and sculpture. Interior and exterior gilding is a specialty and includes cornices, panelled rooms, medallions and other architectural embellishments.

(Top) Detail of a ceiling in the Diplomatic Reception Rooms at the State Department.
(Bottom left) Gilded chair ca. 1820 from public collection.
(Bottom right) Reproduction of antique composition frame.

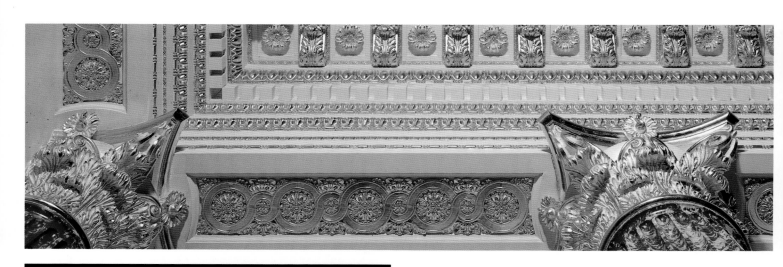

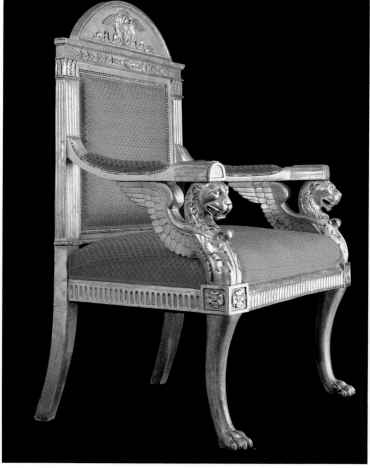

# Johanna Okovic Goodman

**Okovic/Goodman Studio**
**718-B South 22nd Street**
**Philadelphia, PA 19146-1105**
**(215) 546-1448**

Johanna Okovic-Goodman creates limited edition chairs in the Southwest style. These sculptural chairs are designed to be functional. The texture and painterly approach add distinctive quality to a bold design. Brilliant colors creates vitality that whisks the viewer to another place.

All the furniture is hand-crafted from popular; painted with acrylics; and finished with polyurethane.

Goodman's furniture has been exhibited widely in galleries and stores. The artist can create any animal form. Each chair takes a week to complete. The chairs featured are $1,000 each.

Ask about her line of "found chairs", old chairs transformed into folk art objects. Please contact the artist about commissions or to see additional examples of her work.

Upper right, Jaguar (l), Coyote (r) Front View
Lower right, Coyote (l), Jaguar (r) Rear View

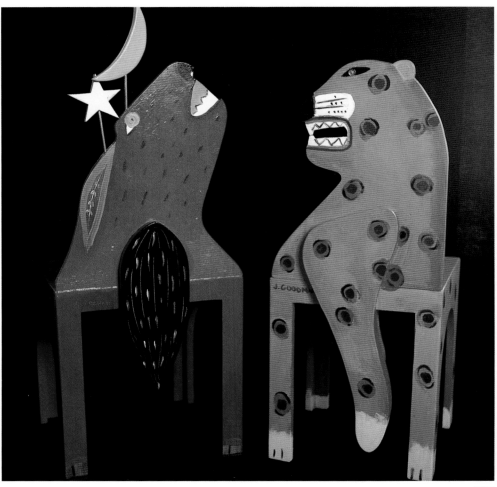

# Peter Handler

**Peter Handler Studio**
**2400 W. Westmoreland Street**
**Philadelphia, PA 19129**
**(215) 225-5555**

Peter Handler designs and produces custom and limited production anodized aluminum, glass and granite furniture for the home and office. Using high-strength clear adhesives to join metal and glass or stone, he creates furniture which is eminently functional, yet esthetically and structurally minimal.

Working with an excellent commercial anodizer, Handler produces a broad range of colors, frequently developing new hues to meet his clients' needs. Anodized aluminum, with its vibrant color spectrum, has a hard, permanent surface that is highly resistant to scratches and stains and which retains its beauty with a minimum of care.

Retail prices range from $1,300 for an occasional table to $5,000 for a conference table.

Delivery time ranges from two to four months. Catalog and aluminum color samples are available upon request.

# Peter Handler

**Peter Handler Studio**
**2400 W. Westmoreland St.**
**Philadelphia, PA 19129**
**(215) 225-5555**

Opposite Page, clockwise from left:
"Pterodactyl" Rocker, 27" × 29" × 36".
"Hydra" Coffee Table, 30"Dia. × 15".
"Pterodactyl" Easy Chair, 24" × 26" × 37".
"Lily Pad" Dining Table, 48"Dia. × 29".
Below, clockwise from right:
"Joy" Dining Table, 36"Dia. × 29".
"Strata" Occasional Table, 26" × 26" × 17".
"Empire" Coffee Table, 40" × 48" × 15".

# John Hein

**87 Woodland Avenue**
**Trenton, NJ 08638**
**(609) 883-4573**

John Hein's wood furniture contains a blend of traditional and contemporary aesthetics. A traditional respect for nature and purity of craftsmanship combined with a contemporary practical structure are the aesthetic principles influencing their design and construction. A clean design reveals the wood's geometrical and graphic characteristics. Furniture is joined with mortise-and-tenon and dovetail joints, and instead of screws to reinforce crucial joints, carved pegs are used. Hein searches for woods containing suggestive patterns, woods he can combine to create low-tone subtle furniture, furniture with gentle surfaces and unobtrusive friendly messages. Most pieces cost between $3,000 and $7,000 depending on size, number of drawers, and complexity of design.

(Top) "Daedalus Cabinet" of walnut, wenge, pearwood, and English brown oak
(Bottom) "Writing Desk" of wenge, cardinalwood, goncalo alves, and Queensland walnut

# Steven Holman

P.O. Box 572
Dorset, VT 05251
(802) 867-5562

Steven Holman's designs combine a respect for the past with an enthusiasm for the future. All work is crafted to the highest standards and manifests meticulous attention to detail. Over the decade he has maintained a studio, Mr. Holman has collaborated with architects and interior designers on residential and corporate commissions, as well as provided quality installation services. A firm price and delivery estimate are established for each commission, most of which can be executed within sixteen weeks. Slides, resume, and pricing information are available upon request.

(Bottom left) Corner cabinet: bubinga, oak, maple, rosewood, black lacquer; 22"d × 34"w × 84"h.
(Top right) Temple table: cherry, curly maple, wenge; 18"h × 27"w × 44"l.
(Bottom right) Coffee table: curly oak, padauk; 17"h × 22"w × 40"l

# Ira A. Keer, AIA

2011 3rd Avenue South
No. 230
Minneapolis, MN 55404
(612) 871-8802

Ira Keer's whimsical furniture is designed to be used. With each piece he aims to elicit an emotion, enticing the beholder into its matrix of concept, craftsmanship and utility.

Keer's furniture designs inject fantasy and playfulness into ageless architectonic elements and period styles. His conceptual furniture drawings, now emerging in three dimensions, have been exhibited in select galleries. His work has been recognized in a wide range of publications and has won numerous design awards.

A practicing architect, Keer's designs are executed by a spirited collaboration with select craftsmen of the Minnesota Woodworkers Guild. This collaboration ensures excellence of design as well as the finest construction, materials and finishes.

He produces both one-of-a-kind pieces and limited edition works. Special orders, collaborations and commissions are encouraged. More information, portfolio upon request.

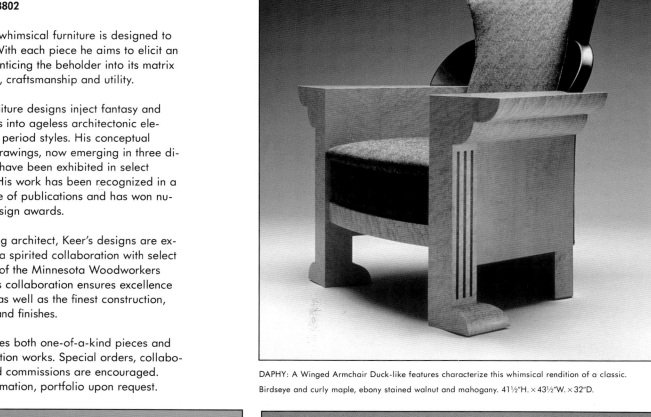

DAPHY: A Winged Armchair Duck-like features characterize this whimsical rendition of a classic. Birdseye and curly maple, ebony stained walnut and mahogany. 41½"H. × 43½"W. × 32"D.

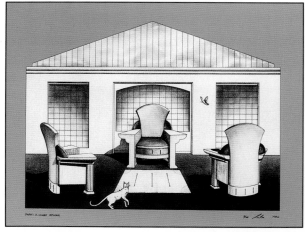

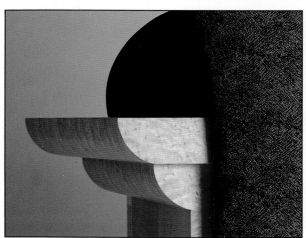

# Darryl Keil

**Darryl Keil, Ltd.**
**47 Portland St.**
**Portland, ME 04101**
**(207) 773-7576**

Darryl Keil's Limited Edition furniture presents elegant functional art forms hand-crafted from unique woods selected for color, grain, and figure. Each piece is available in a variety of these woods which can be personally selected. The line has evolved over 15 years as a designer and craftsman of custom, commissioned work in wood. Delivery is in six to eight weeks with prices and slides of additional designs available upon request.

(top right) Round dining table, bleached maple butt, ebonized maple and black marble center, 60" dia. × 29"h.
(top left) Writing table of ebonized maple and curly koa. 36" × 72" × 29"h.
(bottom) Credenza, tineo and ebonized maple, 18" × 69" × 32"h.

# Laura D's

**Folk Art Furniture**
**Laura Dabrowski**
**106 Gleneida Avenue**
**Carmel, New York 10512**
**(914) 228-1440**

"Who says children's furniture has to be ever so cutesy or as bland as pablum? Not Laura Dabrowski whose chairs are neither"
Corky Pollan
New York Magazine

Laura D. has set out to bring humor and an unmistakable presence to the world of hand-painted childrens furniture. Her durable line of birchwood cows and cats, rabbits and bull terriers as well as bowlegged roosters and many more was inaugurated with the birth of her son Cody. Each piece is done individually featuring bold brush work and fabric like patterns.

Laura D's work can be seen at FAO Schwarz, Macys, Neiman Marcus, and many fine stores and galleries. Prices from $100.00 to 3,200 for a indoor carousel. A color catalog is available for $2.00. Adult sized pieces are available in all designs.

Andrew Bordwin

Andrew Bordwin

132

# Lewis & Clark

**1231 Lincoln Street**
**Columbia, SC 29201**
**(803) 765-2405**

Lewis & Clark's witty and meticulously crafted sculptural furniture has won many awards, including the Formica International Design Competition. Their fresh, often whimsical, vision has earned them showings in the Salon De Mobile, the Victoria and Albert Museum, the Miami Museum of Modern Art, and the Chicago Art Institute (permanent collection). Their designs have appeared in many publications, including *Casa Vogue, Pronto* (Japanese design magazine), *Architecture, Interiors,* and *Architectural Record.*

Typical is the Robe Cabinet pictured, (57"w. × 58"h. × 12"d.), now part of the permanent collection of the South Carolina Arts Commission. The cabinet is finished on all sides. Each one in the series is a different pattern with a base price of $3,000. (Subject to change.)

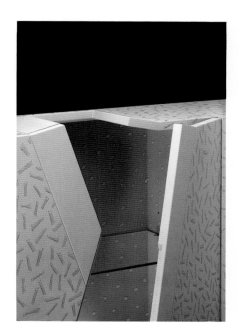

Other sculptural objects for sale include modestly priced lamps and accessories. Slides available for $5. Dealers welcome.

# Some Reflections on Furniture

American art furniture seems to be coming of age. Or, at least, it is expressing its self-confidence, a sure sign of maturity.

Despite the evident talent of so many of its makers, furniture has been the most reluctant of the contemporary crafts in finding a unified identity and a large audience. There are at least four reasons for this.

First there has been and there remains a dearth of critical dialogue within the field. Without a regular forum to provide for a free exchange between artists and critics, the evolution of ideas is slower and more halting. In a world where information flows almost instantaneously, the absence of a national, professional organization and its concomitant literature fosters a kind of isolation and a lack of cross-fertilization evident in no other genre.

Second, furniture making may well be the most labor intensive of the contemporary crafts. Even with assistance, a single piece can take months to complete. Thus, while a fine ceramist can make dozens of pieces in a year, refining his skills dramatically in the process, the four or ten pieces made by the furniture maker in the same time frame means a considerably slower development. This affects the entire field, which is thus slower to mature.

Third, the slowness of the creation process and the high cost of maintaining a woodworking studio forces the artist to sell every piece he or she produces. Particularly at the outset, the artist has too much invested in a single work to hold it in inventory or in a personal "archive." Where the glass, clay, or fiber artist has the luxury of building a repository of past work for personal study and growth, the furniture artist can ill-afford even the space necessary to house his or her work. Most furniture makers have to depend on their photo albums for self-criticism.

Fourth, the fact that furniture remains more strictly tied to use than other media promotes a reliance on the client as patron that few contemporary artists relish. Furniture makers were initially reluctant to embrace the commission opportunity and master the considerable skills necessary for the completion of successful projects.

Today, however, the furniture commission is alive and well as artists rise to the challenge of making their own viewpoints suit their clients' specifications. And so, too, is the art furniture movement alive. The wide variety of furniture styles and interpretations included in this year's GUILD offers clear evidence that the field is growing and maturing despite the inherent obstacles. From whimsy to contemporary interpretation of classic idioms, the level of accomplishment and professionalism remains a tribute to this still evolving medium. Both client and artist can only prosper by joining forces.

**Vanessa S. Lynn**
**Writer/Critic**
**New York, New York**

# John Lewis Glass Studio

**1681 Eighth Street**
**Oakland, CA 94607**
**(415) 893-3224**

The John Lewis Glass Studio creates cast glass sculptures and functional pieces such as tables and benches, which are rendered in a variety of shapes, forms, textures, and colors.

During its 20 years in business, the studio has completed a number of commissions for private and corporate clients, and is represented internationally by galleries and art consultants.

Commissioned works can be delivered in three to six months depending on the scale of the project. Sculptural pieces range from $2,500-7,500; tables and benches range from $7,500-15,000.

Further information is available upon request.

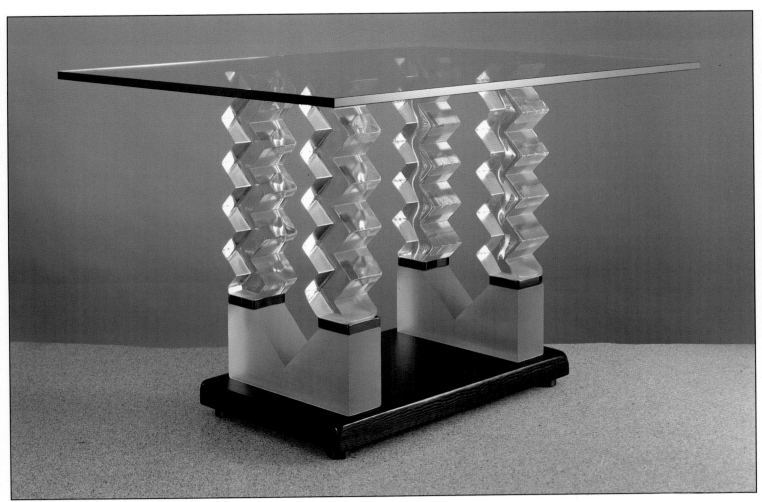

# Monte Lindsley

**Ptarmigan Willow**
P.O. Box 551
Fall City, WA 98024
(206) 392-5767

Monte Lindsley has been designing contemporary willow furniture since 1978. His work has been shown nationally and featured in magazines and newspapers.

Educated as a landscape designer and a forester. He incorporates his love of plants and nature into his work.

His works are constructed in limited individual editions. All his materials are native to the Northwest. Monte personally hand selects, gathers and prepares his materials.

One of Montes goals is to create a more eloquent contemporary look to a traditional craft form. This he achieves through his flowing loop designs and use of specially selected materials. His work consists of bark, peeled and color finishes.

Contact the artist for a brochure. Delivery time runs 4-6 months.

(Top left) Peeled willow mountain forest bed.
(Bottom left) Peeled willow dining set.
(Top right) Peeled willow bed.
(Center right) Bark willow headboard.
(Bottom right) Peeled willow gazebo bed.
Photography by Clark Fisher.

# Mack & Rodel Cabinetmakers

**Kevin Patrick Rodel**
**Susan Catherine Mack**
**Leighton Road**
**Pownal, ME 04069**
**(207) 688-4483**

Mack & Rodel Cabinetmakers, a husband and wife team with over ten years of experience, is committed to the creation of excellent furniture using traditional joinery techniques. Each one-of-a-kind piece is built to the exact specifications of their clients. Scale drawings and prices are finalized before construction is begun. Prices will vary with each piece but generally start around $3,000. Brochure and price list are available upon request.

(Top) Bow-front dresser, cherry, curly-maple and bone. 41″×21″×40½″h.
(Bottom) Queen-Anne desk, cherry, 60″×32″×30″h.

# Bruce MacPhail

**Highland Woodworks**
**Box 22**
**South Strafford, VT 05070**
**(802) 785-4364**

Custom and production pieces.
*Guild* 1, 2, and 4 show my work, or write or
call for a brochure.

(Top right) Queen-size maple bed.
(Bottom) Maple table with 3 leaves to seat 12
persons.

How to write about
These strong young ash?
Their fine wrinkled skin
Dusted with softness
  Dappled with light?
Young elephants
Stride swiftly
Long-legged and silent
Through this northern forest.
  The older ash remain,
  Root-knotted,
  Shade-makers,
  Good for boards.

bgm

# Malakoff & Jones

**Peter Malakoff and Norman Jones**
**Schoonmaker Building**
**10 Liberty Ship Way #4139**
**Sausalito, CA 94965**
**(415) 332-7471**
**(415) 332-2481 FAX**

Peter Malakoff and Norman Jones have designed and built art cabinetry and furniture in the San Francisco area for the past eight years. With their knowledge and appreciation of both ancient and foreign cultures, they demonstrate in their work a distinctive interplay between craft and fine art, with a sensitive attention to detail.

They welcome innovative commissions from the architectural, corporate and private worlds.

Pictures of "Egypto-Deco Pharaoh Cabinet," inspired by objects found in Tutankhamun's tomb. Privately commissioned. Completed 1/8/89. 120"w. (180" w. open) × 90"h. × 28"d. Materials: Sycamore, satinwood, ebony, ivory, gold, lacquer

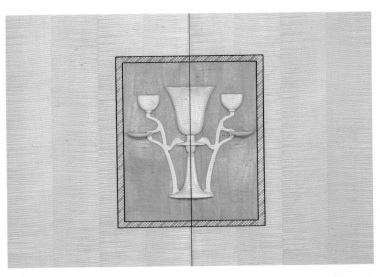

# Jonathan I. Mandell

24 Walnut Hill
Ardmore, PA 19003
(215) 896-6216

Jonathan Mandell creates a stone-like finish on his modular components. The look fits in well with Southwestern or other contemporary decors. As pictured, wall units can be designed to fit any space, from individual pieces through entire rooms. If desired, the components can be equipped with drawers and/or doors. The use of this process is limited only by the imagination of the client. Examples of applications are pedestals, tables, lamps, head frames for beds, desks, dining room tables. The finish is available in a wide range of colors.

Work is priced at $114.00 per sq. ft. with additional fees for lighting, etc.

Jonathan Mandell has a Master of Fine Arts degree from the University of Pennsylvania.

# Jeffry Mann

P.O. Box 3420
Aspen, CO 81611
(303) 925-8651

Jeffry Mann designs furniture using selected, dramatic wood from around the world. His pieces are sculptured and functional. Each is a delight to the eye, the hand, and the body as it is experienced visually, tactilely, and kinesthetically.

He is known for his rocking chairs but welcomes inquiries on commissions of all kinds. Rocking chairs range in price from $2500 to $4000, according to materials and design. Commissions require from 3 to 12 months.

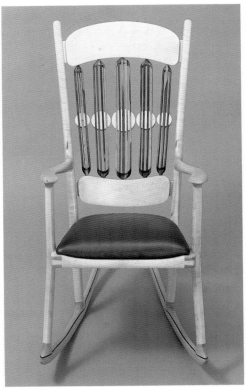

# Peter Maynard

**Peter Maynard and Associates**
**P.O. Box 77, Main Street**
**South Acworth, NH 03607**
**(603) 835-2969**

Peter Maynard is a master furnituremaker. His work integrates a classic sense of proportion with functional simplicity. And this can be applied within a broad range of furniture styles, and the design of architectural ornamentation, facades and detailed interiors.

Whatever furniture style or architectural context is desired, Peter can create it—executing a one-of-a-kind piece that blends harmoniously into the existing environment or developing the entire atmosphere of a room or office.

(Top left) Chinese table, handcarved in solid rosewood.
(Top right) Pembroke table in solid butternut with various inlays.
(Below) Contemporary solid cherry tables, (in front) table with rosewood inlaid drawer, (in back) table in trestle style.

All inquiries welcomed.

# John McAlevey

**Mill Street**
**Warner, NH 03278**
**(603) 456-2135**

John McAlevey designs and builds fine furniture in his studio in Warner, NH. His furniture is made from domestic and imported hardwoods. A variety of finishes are available and while John usually prefers an oil finish he will help you choose one appropriate to your requirements.

John McAlevey draws upon an extensive knowledge of woodworking design and traditional joinery to convey a strength of line and an attention to detail in his work.

Residential and corporate commissions are accepted. The time from initial contact to delivery can be from 3-6 months, depending upon the size of the commission.

Blanket chest ebonized mahogany 16"h. × 26" × 16".

Folding screen left, cherry right, walnut 66"h. × 56"l.

# Neophile, Inc.

**1239 Broadway**
**New York, NY 10001**
**(212) 213-9313**

Neophile (nē·ō·fīl) a lover of the new.

Eric Bergman started Neophile in 1984. The studio produces a comprehensive line of furniture, lighting and decorative accessories. Bergman and his staff draw decorative elements from design styles of the past and apply them in ways that give their work an unmistakable look. All of the pieces are hand-made and hand-painted with durable acrylic enamels, making them suitable for all interior environments. Glass designs are cut and sand-blasted in-house. Each piece is dated and signed with the Neophile signature.

Brochure and price list are available upon request. Delivery time ranges from 6-8 weeks. Custom colors are available on most pieces. Commissions for residential and commercial installations as well as display and special events props are welcomed.

# Darragh Pechanec

P.O. Box 4706
Chicago, CA 95927
(916) 345-1644

Boat designer and shipwright, with a strong background in metal and wood, Darragh incorporates his skills as a craftsman and artist to create a nearly uncanny diversity of design.

Slumped glass, cut granite and marble garnish Darragh's designs forged from solid steel, cast bronze, silver and gold.

Commissions are completed in forty-five working days.

Additional slides and pricing information available on request for $15.00. (Refundable on purchase).
(Top right) Steel chair, 21"w × 25"d × 43"h
(Bottom right) Kitchen work table, solid forged steel & 3/4" glass, 24"w × 48"d × 37"h.
(Bottom left) Kitchen work table, top granite on 3/4" glass, 25"w × 35$8ind × 43"h.

# Norman Petersen

**350 Treat Avenue**
**San Francisco, CA 94110**
**415/431-1100**

Furniture, especially chairs, is like a canvas for three-dimensional expression. Function happens because I am designing furniture, but the visual result is the most important thing for me.

Norman Petersen will accept commissions for both interior and outdoor pieces. At present he is working on a series of desks and tables. His work has been shown in galleries throughout the U.S. and is in the permanent collection of the San Francisco Museum of Modern Art. Contact Norman Petersen's studio for information on pricing and current exhibitions.

born 1941

Stanford University, Academy of Art in in Minich, San Francisco Art Institute

1966–79 Designer, Teacher, Builder in California and France

1979–present, designs and builds furniture in his San Francisco studio.

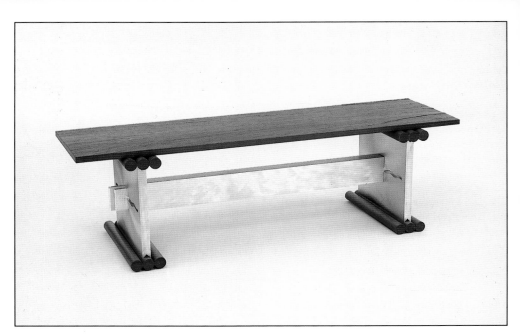

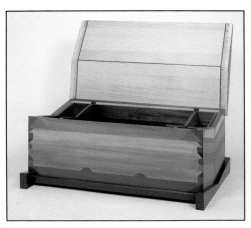

# Norman Petersen

**350 Treat Avenue**
**San Francisco, CA 94110**
**415/431-1100**

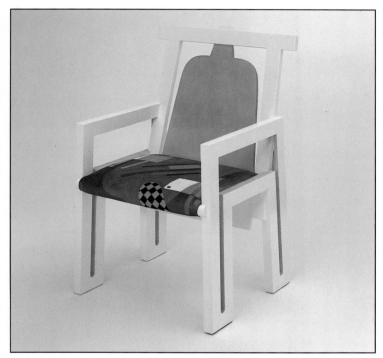

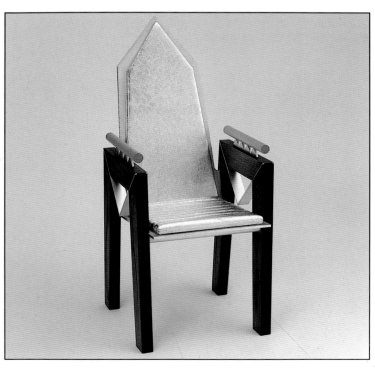

# Ronald C. Puckett

4012 Monticello St.
Richmond, VA 23227
(804) 264-2411

". . .if I had to describe Ron Puckett's work in one word it would be 'handsome'".
—Bebe Pritam Johnson
　Gallery owner
　Pritam & Eames
　East Hampton, NY

Using strong architectural influences and touches of history, Ron Puckett has been designing and building fine furniture for individuals and corporate clients for 15 years.

Puckett has been featured in *Southern Accents, Interior Design, Interiors* and *Metropolitan Home* in the past year. His work has been exhibited in Philadelphia, Washington and New York. He was a contributing artist in the American Craft Museum Auction, selected to participate in the Ziff-Stafford residence, and was a Merit Winner in the Kraus-Sike 2nd American Crafts Awards.

(Below) "Savannah" Lacewood, padouk, stained cherry 32"H × 52"W × 18"D

"Ocean Drive Drawers" Lacewood, wenge, ash
36"H × 52"W × 22"D

"Churchill Cabinet" Bubinga, wenge, ash
6'6"H × 44"W × 22"D

# Bert Ray, A.I.A.

**2472 Bolsover Suite 345**
**Houston, TX 77005**
**Phone (713) 528-5062**

As an architect, Bert Ray approaches the art of wood inlay as rich patterning to enhance an environment.

Working with unstained woods, both exotic and commonplace, he creates one of a kind surfaces for commercial and residential applications: paneling, tabletops, headboards, and screens. A palette of woods from a specific region of the U.S. or the world may be requested.

The work is a personal interpretation of age old techniques of wood inlay, marquetry and tunbridgeware. Each surface is meticulously crafted with veneers created by hand by the artist—as many as 4,000 pieces per square foot. Accents of semiprecious stones or metals may be included.

Collaboration to accomodate client themes or motifs is acceptable. Prices and schedules on request.

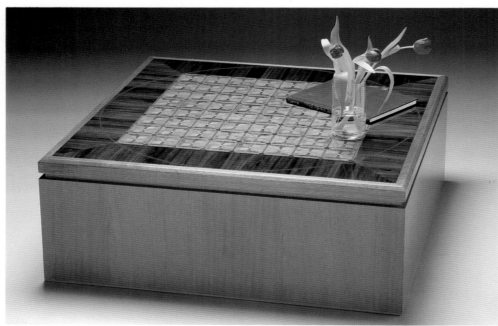

# Carolyn Sale

**Carolyn Sale Ceramic Sculpture**
P.O. Box 78093
San Francisco, CA 94107
(415) 495-6411

Ceramic table bases designed and hand crafted by California artist Carolyn Sale are the ultimate in artistic furniture.

These unique tables strike a perfect balance of contemporary design and function. They capture a full range of colors that are softly blended with each other through a variety of air-brushing techniques. An exterior transparent glaze adds durability.

Delightfully elegant, these sculptural tables are a dramatic addition to any home or office.

Production time is approximately 12 weeks. Prices begin at $2,000.

# Wm. B. Sayre, Inc.

**One Cottage Street**
**Easthampton, MA 01027**
**(413) 527-0202**
**(413) 527-0502 Fax**

Fine commissioned furniture executed to the designs of specifying architect, interior designer, or residential customer.

Working in the finest hardwoods available, collaborating in a wide range of other media to produce heirlooms of distinction and innovation.

Full design services available. Complete production facilities.

Brochure available upon request.

© 1989 Wm. B. Sayre, Inc.   Jatoba.   Designed by Wm. Sayre.

Leather on-lay in Nigerian goat leather.

# Martha Sears

263 Concord Rd.
Longmeadow, MA 01106
(413) 567-7433

Martha Sears creates provocative table sculptures using mixed media- ceramics, laminated wood and glass. Visually intriguing and challenging one's sense of balance yet structurally sound. Her pieces range from coffee tables to runners to conference tables.

Martha Sears' indoor/outdoor architectural pieces are an enticing palatte of primitive and rustic qualities with strong modernistic characteristics.

Prices range from 1500.00-5000.00

A portfolio is available upon request. Commissions are accepted.

(Top left) "Table Study I", mixed media, 41"×8"×10"
(Top right) Detail: Table Study I
(Bottom)"Yes, It's Level II", mixed media, 30"×4'×8'

# Gregory Sheres

**Greg Sheres Studio**
**1710 W. 23rd Street**
**Miami Beach, FL 33140**
**(305) 858-5577**

Greg Sheres brings fine art to furniture. For a canvas, the artist uses such materials as emerald pearl granite imported from Sweden and travertine marble imported from Italy. Every table is cut by the artist's own hand; an original painting is then applied to the stone, and then finished with lasting layers of acrylic resin. Heavy stainless steel is then shaped, molded and welded to form a one of a kind base as inspired by the table top.

The artist works closely with clients to incorporate their custom specifications.

Allow 2–3 months for completion of project.

Brochure available upon request.

Prices range from $1,900–$11,000.

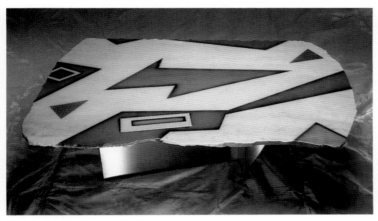

Travertine cocktail table; 60″ × 36″ × 17″

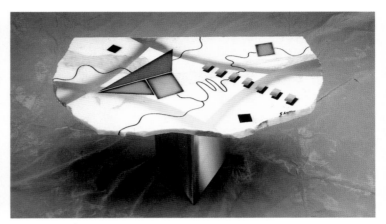

White marble end table; 32″ × 22″ × 19″

Granite cocktail table; 68″ × 38″ × 17″

# Spadone • Rieger

**Furniture Design**
**53 Summer Street**
**Kennebunk, ME 04043**
**207-985-7214**

The partnership of Spadone • Rieger, design and produce furniture for both the residential and corporate environment. Their one-of-a-kind and limited production commissions are generated from a design fee, which address the specific requirements and budget parameters.

With educational backgrounds in furniture design and Architecture, Peter and Stephen display a wide range of skills and versatility which enables them to work with architects, interior designers, furniture manufacturers and individual clients.

Each year Spadone • Rieger exhibit their work at major craft shows in N.Y.C. and display work in galleries along the east coast.

A brochure and portfolio information is available upon request.

# Bill Stankus

611 Bradford Parkway
DeWitt, NY 13224
(315) 446-6761

Bill Stankus is an American craftsman whose designs are imbued with the beauty and strength of the best traditional joinery. Disdaining mass-production techniques, Stankus works with an intuitive understanding which transfigures the original materials.

Unique traditional and contemporary pieces are executed in the finest manner and enriched by his ideals and reverence. Ever cognizant, his client's personality and preferences are always given the utmost consideration.

Prices begin under $1,000. Most orders can be met within eight weeks after design approval.

For more information, contact Bill at his workshop.

(Top) End tables, walnut; bowl, mahogany, oak, walnut
(Bottom left) Chair, walnut, zebrawood
(Bottom right) Game table with reversible top, walnut, ebony, maple

# Thomas W. Stender

**9339 Boston State Road**
**Boston, NY 14025**
**(716) 941-6388**

Thomas W. Stender makes one-of-a-kind and limited edition hardwood furniture. Distinguished by their sensual and lyrical forms as well as by their gestural qualities, his award-winning designs have been exhibited nationwide. He collaborates with architects and interior designers to furnish specific environments.

Prices begin about $1000. Price list and current slides available on request.

(Top) "Wave Goodbye," hall table, curly maple and cherry,12½"w × 61"l × 31½"h, edition limited to one hundred.
(Bottom) "Canilune" chair, padouk, birdseye maple, lacewood, 52½"h, edition limited to two hundred

# The Century Guild

Nick Strange
P.O. Box 13128
Research Triangle Park, NC 27709
(919) 598-1612

By commission: design, fabrication, installation of exceptional contemporary or traditional pieces for corporate, residential, ecclesiastical spaces. Brochures available upon request.

Examples in the gothic style: solid mahogany queen-size four-poster ($7,500.00); architect-designed sanctuary chairs ($9,500.00 the set); tabernacle, 28″ high by 21″ wide ($5,000.00).

# Ford Thomas

**Benchworks**
**108 Main Street**
**Baton Rouge, LA 70801**
**(504) 336-9762**

Suitable for residential or corporate environments, the furniture crafted by Ford Thomas has been commissioned by individuals, designers and architects for more than ten years. Thomas graphically communicates his ideas in a realistic manner which makes the client feel secure from the beginning of the project to the end product. All installations are done by the craftsman, when shipping is not appropriate. Versatile, durable, and guaranteed, the one-of-a-kind or limited edition pieces start at $500 retail. A complete color photograph or slide portfolio with price list is available upon request. Commissions or collaborations are welcome.

(Top left) Two Drawer Desk. Figured Walnut, Swiss Pearwood, Ebony Inlay. 30"×60"×29". (Top right) Chair With Free-Edge. Cherry. (Available without free-edge) 20"×21"×36". (Bottom) Up-Leaf Table. Maple with Walnut Hinges. 48"×72"×29" (Open) 24"×72"×30" (Closed).

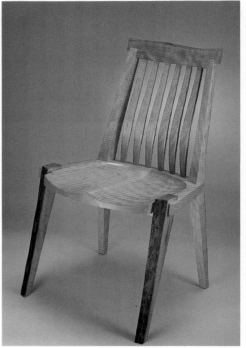

# Vaunt Limited

**Misty Todd-Slack**
5135 Ballard Avenue NW
Seattle, WA 98107
206-782-0133

Vaunt Limited uses a combination of natural and man-made materials including various metals, wood, glass, and plastics to create a classic yet contemporary line of furniture, suitable for contract or residential settings. Crafted with careful attention to detail, they require minimal care. Custom or limited production pieces are available.

Price varies depending on size and materials used. Photographs and delivery schedules available on request. Consultations and collaborations are welcome.

Table/desk: Birdseye maple, patinated steel, burnished stainless (72"l × 30"h × 42"w). Hanging drawer systems are avail. for desks.

Credenza. Birdseye maple, patinated steel, burnished stainless (30"h × 22"w × 60"l).

# Larry Alan White

**August Anonymous Studios**
**1825 Rodriguez**
**Santa Cruz, CA 95062**
**(408) 476-3269**

Larry Alan White's ability to envision and craft contemporary, functional objects of art has earned him the respect and praise of both clients and peers.

A seven-year apprenticeship with preeminent woodworker Sam Maloof influenced White's background in fine arts. His most widely known pieces dramatize an extraordinary balance of mediums—unique combinations of domestic and foreign hardwoods, elegantly coupled with aluminum, copper, glass and other unexpected materials.

With projects ranging from jewelry and furniture to the building of custom homes, White is equally comfortable as sole designer or as a team collaborator.

His work has been exhibited nationally and is included in both private and public collections.

(Top) Tri-Point Series #4, 24"w. × 16"h., wenge, ebony, Osage orange, aluminum. (Bottom) Tri-Point Series #6, 24" × 16"h., wenge, ebony, blood wood, Osage orange, aluminum.

# Floor Coverings and Textiles

# Allegro Rug Weaving Company

Sally Vowell Gurley
512 Main Street, 13th Floor
Ft. Worth, TX 76102
(817) 877-4776

Sally Gurley and the Allegro studio weavers offer quality with design and color flexibility to meet your personal and spatial needs. Select a One-of-a-kind rug, choose from the Studio Line, or a combination of the two.

All rugs are weaved with 100% wool, New Zealand Romney and Engish Carpet wool blended for quality, durability, and resiliency. All colors are custom dyed at Allegro with natural dyes. Size is unlimited. The maximum unseamed width is 10 feet.

Contact Allegro for a complete brochure, price list, and yarn cards.

Sample sets are available. Strike-offs and computer images may be ordered.

(Top) "Welcome", One-of-a-kind Rug, 4'6"×12'6"
(Bottom left) "Re-200", Allegro Studio Line Rug
(Bottom right) Allegro Studio Line Twill, full scale texture

# Art Underfoot, Inc.

**Cathy Comins, president**
**12 Godfrey Road**
**Upper Montclair, NJ 07043**
**(201) 744-4171**

Art Underfoot offers a remarkable collection of American handmade rugs and tapestries for those seeking exceptional artistic statements for the floor and walls. This distinguished private service features exquisite, <u>newly-made</u> traditionally hooked area rugs ($85-265 per sq. ft.); vibrant, custom <u>room-size</u> braided ($37-54 per sq. ft.) and woven rag rugs ($28-43 per sq. ft.); and modern, abstract tapestries ($150-555 per sq. ft.).

The collection represents over seventy folk and fine fiber artists, encompassing hundreds of originally-designed, patterned, and commissionable works, several of which have been featured in *House & Garden* and *Country Living*. Art Underfoot can provide technical specifications and the personal history of each carpet, custom-design services, quality padding, archival mounting, and conservation information.

Please <u>call</u> for a brochure, investment profiles, photographs, and the assurance of individualized attention.

"Halsa," (detail) traditionally hooked rug, Theresa Strack 1982

"Charlton Idyll," traditionally hooked rug, © Jule M. Smith 1986, hand-dyed wool fabric, 44"×77"

Braided rugs, © Jan Jurta 1988, wool, 7' round, 5'×3' ovals

"Rhyme & Reason," woven rag rug, © Harriet Giles 1987, cotton/cotton-blends, 10'×14'

# Pamela Bracci
# Kathy James

BRACCI and JAMES
**Bracci**
81 Hamilton Avenue
Haverhill, MA 01830
(508) 374-4955

**James**
81 Sherwood Forest
Exeter, NH 03833
(603) 778-3885

Bracci and James offer you a ready-made collaboration in their handpainted and hand-woven fabrics. Separately, each one's fabrics are classic, contemporary and richly colored, but collaboratively they are an unbeatable combination. Since they enjoy their collaboration, they welcome commissions for custom designed fabrics and collaborations with other artists who use fabric in their work. The special feature of handmade cloth is the flexibility it offers in design and color, and when you begin with two fabrics that have already been designed to work together, you increase your visual variety.

Both are graduates of the Program in Artisanry, when it was at Boston University. Bracci has been doing design work for the Frank Lloyd Wright Foundation and James' cloth is in the permanent collection of the Appalachian Center for Crafts in Tennessee. Additional information on fabrics and pricing are available by writing or calling Pamela Bracci or Kathy James.

# Carolyn and Vincent Carleton

**Carleton Designs**
**1015A Greenwood Road**
**Elk, CA 95432**
**(707) 877-3540**

Fine American Handmade Rugs

Carleton Designs has offered custom hand-dyeing and handweaving to designers, collectors, and architects for the past ten years. Their studio produces the only hand Jacquard woven carpets in the U.S. today. Retail price is $128 per square foot with net terms available to the trade.

Major commissions: Roger Baugh, New York; Kohler Corp., Wisconsin; Intradesign, Los Angeles; Brunswig Building, Chicago; Rita St. Clair, Baltimore; Richard Himmel, Chicago.

Awards and Exhibitions: American Craft Museum, St. Louis Center for the Visual Arts, Sacramento 'California Works', ROSCOE Product Design Award for Best Contemporary Rug.

Publications: Architectural Digest, Interior Design, House Beautiful, American Craft.

(Top left and right) Inverse sides of "Saf", 9' × 13'
(Bottom) Detail of "Flamestitch", 12' × 14'.

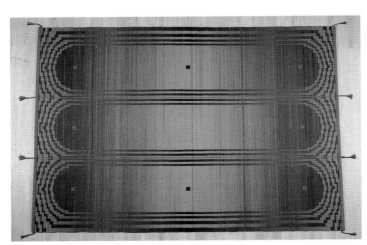 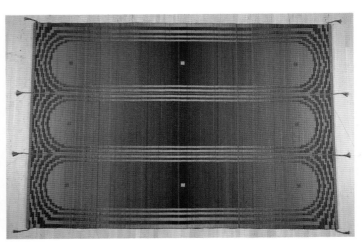

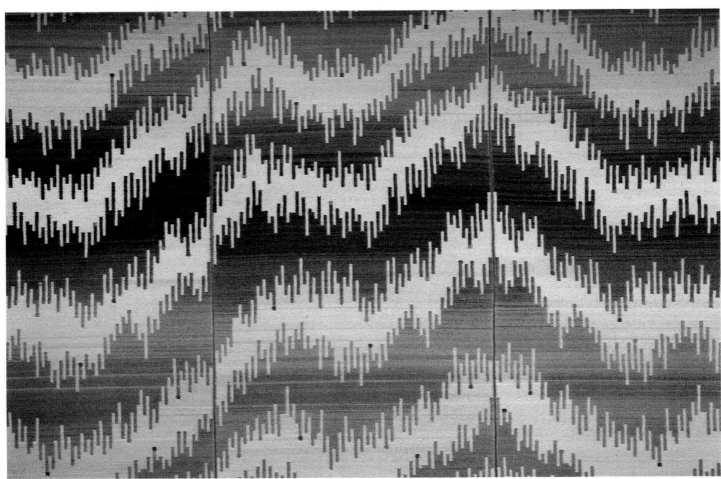

# Kathy Cooper

**Orchard House Floorcloths**
**Rt. 5 Box 214**
**King, NC 27021**
**(919) 994-2612**

Kathy Cooper specializes in custom designed floorcloths. Large sizes are available and priced per square foot. Cooper uses a wide range of imagery in her work including abstract, floral and whimsical depictions of animals and vegetables.

Floorcloths are intended for practical use on hard-surface floors, or may be hung on walls. Made of heavy canvas, each floorcloth is hand-painted and receives several coats of varnish for a durable, yet flexible, surface.

Colors will not fade. Floorcloths can be cleaned with mild soap and a damp sponge or mop. Periodic waxing is recommended to protect the varnish.

Cooper's canvases have been featured in New York magazine, Country Living, House Beautiful, Metropolitan Home, Better Homes and Gardens Decorating and Country Homes.

A catalog is available.
"Diagonal Checks with Confetti Center"
© 1988 7' × 9' Private residence,
Winston-Salem, N.C.

# Martha Cropper

**Rags to Riches**
**437 Murphy Street**
**Murphysboro, IL 62966**
**(618) 687-3753**

Martha Cropper is one of the few contemporary folk artists still using traditional methods to produce hand woven rag rugs. She weaves recycled fabrics on antique looms to produce heirloom quality rugs for traditional and contemporary settings. This dedication to traditional production methods produces exceptional quality and durability. Rugs are priced by the square foot, (starting at $10/square foot), depending on the complexity of the piece. Samples are woven for each custom rug, with the final product completed after client approval.

(Below) Corduroy Christmas plaid; (right) denim and pastel hit-n-miss.

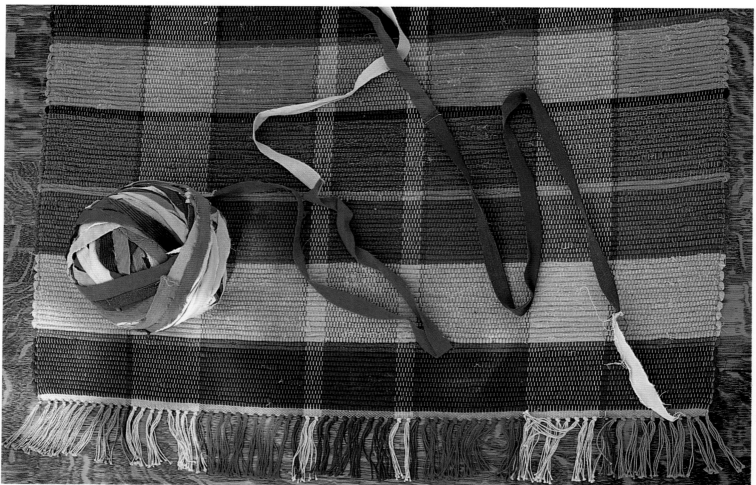

168

# Gloria E. Crouse

**Fiber Art**
4325 John Luhr Rd., N.E.
Olympia, WA 98506
(206) 491-1980

Gloria Crouse creates highly textured art rugs and dimensional wall pieces using variations of hand hooking and sculpting. Unique combinations of metal, plastic, paint with yarn and yardage add further contrasts in these floor and wall-pieces. Recent works emphasize irregular, asymmetric forms, often in two or more adjustable sections or three-dimensional wall sculptures.

Her work has been exhibited nationally and internationally for 20 years and has been part of many private and public collections including Weyerhaeuser; SAFECO Insurance; Sea-Tac International Airport; Pacific Northwest Bell; and Sea-First National.

Prices for commissioned works average $100–$150 per sq. ft. (wholesale). Allow a minimum of three months for delivery. A portfolio of works is available for $5 (refundable).

(Top) "Executive" — 6½' × 7½',
Hooked/Sculpted Wools on Linen; Latex backed
(Bottom)"Pieces of Nine" —
6½'h. × 58"w. × 2"d.; Hooked/Sculpted
Wool/Silver Metallic

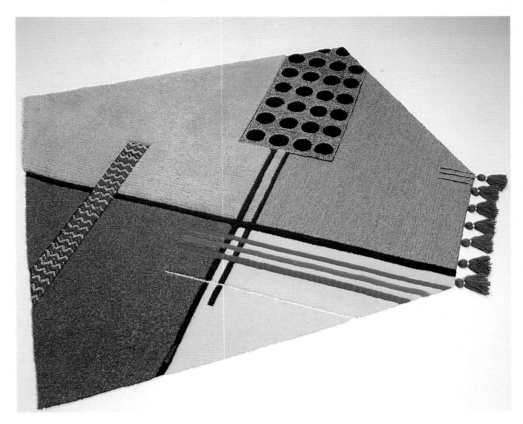

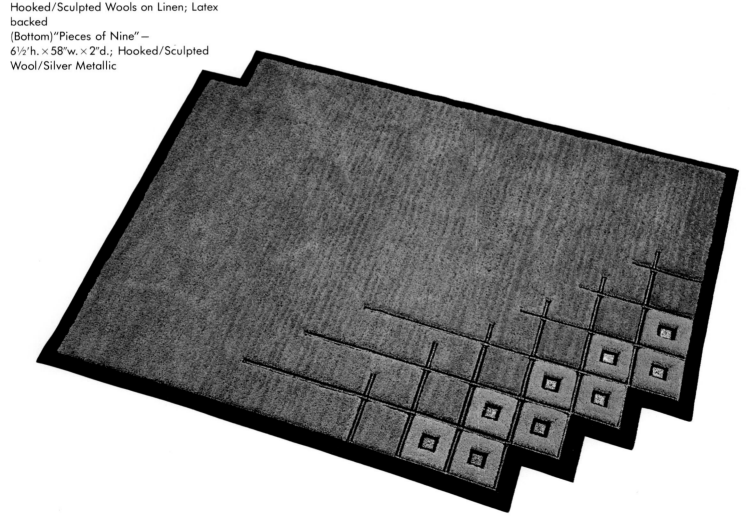

# Anne Lanford Dalton

**Designer/Artist in Fiber**
**1312 Shenna Blvd.**
**Fort Worth, TX 76114**
**(817) 625-9558**

Dyed and handwoven silks in washes of color are the specialty of Anne Lanford Dalton. Applications of Dalton's silks range from large sculptural fiber art installations, to upholstery and interiors textiles, to production lines.

Dalton earned a Master of Fine Arts Degree in Fibers/Printed Textiles from Texas Woman's University and has 16 years experience weaving and dyeing. Her minor field of study during postgraduate work was interior design.

Working from design problem, to concept, to presentation, sampling, and approval, to completed project, Dalton develops custom designs to address client needs, including custom palettes. Every project is completed with care and expertise.

Pricing, delivery, and terms are determined by the size and scope of a project. Please inquire regarding custom projects, works available, and production lines.

"Convexo-Concave" 8'h. × 8'w. Dyed silk, handwoven

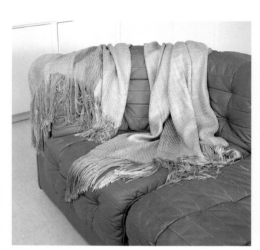

Detail of silk table runner, bottom left

170

# EKO

**Ellen Kochansky**
**1237 Mile Creek Road**
**Pickens, SC 29671**
**(803) 868-9749**

Years of experience in the fiber arts enhance Ellen Kochansky's new line of quilts and related accessories. She specializes in rich variations of color, texture and pattern, developing a contemporary interpretation of a traditional art.

Fabrics are predominantly cotton, but accent materials are an assortment of fibers and blends. Most of the fabrics are stain resistant and designed for interior furnishing. Dry cleaning is recommended. Workmanship is fully guaranteed for one year from date of purchase.

Seven styles are available, with new introductions anticipated seasonally. Retail prices range from $390 (twin comforter) to $560 (king comforter). Spread length (21" drop) is also available. Allow 4-6 weeks for delivery. Pillow shams, throws, and yardage may be ordered. Call or write for a color brochure.

(top left) "Dreams"
(top right) "Wine"
(bottom left) "Canyon"
(bottom right) "Snow"

Blake Praytor

**171**

# Arlyn Ende

Route 1, Box 25
Bradyville, TN 37026
(615) 765-5682

Graphic style, witty illusionism and elegant craftsmanship are the spirit and substance of Arlyn Ende's inventive approach to hooking. Her richly colored rugs and tapetas are as engaging to the eye as the sculpted surfaces are inviting to the touch.

With the capacity to handle commissions of virtually any size, the artist collaborates with individual clients and design professionals for specific spaces. She also makes available several limited edition designs.

Arlyn Ende was awarded Grand Prize in the 1989 American Crafts Awards for her hooked rug "Tidal Pools", pictured in GUILD 4. Her textiles are exhibited nationally and are included in numerous corporate and private collections in the U.S.

Price range is $2,000 to $20,000

(Right) "Motif 2", 6′×7′ © 1989. Collection: Mr. & Mrs. Gary Dryden
(Below) "The Ort Rug" for the dining room, 15′8″×9′6″ © 1989. Collection: Alice Zimmerman and Sanford Ross

# Laurie Ann Kovack

**Textile Design**
540 1st Avenue South #204
Seattle, WA 98104
(206) 621-8577

Classic designer fabrics are woven rich in color, texture, pattern and creativity.

Commissioned textiles are designed to integrate with their architectural setting, and to meet the design goals of the client. Collaboration with a design team is welcomed.

A full range of woven textiles are produced for interiors. These include rugs, banners, and accessories. Yardage is a specialty, for upholstery and window treatments.

The highest quality materials are used, primarily wool, silk, linen, and cotton. Regular maintenance by vacuuming and dry cleaning will ensure long life.

Yardage begins at $30 a square foot. Standard delivery is three months from design approval.

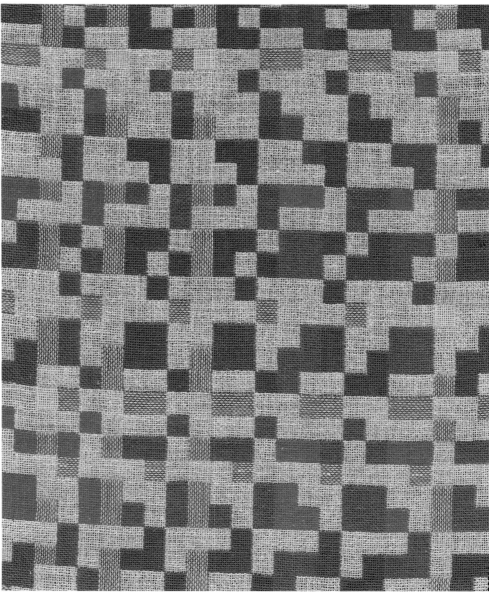

# Martha Donovan Opdahl

714 Highridge Avenue
Greencastle, IN 46135
(317) 653-4052
(317) 658-4345

Martha Opdahl's abstract images are elegantly composed tufted carpets and tapestries. Her penchant is for large scale, painterly compositions depicting complex spatial relationships. A unique palette of hand-dyed mottled hues and *ikated* color dots distinguish her work.

An M.F.A. graduate from Indiana University (1985), Opdahl exhibits nationwide. Recent awards include Indiana Arts Commission grants. Her work is in numerous private and corporate collections.

Premium materials—New Zealand wool—and painstaking craftsmanship characterize her work. Commissions are $250 per sq. ft. Allow 4-6 weeks for completion of a 7' × 7' piece (see *Midsummer Medley*, top; *Chromatic Fugue*, bottom). Prices/slides of available work upon request.

Galleries representing Opdahl are Helen Drutt, New York and Philadelphia; Hodges Taylor, Charlotte, NC; Patrick King Contemporary Art, Indianapolis; and Pro-Art, St. Louis.

# Jan Paul

**Textures by Jan**
**13050 N.E. 112th Street**
**Kirkland, WA 98033**
**(206) 822-9480**

Jan Paul designs and weaves one of a kind rugs using unusual fibers including sheepskin, leather and cotton or wool fabrics. Rugs may be flat woven or pile and two or more materials may be combined in the same rug.

Prices range from $60 to $250 per sq. ft. depending on materials and technique, with a $200 design fee. Most work is by commission.

Internationally exhibited, Paul has won numerous awards and is represented in public and private collections through out the world.

(Top right) Cotton and leather pile rug, 4½' × 7½'
(Bottom right) "Milford Track", woven sheepskin rug, 5' × 8'
(Bottom left) "Rug of Many Coats", leather pile rug, 3' × 5'

# Sissi Siska

154 Second Street
Hoboken, NJ 07030
(201) 963-9673

Inspired by the contrast of city life and tropical utopias, Sissi creates paintings on silk. Her unique creations combine ancient batik and modern resist methods. This perfect blend of artistic tradition and contemporary sensibility adds drama to any environment.

An award winning artist, Sissi has twenty years experience designing textiles and has been shown world-wide. Her work was exhibited at Artpark in Lewiston, N.Y. during a recent residency, where a large environmental painting was produced on-site.

Sissi designs large-scale pieces and wall hangings on commission to meet the specifications of private, corporate or architectural settings. Smaller paintings feature museum quality framing.

Further information and current exhibition schedules available upon request; work may also be viewed by appointment.

(top) "Leland's Garden" 30" × 32"
(bottom) "Butterflies" detail, 20" × 20"

# Sheree White Sorrells

**Whitewoven Handweaving Studio**
**201½ North Main Street**
**Waynesville, NC 28786**
**(704) 452-1864**

Sheree White Sorrells produces area rugs in original and traditional designs, and accepts rug commissions for private and commercial interiors.

Custom samples are available within job specifics for refundable $75-$125. Rug sizes may vary in length, with eight feet maximum width without seams. Square foot price $16-$32; production time average one to three months, custom color-matching in all natural fibers 15-30%. Client offered final approval on price and design before production, contract required.

Professional portfolio available for $60.00, refundable on first commission. Inquiries welcomed without obligation.

# Linda Hali Zucker

185 Front Street
Fair Haven, CT 06513
203-865-8990

Linda Hali Zucker designs and executes the spirited graphics and gemlike colors of Z Studio silk products using fiber reactive dyes with gutta serti.

These products range from one-of-a-kind works, such as folding screens and frameable fabric pieces, to limited edition scarves, throws, tablecloths, and pillows. Z Studio fabrics are meticulously handpainted.

All silk qualities may be washed or drycleaned.

Prices range from $75–$3,000. Descriptive price lists and silk quality swatches available on request. Commissions and Custom orders accepted with estimate and leadtime submitted per job.

(Top) "Still Life Border" cloth, 45" × 45" crepe back satin
(Bottom) "Zebra Party" reversible folding screen, each panel 6'h. × 23"w., fabric: shantung dupioni, frame: laquered pine

# Tapestries

# Carol Atleson

465 Ruskin Rd.
Amherst, NY 14226
(716) 834-9384

For over twelve years Carol Atleson has been weaving imaginary landscapes wonderfully rich in color and texture. Her unique inlay weavings explore relationships of color and space, evoking feelings of places remembered or imagined. Tightly woven, the fused double layer tapestries are exceptionally durable and easy to install and maintain. They have been exhibited nationally and have been chosen for residential, corporate and public spaces.

Commissioned works, available in single or multiple panels of variable lengths, can accommodate any size and color specifications. A minimum of two months is required from the initial color studies to completed weaving. Retail prices start at $130 per square foot. Please contact the artist for slides, resumé and further information.

(Top) "Sea Escape", mixed fibers,
43"w. × 60"h.
(Bottom) "Stoned Henge", mixed fibers,
43"w. × 61"h.

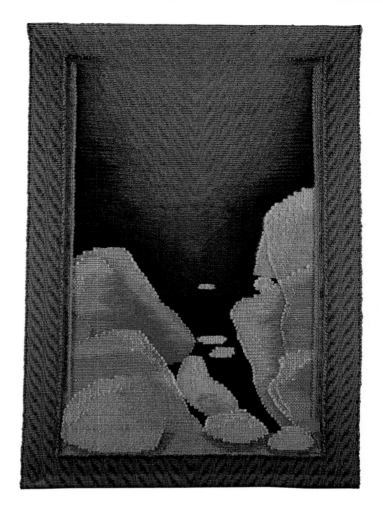

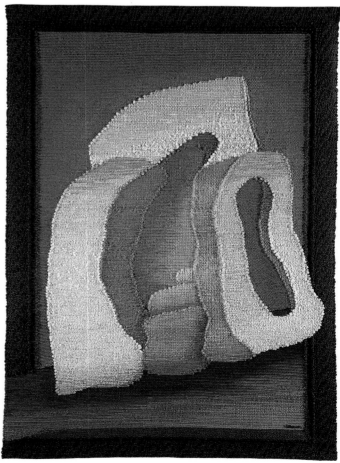

# Lynda Brothers

**Represented by Laurie McKeon**
**McKeon Art Consulting**
**1404 Foothill Road**
**Ojai, CA 93023**
**(805) 646-7917**

Lynda Brothers designs and weaves tapestries for corporate and residential spaces. Her versatile techniques encompass sophisticated abstract and representational themes.

She has experience in large scale collaborations, up to 3,375 square feet, with architects and designers. Collectors of her work in the United States, Africa and Europe include: Medical Advertising and Design, Fuji Bank, Coldwell Banker, Pacific Telephone, Marriott Hotel. The artist completes approximately 20 square feet per month. Prices range from $200-$450 per square foot. Installation available.

*Photo #1 Commissioned tapestry, wool and mohair, 69"×113", St. George's Farm @1988*

*Photo #2 Commissioned tapestry, wool and mohair, 60"×180", Ojai Valley Inn and Country Club @1987*

182

# Lucretia Davie

6 Tuxford Road
Pittsford, NY 14534
(716) 586-8467
25 Ocean Bay Club Dr.
Ft. Lauderdale FL 33308
(305) 782-8598

Lucretia Davie creates Art Tapestries for Architectural, Commercial and Residential. As Seurat would paint with dots of color, Lucretia Davie uses muted and natural linens in the warp, to give depth to the tapestries. Bas Relief technique incorporates natural elements which are inserted during the weaving. Weft yarns are dyed, spun and blended for custom coloring and unique effects. The Davie studio has been commissioned by Xerox, Citicorp, Curtice-Burns. The on-location photos show examples of the three markets served by the Davie Studios. The artist is represented in Paris, France, Boston, Nantucket, Wellfleet, Alexandria, Ft. Lauderdale, West Palm Beach, Palm Desert and Los Angeles.

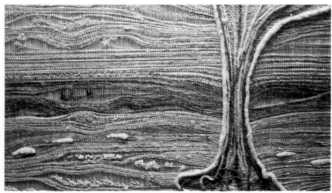

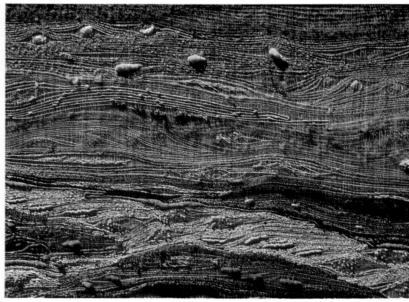

183

# Su Egen

**Egen Weaving Studio**
**2233 E. Hawthorne Street**
**Tucson, AZ 85719**
**(602) 325-0009**

For 20 years Su Egen has been creating bold geometric tapestries which integrate well into their surroundings. She is known for masterful color and yarn blending which delivers an outstanding effect in close and distance viewing.

Woven with the finest Scandinavian yarns, these works are durable and practically maintenance free.

Prices range from $100-$300 per sq. ft. including yarn samples and drawings. Allow a minimum of three months for delivery.

Collaborations with architects, designers, and private individuals are welcomed.

(Top left) "I Two" 35"w. × 36"h.
(Top right) "Converging on the Center" 3'w. × 5'7"h.
(Bottom) "Crossroads" 10'6"w. × 4'9"h.

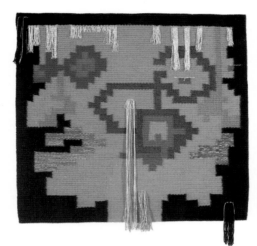

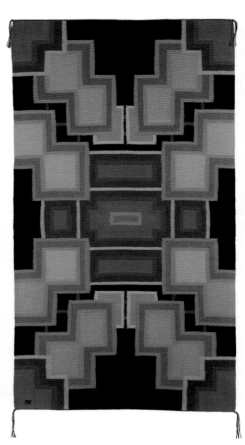

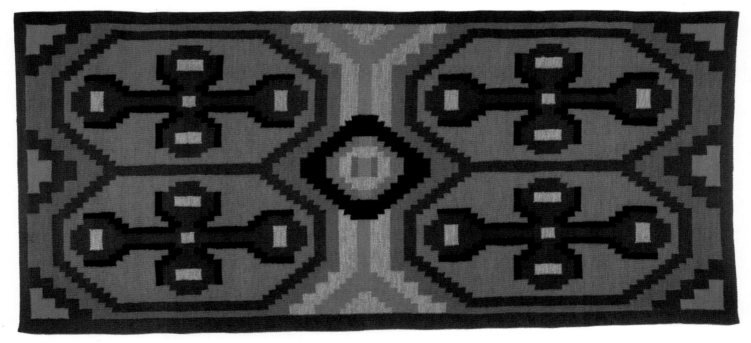

# Alexandra Friedman

7 Sequassen St., Fifth Floor
Hartford, CT 06106
(203) 548-1996

The tapestries from Alexandra Friedman's Studio are creatively designed and traditionally hand woven to accomodate the specific needs of the corporate or residential client. They are woven with 100% premium quality wool on a linen warp which makes them very durable and easy to maintain.

Scale drawings and a yarn color sample will be provided for prospective commissions. A design fee of $150 will be applied toward the completed tapestry.

Prices range from $125-175 a square foot depending on the complexity of the design. Delivery time is six to ten weeks from the time the design proposal is accepted. Further information is available on request. Collections: Aetna Life and Casualty Co.; Mechanics Savings Bank, Connecticut; Connecticut Bank and Trust Co.; Connecticut Business and Industry Assoc.

Photos: (Top) Summer Shadows, 68" × 51",
Mechanics Savings Bank
(Bottom) Beach Towels, 71" × 58"

# Sarah D. Haskell

30 North Main Street
Newmarket, NH 03857
(603) 659-5250

Sarah D. Haskell designs and weaves textural impressionistic tapestries in landscape and seascape themes. The tranquil balance of images and colors brings warmth and dimension to residential as well as corporate interiors.

The landscape/seascape scene can be a solo panel or extended over several panels to create a panorama. The tapestries are woven primarily in hand dyed wools, with accents in rayon, lurex, cotton, linen, and silk.

Haskell's tapestries are in the collections of IBM, Digital Equipment, Sanders Corp., and several New England Banks.

# Silvia Heyden

2729 Montgomery Street
Durham, NC 27705
(919) 489-0582

After graduation from the Art Institute of Zurich, Switzerland, Silvia Heyden spent thirty years to explore the unique medium of tapestry weaving.

The results are contemporary tapestries with the rhythm and spontaneity of preclassical weaving.

Recent commissions include: North Carolina Art-in-State Buildings competition; Choate Rosemary Hall, Wallingford, CT; Doral Saturnia, International Spa, Miami, FL; Duke Power Building, Charlotte, NC; Alumni Center, Williams College, Williamstown, MA.

The Artist welcomes collaborations with architects and designers on commissioned projects.

'Red Exaggerated Weave' Linen tapestry 54'inw by 56"h.

# Victor Jacoby

**1086 17th Street**
**Eureka, CA 95501**
**(707) 442-3809**

The tapestries of Victor Jacoby are woven from fine wools and cottons using classical tapestry techniques. They have been shown in solo and group exhibits in galleries and museums throughout the United States and in Canada. Jacoby has completed many commissions, among others tapestries for AT&T, Kaiser-Permanente and Marriott Corporation.

Commission Information: $130–$150. per square foot
(Top) "The Twelve Apostles," 30"×31" © 1989
(Bottom) "Calendula," 41"×41" © 1987

# Michelle Lester

**15 West 17 Street**
**New York, NY 10011**
**(212) 989-1411**

Michelle Lester's watercolors and drawings have been the basis for her studio's production since 1971. The original works-on-paper are available and can be co-ordinated with her tapestries.

Themes are varied—from landscapes and florals through abstractions on other themes.

Clients include Honeywell, Neiman Marcus, Texaco, IBM, General Electric, TRW, and R.J. Reynolds

(Top) "Red Hot," 4' × 7" © 1987
(Bottom) "Leaves of Grass" © 1987
photos by Gustavo Gonzalez

# Carolyn McClain

**Artist in Fiber**
**3150 Raindrop Drive**
**Colorado Springs, CO 80917**
**(719) 591-9580**

The strong textural statement of Carolyn Mc-Clains's soumak tapestries is enhanced by her use of multiple shades and hues of color creating a wall piece of depth and substance. Landscapes provide the inspiration for Mc-Clain in abstract of realistic form.

All pieces are woven using linen warp and predominately wool weft. A minimum of 90 days is required to complete a commissioned piece. Single-width tapestries may be commissioned up to eight feet.

Prices range from $90-$150 per sq. ft. depending on complexity.

Portfolio and resume available on request.

(Top) Detail, "From Summer to Fall", soumak
(Bottom) "From Summer to Fall", 62" × 43", soumak

# Dianne McKenzie

P.O. Box 337
The Sea Ranch, CA 95497
(707) 785-2567

Dianne McKenzie's studio designs and weaves large-scale tapestries for corporate collections, public art installations and residential interiors. Over the past 13 years, clients have included: Bank of America; San Francisco Design Center; Gibson, Dunn and Crutcher, attorneys; Washington National Insurance; and other private collectors. McKenzie also collaborates with fine artists, interpreting their work into her tapestry style. Artists currently include painters Millard Sheets and Marguerite Fletcher.

Her tapestry technique employs weaving various yarns to create a three-dimensional textured relief unique to her style. All yarns are custom dyed, lightfast and moth proof. Production time runs 3-4 months for a 6' × 8' tapestry.

A selection of tapestries, portfolio, commission procedures, pricing and additional information are available upon request.

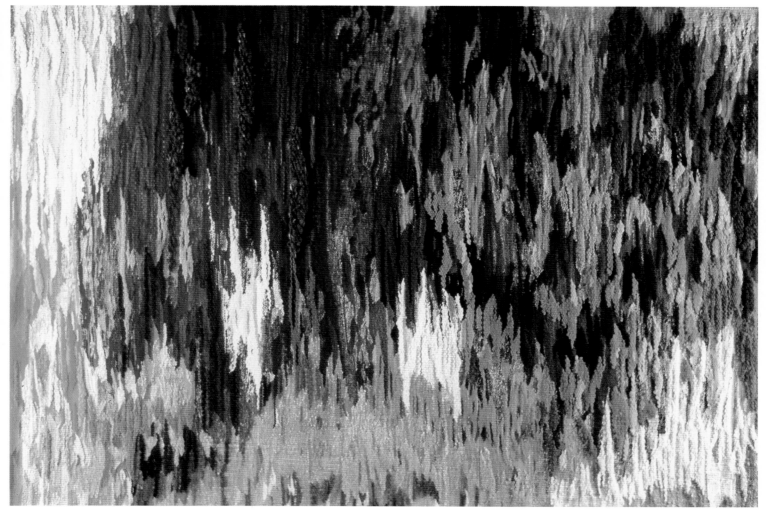

"Moving On" 6' × 8' 1989 private collection of the Brunsells

# Widney Moore

**6968 N. W. Cardinal Drive**
**Corvallis, OR 97330**
**(503) 745-7747**

Widney Moore's tapestries are stunning in their utilization of a vibrant, rich color palette. Her larger than life florals and landscapes are enhanced by their subtly textured surfaces, achieved through the use of a variety of wool yarns. Widney is experienced with large, architecturally scaled works, and has successfully collaborated with architects, art consultants, and corporate personnel. She is committed to on-time delivery and a professional presentation of proposals.

Widney's tapestries are included in numerous private and corporate collections, including Boise Cascade Corporation, Pet Corporation, Morrison-Knudsen, and Peat-Marwick.

Retail prices are $150 per square foot, with a $200 design fee.

A slide portfolio of prior commissions and currently available work is available upon request.

(Top right) "Sawtooth Poppies", 60" × 60"
(Bottom right) detail, "Blue Syringa"

"Blue Syringa", lobby, Coeur d'Alene Resort Hotel, Coeur d'Alene, ID, 7' × 21'6"

192

# Cynthia Neely

**Designer/Weaver**
**Contemporary Rugs and Tapestries**

**13508 Highway 9**
**Snohomish, WA 98290**
**(206) 668-2454**

The soft appeal of color and texture, combined with strong design, is the hallmark of Cynthia Neely's award-winning work. Specializing in woven hangings for the home, office and corporate environments, she custom designs by commission, working with the client to complement architecture and decor.

Handwoven with a select blend of wool, silk and linen, her tapestries are available in custom sizes and colors and are delivered ready for easy installation.

Neely's work has been widely published and exhibited and is included in the private and corporate collections of, among others, Frances Lear (LEAR's Magazine); Eli Lilly, Indianapolis, IN; American Insurance Association, Washington, DC.

Price information and slides are available on request with a refundable slide fee of $1.00 per slide. Call for availability of completed work.

(Top) "Morning Light" 4' × 4'
(Bottom) "Threshold" 4' × 4'

# New York Tapestry Artists

P.O. Box 1747
Old Chelsea Station
New York, NY 10011
Betty Vera, (212) 924-2478
Bojana H. Leznicki, (201) 857-4602
Ilona Mack-Pachler, (212) 627-0835

NYTA is an international group of professional artists based in New York City. Its members weave tapestries from their original designs both individually and collaboratively. The work ranges in size from residential to large corporate installations. The tapestries are durable, easy to install, and require minimal maintenance. Group or individual portfolios and additional information are available on request. Studio visits by appointment.

Artists represented on this page: (top) Betty Vera, *Late Winter,* 46"h. × 63"w., 1989, cotton, linen, and silk; (bottom right) Bojana H. Leznicki, *Tender Is the Sunset,* 60"h. × 54"w., 1989, wool and silk; (bottom left) Ilona Mack-Pachler, *Scars,* 48"h. × 17"w. 1989, wool, silk, and lacquered wood.

All photos on this page taken by Earl Ripling.

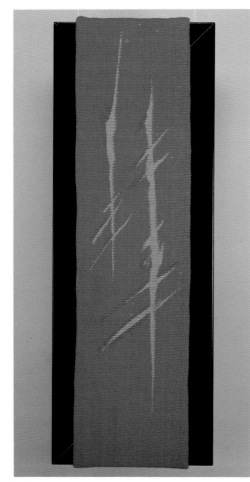

# New York Tapestry Artists

P.O. Box 1747
Old Chelsea Station
New York, NY 10011
Mary-Ann Sievert, (914) 225-9398
Susan Martin Maffei, (212) 989-3860
Rita Romanova Gekht, (212) 645-1031

NYTA has exhibited in New York and other major cities, and its members are represented in both corporate and private collections. They execute tapestries in a variety of styles and techniques, from traditional to experimental. Prices depend on size, materials and complexity of design. Completed work is available for purchase, and most of the artists also design and weave commissioned tapestries. Inquiries regarding NYTA or individual artists are welcomed.

Shown on this page: (top) Mary-Ann Sievert, *A.W.S. at Sea*, 78"h. × 42"w., 1989, wool; (bottom right) Rita Romanova Gekht, *Turnaround*, 42"h. × 60"w., 1989, wool; (bottom left) Susan Martin Maffei, *Mon Frère Moi Même*, 28"h. × 19½"w., 1988, wool.

All photos on this page taken by Earl Ripling.

# Mary Lynn O'Shea

R.D. #1 Box 1684
Vergennes, VT 05491
(802) 758-2349

Mary Lynn O'Shea is well known for her floral tapestries. These tapestries may be abstract or realistic and incorporate a wide variety of materials and textures. This gives the work a sense of depth and reflected light. O'Shea has exhibited her work nationally in corporate, public and residential spaces. She uses a traditional slit-tapestry technique with linen warp and a weft of mixed fibers. The pieces are durable and easy to install with velcro mounting. They are available from the artist's studio or by commission. The price is determined by the square foot and the amount of detail required. Slides, resume and prices are available upon request.

Top Right—"Helen Elizabeth," 58″×68″
Top Left—"Hibiscus," 48″×72″
Bottom—"Papaver Orientale," 60″×86″

# Myra Reichel

121 East Sixth Street
Media, PA 19063
(215) 565-4239

Myra Reichel has a selection of tapestries, drawings, and slides of previous work in her studio. She collaborates with other artists or weaves the client's own ideas in the traditional manner with her artistic interpretation happening in the weaving process. Myra Reichel has been a weaver since 1971. She uses wool, cotton, silk, plastic, synthetics, and metallic yarns in her work. Vacuum to clean. Prices listed are retail.

(Top) "Fairytale" 10 panel installation at The Fox Company, Chesterbrook, PA. Unframed 2' × 2' $400. 9' × 9' panels $7200. Any number of rearrangeable panels can be ordered in any size and color combination. © 1986. (Bottom) "Dinosaur Egg" 4 panels shown joined 51" × 71" $5000. 1 panel 8½' × 12' $16000. 4 panels total size 18' × 24' $52000. © 1987.

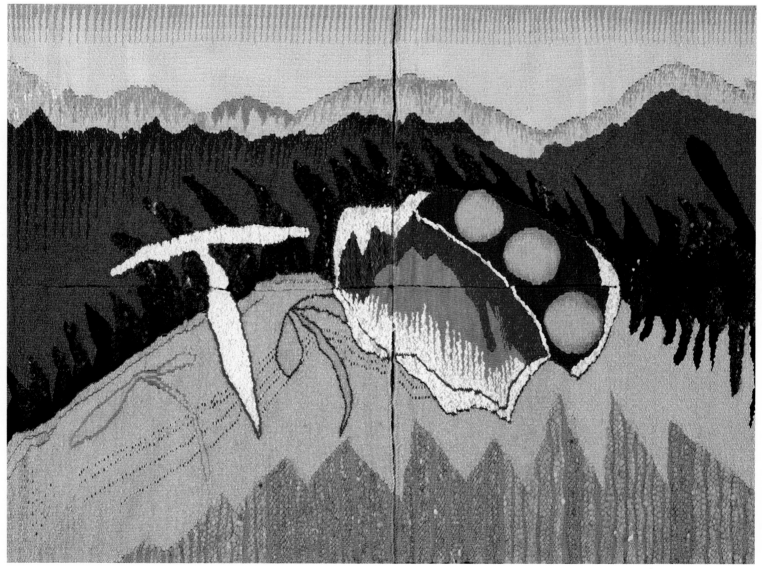

# Julia Schloss

**Handwoven Originals**
**6005 28th Street N.W.**
**Washington, D C 20015**
**(202) 363-4718**

Award winning fiber artist Julia Schloss creates one-of-a-kind originally designed handwoven wall hangings for corporate, institutional and private spaces.

Her handwoven wall hangings are included in over 40 collections, and are installed in banks, hotel suites, conference rooms, lobbies, hospital meditation and recovery rooms, private offices and private residences.

Ms. Schloss accepts commissions and also has available a varied selection of completed work.

Retail prices range from $100–$150 per square foot. Slides and information are available upon request.

"Northern Peaks" 99" × 56" wool on linen

"Pinnacles III" 80" × 56" wool on linen Kaiser Permanente, Kensington, MD

# Elinor Steele

**65 Flint Pond Drive**
**Hollis, NH 03049**
**(603) 465-2601**

Elinor Steele creates handwoven tapestries of contemporary design using both traditional and innovative techniques.

Her flat tapestries display a meticulous approach to composition and craftsmanship. "Formed" tapestries are sculpted by stuffing all or part of the tapestry to create a low relief of rounded pockets and vertical stripes.

Steele has exhibited nationally for 15 years and has created works for many homes, offices, and corporations including IBM and Prudential Insurance Company.

Commissions of any size are invited and may incorporate design elements from the surrounding architecture and furnishings. Prices per sq. ft. range from $125–200 for flat tapestries and $175–250 for formed tapestries.

(Top) "Refraction on a Silicon Wafer," formed tapestry, 30" × 48". Collection: Vermont Technical College
(Below) "Deja Vu," flat tapestry, 59" × 54", Private Collection.

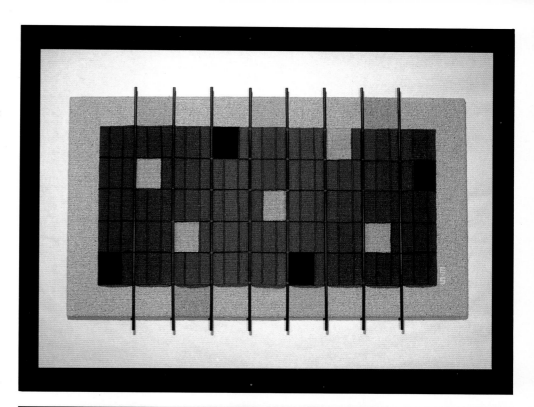

# Wendy Teisberg

**Zephyr Studio**
**1460 Simpson St.**
**St. Paul, MN 55108**
**(612) 644-7028**

Wendy Teisberg's tapestries reflect her interest in clarity of form and the economical style of the Bauhaus.

Teisberg's woven images come to life through grouping lines of rayon threads to create a rich luminous surface. Her work is characterized by hand painting these rayon threads in vibrant color gradations.

Prices range from $100–$130 per sq. ft. wholesale and do not include installations costs. Depending upon size, commissions require approximately 2 months to complete.

A slide portfolio is available for duplication.

(Top) "Waterfall, hand painted (detail)
(Bottom) "Waterfall, hand painted
5'w. × 11¼'h.

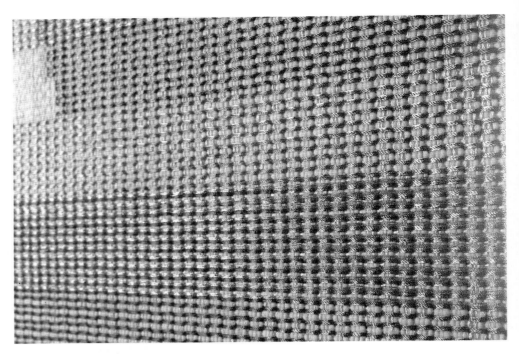

# Nancy Wines-DeWan

**Contemporary Maine Textiles**
**P.O. Box 861 Sligo Road**
**Yarmouth, ME 04096**
**(207) 846-6058**

Nancy Wines-DeWan creates woven tapestries for public spaces, churches, and private residences. Her designs, inspired by the Maine landscape, are studies in texture and subtle colors. Natural fibers are featured in her work, especially mohair from her herd of Angora goats. The hand-spun and hand-dyed fiber can be dyed to match color samples provided by the client.

Her work is in the collection of the University of Nebraska's College of Nursing; Northwestern Bank, Omaha, Nebraska; the Salter Corporation, Augusta, Maine; and many other institutional and private collections.

Prices start at $100 per square foot. Please contact the artist for additional information regarding commissions.

(below) "Tidal Triptych," Private Collection, Falmouth Foreside, Maine. 108"w. × 48"h.

# Charlotte Ziebarth

**3070 Ash Avenue**
**Boulder, CO 80303**
**(303) 494-2601**

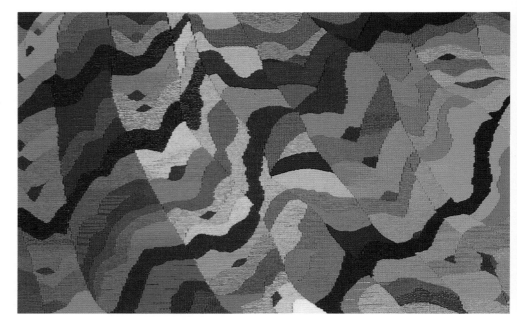

Tapestry designs of Charlotte Ziebarth reflect a broad range of abstract imagery; microscopic organic patterns, land form images, Southwestern and Middle Eastern rug interpretations, representational landscape murals. Interest in color and pattern are reflected in all these styles.

Specially hand-dyed wool yarns enable matching colors exactly to commission environments. High quality dyes yield excellent lightfastness. Tapestries are designed for easy installation and maintenance.

Ziebarth has been weaving for 15 years. Her pieces are included in many private and corporate collections. Slides of completed works are available upon request.

(Top) "Kaleidoscope" 36" × 58"
(Bottom) "Crystal Magnification" 32" × 48"

# Art Quilts

# Teresa Barkley

24-40 27 Street
Astoria, NY 11102
(718) 545-4281

Teresa Barkley designs and creates distinctive wall quilts of the highest quality craftsmanship, drawing on 15 years of quilting experience. Her unique designs result from the use of cotton prints and photo transfers combined with canvas money bags, fabric labels, feed sacks, linen pages from vintage children's books, and commemorative handkerchieves. These found object fabrics are pieced together in designs that are frequently in a postage stamp motif. Such stamp designs may be inspired by actual stamps or be totally ficticious. Barkley's award winning quilts have been exhibited internationally and are represented in corporate, university, and private collections. Prices range from $2,000.-$20,000. Commissions accepted.

(Top) "The Dawn of Television," Mother Goose vintage linen pages, cottons, heat transfers, 45"w × 54"h.
(Bottom) "How To Get a Husband Stamp," Tea towels, handkerchief, damask napkin, cottons, heat transfers, 50"w × 53"h.

Both photos by: Stuart Bakal-Schwartzberg, 40 East 23 St., NYC 10010 (212) 254-2988

# Doreen Beck
# Dink Siegel

100 West 57 Street #10G
New York, NY 10019
(212) 246-9757

They are a husband-and-wife team, who have gravitated to Art Quilts as a way of capturing the world around them, especially New York, where they met and live.

If you want them to capture your worlds for you, talk to them. They have large sympathies and imaginations, and good research skills.

He does the sketches. She does the fabric work—selecting, piecing, layering, appliqué-ing, occasionally embroidering, and outline quilting for bas-relief.

One of their smaller hangings (approx. 5′ × 4′) takes about 6 months from conception to finish, and costs about $377.50 per square foot.

They are very simple to hang using rods slipped through fabric sleeves attached to the backing.

# Karen Bovard

**Spectrum Quilts**
**102 Highland Avenue**
**Middletown, CT 06457**
**(203) 346-1116**

Karen Bovard creates contemporary wall quilts which combine bold design with intricate hand detailing. Many use innovative adaptations of traditional techniques or motifs from a variety of cultures; some are whimsical, and include detachable or three-dimensional forms. Striking from a distance, the quilts also include fine needlework appreciable upon closer viewing.

Her work is easy to install and care for, and durable. She works by commission and enjoys collaborating with clients for site-specific works. Work is priced by the job at $80-$150 per square foot depending on size and intricacy, with a $250 design fee.

(Top) "Riotous Bloom," 44"×57", machine pieced, hand quilted, hand appliqued, with Arabic and Hawaiian influences

(Bottom) "Armor of the Mystic Warrior," 40"×44", machine pieced, hand quilted, with Japanese motifs

# Jo Diggs

**Jo Diggs Appliqué**
P.O. Box 6609
Portland, ME 04101
(207) 773-3405

Multi-layered appliqué in cotton or wool by Jo Diggs is graphic and representational in a simplified, stylized manner. Her work has been described most often as "serene"; floral and landscape motifs predominate in beautifully worked wall pieces and art garments. The soft richness and visual warmth of wool tweed, plaids and solids add a unique new dimension to appliqué and quilting.

Pieces can be free-hanging, stretched, quilted or combinations thereof. Work is usually hand-stitched, hand-quilted. Machine stitching is recommended for very large projects.

Production time varies with current work in progress and size of commission. Slides of work on hand available; prices per square foot quoted for cotton and/or wool, quilted or unquilted. Resumé and references on request.

(Top) Calico Revision
(Bottom) Mars Garden, 77"w. × 59"h.

# Prosser Fink

548 Warren Avenue
Swansea, MA 02777
(508) 336-5166

Prosser Fink designs and creates one-of-a-kind fine art wall quilts for corporate and private settings using hand dyed and hand printed materials. Some of the dyeing techniques include hand painting, batik, tie-dye, and linoleum print. These techniques and materials vary according to the subject matter of each piece.

Prosser has exhibited work internationally in galleries and museums and has been included in collections in U.S. hotels and corporations.

Wholesale prices start at $50 per square foot and may rise depending on the complexity of the design.

A portfolio is available upon request. Commissions are accepted.

(Right) "BLOOM"; Approximately 4½'h. × 5½'
(Bottom) "SILVER LINING"; 5'h. × 12'

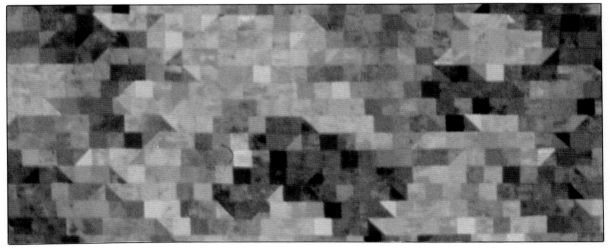

# Vicki L. Johnson

225 Muir Dr.
Soquel, CA 95073
(408) 476-7567

The quilts of Vicki Johnson combine painted images with traditional pieced patterns. They are inspired by coastal scenes and marine life. By using innovative techniques she achieves a surface rich in detail and color. Prices average $100 to $250 per square foot depending on the size and intricacy of the design.

Left top: A Bright Winter Day in Mendocino © 1985 — 65" × 82"
Right top: The Next Friontiers © 1989 — 42" × 62"
Below: Monterey © 1987 — 58" × 58"

# Carol Keller

**60 Burnside Avenue**
**Somerville, MA 02144**
**(617) 666-1302**

Inspired by architectural forms and textile patterns, Carol Keller works in natural fibers to create detailed quilted surfaces. Her quilts have been exhibited nationally and are included in private collections. Keller's work has also been used as book cover illustrations.

Average completion time is two months. Prices range from $150 to $200 per square foot with an additional sketch fee. She will supervise installation and provide care instructions.

(Top) "Summer/Winter Weave Revisited", cotton and silk. Overall size of the three panels is 87"w. × 47"h.
(Bottom) "Interaction", cotton and silk. 11" square.

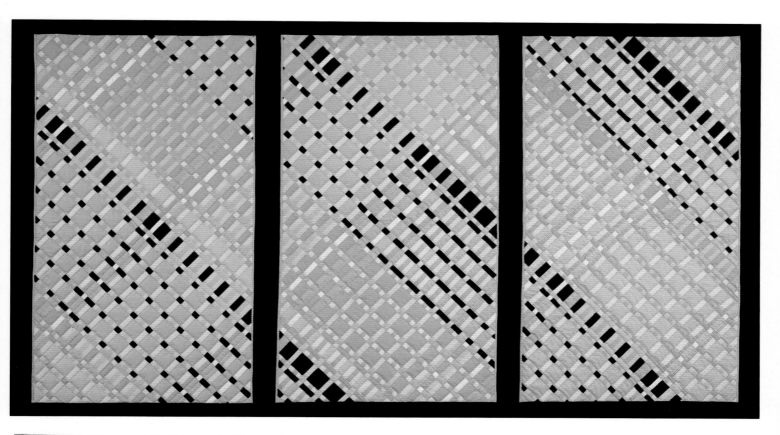

# Personal Signatures

Not only can you go home again, you do go home again—and again and again. More and more people are doing just that. As Americans search for a sanctuary in this fast-paced world, we are looking home-ward to find it. The home has taken on a new significance as we are spending increasing amounts of time there—enjoying family, entertaining friends, sometimes working, and often just relaxing.

The home seems to be providing something beyond being a simple refuge; it is the place that we can make a footprint, put our stamp, inscribe our personal signature. The home is a singular place now as we put more time, energy, and money into personalizing it.

One of the major manifestations of this movement has been a return to the crafts world for things that are products of the head and the hand and the heart, objects that are unique, work that bears the personal signature of the artist. The evident presence of the human hand draws us back to values believed to be lost, as we turn away from the trendy in search of the enduring. We have re-discovered the love of materials, the joy of singularity, the pleasure of a thing well made.

There are many reasons for this placement of signatures in the places where we live. The most important is that our living spaces are being designed and crafted with the goal of articulating a personality rather than a pre-ordained, systematic decorating style. Today's homes speak chapters, if not volumes, about someone's life style. People are more becoming more self-confident about their own tastes, and somewhat more assertive as well one suspects.

You are likely to see crafted objects all over the house, dominating a room or providing a vital imaginative detail. There are the hand-carved wooden spoons, the woven throw on the sofa, the quilt on the bed, and the wall hanging over it. Even the brass candlesticks on the dining room table are more than likely the signed product of some craft artist whose taste and sensibilities match those of the owner of the home you are visiting.

The craft artists of this country are, metaphorically at least, stocking a veritable "Alice's Restaurant" for us. It is inconceivable that there is not an artist out there for every taste, for every need, for every home, for every niche in every home. They were there while the world of design was homogenizing, and they are still there. And now they are back in demand, because more and more of us want them and their work. Anonymity angst seems to be passing. Keeping up with the Joneses may not be entirely passe, but being just like the Joneses certainly is. We no longer seek the safety of sameness, because we are no longer worried about being thought "different."

We are regaining our senses and our humanity. And we are making homes that fit us, that suit us, that reflect us. Our homes are hand-crafted and signed. What we seem to be saying is "This is not just mine. This is me."

**Bill Kraus**
**Chairman, Kraus Sikes Inc.**
**New York, New York**

# Linda Ruth MacDonald

191 Wood Street
Willits, CA 95490
(707) 459-4563

Echoes of architecture, organic themes, illusionistic forms, subtle color gradations, and elaborate freeform hand quilting inspire and present Linda MacDonald's creative vision. Such diverse techniques as airbrushing, hand painting, custom dying, and machine quilting are also integrated into many of her multi-layered compositions.

MacDonald's award winning quilts have been widely published and exhibited throughout the world. She is represented in many public and private collections.

Slides and resume available upon request.

Collaborations and commissions welcomed.

Prices begin at $130 per sq. ft.

(Below) "Salmon Ladders", 92"×92", hand quilted, painted and custom dyed cotton fabric. Photographer: Sharon Risedorph

# Linda S. Perry

**96 Burlington Street**
**Lexington, MA 02173**
**(617) 863-1107**

Linda Perry's quilts reflect her interest in Japanese design and classical mythology. Most include hand dyed and hand painted fabric. She has been working with fiber for more than 10 years and received her training at the University of California at Berkeley, Harvard University and the School of the Museum of Fine Arts in Boston. Perry's quilts are included in private and public collections in Massachusetts, Florida, California and Illinois. Her art quilt "Berkeley Blue" received first prize at the American Quilter's National Show. Works range in price from $1,000–$5,000. Commissions require a minimum of 10 weeks. Please contact the artist for additional information and slides of current work.

(Below) "Leda", 38" × 47", cotton, silk

# Joan Schulze

**808 Piper Avenue**
Sunnyvale, CA 94087
(408) 736-7833

Work from Joan Schulze's studio includes large scale art quilts and medium sized painterly layered collage/constructions. Working in the fiber medium since the early 70's, Joan has designed and executed works for both private and public spaces. The artist has an experimental attitude towards quilts and enjoys working with clients who have unusual requirements such as curved walls or spaces which are enhanced by two-sided work.

Collaborations with architects, designers and individuals usually take 1–3 months after the design is approved. Collages are $800– $3,000; quilts are $200 a sq. ft. Slides and resume are available on request.

"Wind Trigonometry", 1988, 6'h. × 4'6"w. Private commission.

# Ann Trusty

**Hulsey/Trusty**
**Route 9D**
**Garrison, NY 10524**
**(914) 424-3544**

Ann Trusty's quilts are distinctive for their brilliant and unexpected color and energy. The quilts have been exhibited in Paris, throughout France, Turkey, Japan and in Boston and New York City. Please contact the artist for information on commissions and slides of available work.

(Top) Light Dance, 6' × 6'
(Bottom) Verdigris Vertigo, 6' × 6'

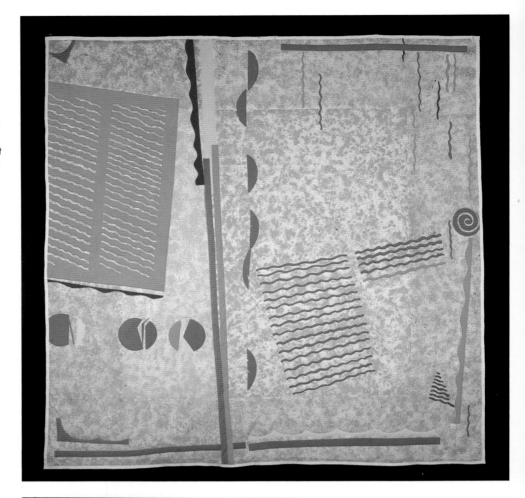

# Fiber
# Installations

# B. J. Adams

**Art in Fiber**
2821 Arizona Terrace, N.W.
Washington, D.C. 20016
(202) 364-8404 (studio)
(202) 686-1042 (home)

Adams' fiber art is bright or subdued, free-flowing, or crisply geometric, two-dimensional or highly textured. Framed single pieces, modular units or entire walls range in size and are suitable for commercial or residential installations.

Works have been purchased or commissioned by medical and government facilities, corporations and individual collectors.

Adams will collaborate with clients, art consultants and interior designers to meet their specific scheduling and budget requirements.

Brochure available.

(Top left) "Structure & Enclosure", 14" × 18" framed, machine stitchery
(Top right) "The Freedom of Non-Definition", 37"h × 28"w, pieced, stitched, and manipulated fabrics.
(Bottom) "Grid" Series, 3 panels, 2'h × 6½'w, machine stitchery over many fabrics.

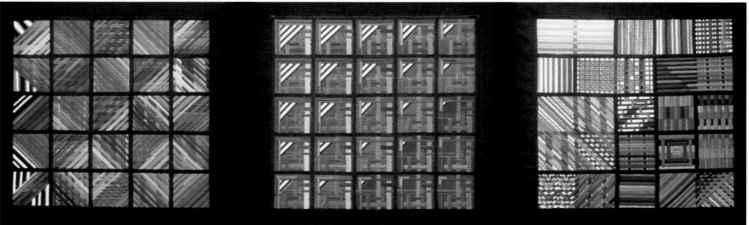

# Robert W. Alexander

**Industrial Strength Art**
P.O. Box 599
Morganton, GA 30560-0599
(404) 374–5792

His works are true 'Fiber Art', powerful so-phisticated expressions of man's oldest materials used in creative new ways.'
—Richard Langman, Langman Gallery

Bill Alexander's hand-wrapped hangings mix durable industrial fibers with metals and exotic materials. Ranging from large scale installations to exquisite miniatures, these art-works are the intersection of creative energy and careful design.

Prices range from $50 to $1000 per square foot. Commission costs include design, shipping/delivery, and installation.

Slides/materials by request.

(Below top) 'Mothers And Children' detail, wool, acrylic, silk.
(Bottom left) 'Virtual Light', 68' × 8'6" × 1', TVA Complex, Chattanooga, TN.
(Bottom right) 'Shield, (Dying Slave)', 60" × 36" × 8".

Gary Bogue

Tracy Knauss

Gary Bogue

220

# Barbara Barron/ Al Granek

1943 New York Avenue
Huntington Station, NY 11746
(516) 549-4242
(516) 549-9122

Barbara Barron and Al Granek specialize in creating site-specific wallhangings for commercial and residential interiors. Working partners for ten years, they have successfully used the medium of wrapped fibres to create dimensional fibre sculptures world wide. They collaborate with architects and designers to meet individual needs for size, color, texture, and budget.

Pricing information, brochures and slides are available upon request.

Delivery time: 4-6 weeks. Prices range from $65-275 per square foot. Complete installation and maintenance services available.

Barron and Granek are pleased to include as their collectors: Burt Reynolds, Trump Plaza, A.T.&T., Shearson Lehman Hutton, The Penn Central Corp., United Virginia Bank, Australian Film Institute

"Flight" 9' × 6' Amagansett, Lond Island, New York

"Fantasia" 20' × 4½' Kimberly Clark Corp., Paris, Texas

# Nancy Boney

**97 King Street**
**Fanwood, NJ 07023**
**(201) 889-8219**

Vitality, strength of design, and richness of color are central to the appeal of the fabric wall hangings and wall sculptures of Nancy Boney. A pleasant diversity of fabrics are used to suggest the natural environment as well as abstract ideas. While they stand on their own, some of the smaller pieces are especially effective in groupings.

Installations of Boney's work are found in professional and corporate offices, hospitals, churches, and private homes. Retail prices begin at $650 for sculptural wall pieces, and at $80 per square foot for wall hangings. Delivery is 4-8 weeks. Works are protected with scotchgard and are easily installed and maintained. Commissions and collaborations are welcomed.

(Top) Wall Sculpture, "Oriental Splendor", 36"w × 21"h × 11"d.
(Bottom) Appliqué and constructed wall hanging, "Imperial Spirit," 8'w. × 4½'h. Priv. home.

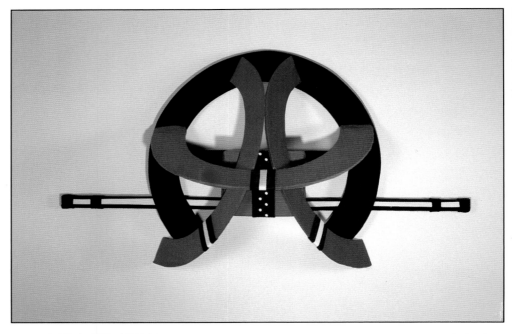

# Dana Boussard

2 Heart Creek
Rt. #1
Arlee, MT 59821
(406) 726-3357

Dana Boussard has professionally collaborated, fabricated and installed over 35 commissioned works for corporate and state buildings including: fourteen 10′ × 6′ pieces for the Anchorage International Airport; The Denver National Bank; Beneficial Corporation, Delaware; Wells Fargo Bank, Los Angeles; SAFECO Insurance, Seattle, and the largest, a 10′ × 60′ wall, Boise, Idaho City Hall. Professional drawings included, completion of the painted fibre constructions takes from 3 months to a year with time proven durability.

She has exhibited extensively, with works in private and museum collections.

Please contact the artist for information about commissions and slides of available work. Prices: $3000, up.

"We Met With Oh Such Separate Dreams", 53″ × 116″

"X Marks The Spot", 78″ × 58″

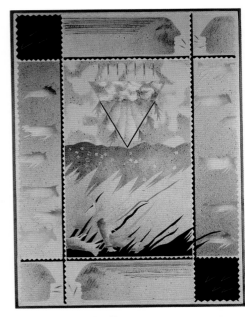

"Between Places", 63″ × 47″

"Save A Piece Of The Sky", 6′ × 18′6″

223

# Judith Content

**Judith Content Fabrics and Designs**
**527 Bryan Avenue**
**Sunnyvale, CA 94086**
**(408) 739-4151**

Judith Content creates hand-dyed, quilted silk tapestries for corporate and residential environments. She achieves rich colors and textures dyeing a wide variety of silks in an adaptation of the traditional Japanese "bomaki" technique. Dyed silks are assembled into fully lined, quilted panels which are suspended from acrylic rods and brackets for display. The completed pieces range in size from single panels to large-scale, multi-story installations. Judith Content welcomes commissioned work and can provide hand-painted maquettes for site-specific projects.

Corporate collections include Pacific Bell, Marriott Hotels, American Express, and Chevron Corporation. Her work has been shown internationally through the American Craft Museum, including exhibits in Japan, Canada and Great Britain.

Please contact the artist for information concerning commissions or slides of available work.

(SLIDE #1) "Tracery" Each panel 3' × 5' Private collection

(SLIDE #2) "Cascade" One of two 12' × 16' pieces in lobby of Stoneridge Corporate Plaza, Pleasanton, CA.

Printed in Japan  © 1990 The Guild: A Sourcebook of American Craft Artists

# Sandy D'Andrade

**67 Pleasant Ridge Drive**
**Poughkeepsie, NY 12603**
**(914) 462-0859**

Known for striking nature scenes, Sandy D'Andrade designs and creates one-of-a-kind wall pieces, floor screens and sliding door systems. She incorporates unique handknitting techniques of free-form cabling and intarsia, allowing versatility of function and imagery. Each panel is meticulously handcrafted for strength, durability and easy care. Fine woodworking elements of floor screens and door systems are executed in collaboration with noted woodworker, Anthony Beverly.

D'Andrade's work has been internationally exhibited and is in the permanent collection of the Chicago Historical Society, as well as numerous private and corporate collections.

Commissions are welcome. D'Andrade works with clients, designers and architects to meet color and space requirements. Slides and prices are available upon request.

(Below) B/W Forest Floor Screen, wool panels, mahogany frame with inset brass hinges, 90"w. × 84"h.

# Ann Epstein

3616 N. Maple Road
Ann Arbor, MI 48105
(313) 996-9019

Ann Epstein's painterly ikat-woven hangings integrate color and texture to express the interior landscape and universal emotional themes of our everyday lives. The one-of-a-kind multi-panel weavings are of fine, hand-dyed, cotton yarns in complex twill patterns.

Panels can be combined to meet any space requirement and the color range is unlimited. Prices are approximately $125 per square foot wholesale; drawings and installation costs are extra. Ready-made works are available and most commissioned pieces can be completed within several months.

Ann Epstein's work has been exhibited nationally, and has been featured in *Fiberarts* and *Surface Design Journal*. The artist accepts both residential and corporate commissions, and is pleased to work with architects, designers, art consultants, and gallery agents.

(Top left) "Distancing", 45"×69"
(Top right) "Home Fires" detail
(Bottom) "Home Fires", 44"×69",
(Agent) Sorenson

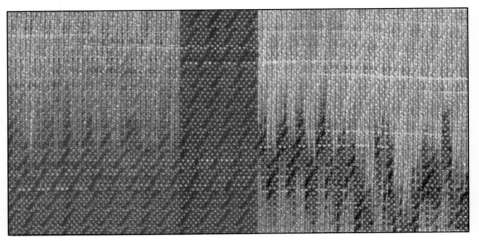

# Fowler & Thelen Studio

**Laurie Fowler & Bill Thelen**
**201 Fairbrook**
**Northville, MI 48167**
**(313) 348-6654**

Reflecting their fascination with form, movement and texture, Fowler & Thelen have developed an innovative design approach which incorporates fiber, suede and metal on three-dimensional steel constructions. Weaving directly on the steel armature allows for a unique exploration of the relationship between sculptural form and the handwoven surface. This integrated approach ensures exceptional durability, minimal maintenance and ease of installation.

Fowler & Thelen have worked for 12 years in close communication with clients, designers and architects, and they specialize in site-specific commissions. Architecturally-scaled renderings and color samples are available for limited edition pieces and commissioned originals. Prices range from $350–4,000. Minimum delivery is 4–8 weeks Supervision of installations by the artists is available. Please call or write for an informational portfolio.

Detail of bottom photo

"Rhyme", 36"h. × 82"w. × 10"d.

# Linda H. Garbe

P.O. Box 443
Bloomington, IL 61702
(309) 728-2237

Linda Garbe creates unique pieces for unique environments. Tubes and cords are covered, wrapped, painted and enhanced to create strong textural pieces.

The goal of every commission is to work with the client to create a piece that complements all aspects of the architecture and interior design.

There is a design fee for all accepted commissions. Proposals include sketches and material samples. Pieces can be treated with fire retardants and scotchguarding. There is no size limitation. Prices begin at twenty-five dollars a square foot plus the cost of materials. The production schedule is based on the size and complexity of each commission.

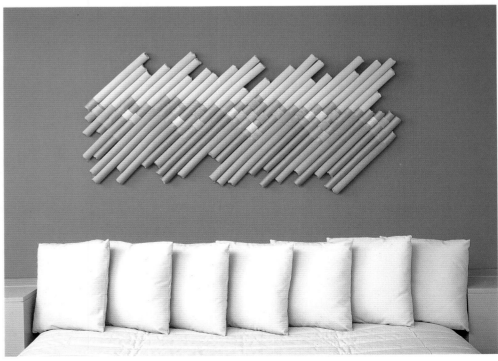

# Jacquelynne Garner

**Artist-Designer**
4312 Proctor Place
San Diego, CA 92116
(619) 692-3689; 291-4104

Jacquelynne Garner paints on silk—crepe de chine, china silk, pongee, charmeuse, chiffon. Stretched paintings, draped paintings, silk folded behind glass, soft paintings, banners, sculpture and scarves (12" and 15" by 45" and 72"; 45" square; $45-$300, handrolled. Scarves come in a very wide variety of technics including "Raku" silks. Many wearables can also be wall pieces. She has had one-woman and group shows in Southern California and Europe, and work in galleries in La Jolla, Del Mar, Beverly Hills, San Diego and Santa Fe. She is seeking new galleries for both wall pieces ($150 to $3,000) and wearables. Especially exciting is the prospect of installation commissions (a silk wall? Three dimensional?)

Subject matter and style is diverse—abstractions, figures, faces, cartoons. All work can be drycleaned, including paintings stretched on wooden frames. The work is lightweight and can be mailed easily and ironed before showing or stretching.

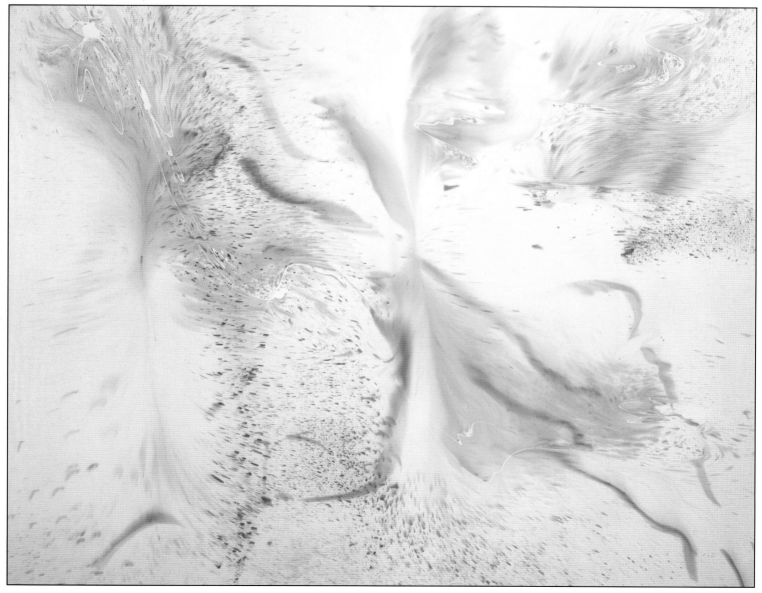

# Marie-Laure Ilie

M-Laure Design Studio/Cocoon
1241 Kolle Avenue
South Pasadena, CA 91030
(213) 254-8073

Ilie's hand-painted silk wall hangings recreate the masterpieces of the ancient world, using the styles of Medieval Europe, the Middle East, the Orient and American Colonial. A delicate crackling pattern gives an antique appearance to these designs.

The same antique effect also graces the floral compositions and creates a look of rare sophistication.

Commissioned works can reproduce the client's required decorative theme, whether of a historical period or of a cultural region. They can also adapt to specified colors and sizes.

Available either for framing or for hanging with a rod. Colors are fade proof.

Prices are $80 per sq. ft. Commissions require one month after approval of sketches.

Additional photos, slides, or samples are available upon request.

# Marie-Laure Ilie

**M-Laure Design Studio/Cocoon**
**1241 Kolle Avenue**
**South Pasadena, CA 91030**
**(213) 254-8073**

Ilie creates large abstract tapestries by layering transparent organza on top of a hand-painted silk background. The rich colors and textures of this appliqué technique enhance the inherent sophistication of silk. These fabric paintings come ready to hang like tapestries. They can also be framed.

For the past 15 years, Ilie has exhibited extensively in the United States and Europe, in galleries, universities, and museums. In addition to many private collections, selected corporate collections include the Bank of America, the Bank of New Zealand, Neiman-Marcus, Marshall Field and Company, Gale Research Company.

Prices range from $120–$150 per sq. ft. Commissions are welcome. Colors are fade proof.

Ilie also creates wall reliefs made of transparent nylon mesh.

Additional photos, slides, or samples are available upon request.

"Resonance", 50" × 67"

"Apparition", 58" × 88"

# O. Jolly

**57 Greene Street**
**New York, NY 10012**
**(212) 966-0185**

O. Jolly uses non-traditional techniques to create highly textured tapestries, often conceptual in nature. Finished works are fade-resistant, mothproof, easily installed and maintained.

Although completed pieces are available, O. Jolly accepts commissions. The design fee, deductible from the price of the completed project, provides the client with sketch, color study, and textile swatch. Retail prices range from $275-$400 per sq. ft. Delivery time is dependent upon size of the piece and current schedule, with a medium sized (3 ft. × 6ft.) piece taking 2 months to complete.

Write or call for current slide portfolio and further information or to arrange an appointment at our showroom.

(Top) "Means Ends Reversal"
60"w. × 36"h. × 2½"d.
(Bottom) Detail

# Lori Kammeraad

**Thornapple Designs**
**2822 Thornapple River Dr. S.E.**
**Grand Rapids, MI 49546**
**616-942-7042**

Lori Kammeraad is a weaver interested in creating textured flowing surfaces woven into abstract designs. Each wall hanging is made from custom dyed wool and can be coordinated with interior colors.

The artist has been weaving for the past 12 years and is now represented in over 100 galleries in the United States.

Commissioned weavings are completed in 2–3 months. Prices range from $300 to $1000 depending on the size and complexity of the work.

Brochure and price list available upon request.

(Top) "Newsprint," 44"×55".
(Bottom) "Llama," 44"×60".

# Janis Kanter

**1923 West Dickens**
**Chicago, IL 60622**
**(312) 252-2119**

Incorporating mixed media, such as neon tubing, with the use of varied fibrous materials, visual impact and movement become the distinct elements of Janis Kanter's fiber installations.

Using only the finest quality wool, linen and metallic yarns, these contemporary art works, contrasted through a traditional craft medium, are easy to maintain and are highly durable for most interior spaces.

Collaborations with architects, designers and individuals are welcome. Prices range from $100-150 per sq. ft. Recognizing that each client's needs are different, Kanter will meet directly with the client to work out the details of a commission.

Finished works are also available.

"Waterfall of My Mind" 4'w × 6'h. Collection of Art Enterprises © 1989.

"Bill's Place", 12'w × 8'h. Private Collection © 1989.

234

# Ellen Kochansky

1237 Mile Creek Road
Pickens, SC 29671
(803) 868-9749

Ellen Kochansky's collage works depart from the traditions of quilting to humanize and soften corporate and residential settings. Original techniques involve laminating, over-dyeing, transparent fabrics, airbrushed fabric dye and pigments. Eleven years commission experience. Portman Hotels, IBM, Florida National Bank, and other collections.

Required lead time averages two to three months for completed work. Proposal (10% fee) consists of actual color fabric swatches, scale color rendering, and contract confirming date of delivery, price, terms, installation arrangements and care procedure.

Extraordinarily durable and light resistant for the textile medium, works may be conveniently removed from supports for occasional dry cleaning. Easily installed mounting system provides formality and security. Call or write for current scheduling, price, slides, and brochure.

"Reverberation" 4' × 6' Neal, Prince & Partners, Architects

Robert Starling

# Janet Kuemmerlein

**Kuemmerlein Fiber Art Inc.**
**7701 Canterbury**
**Prairie Village, KS 66208**
**(816) 842-7049 (studio)**
**(913) 649-8292 (home)**

Janet Kuemmerlein's fiber relief murals and fiber vessels range in size from 2′ × 3′ to 4½′ × 50′. Her original technique was developed over a period of twenty years. She uses fabrics and yarns in a combination of hand and machine stitching. Her work has won numerous Art in Architecture Awards, Religious Art Awards and Artist-Craftsman Awards.

Kuemmerlein studied at the Center of Creative Studies, Detroit, Michigan and Cranbrook Academy of Art, Bloomfield Hills, Michigan.

Her work is included in the permanent textile collection of the Chicago Art Institute; The Museum of Contemporary Crafts, New York, New York; The Smithsonian National Collection of Fine Arts, Washington, D.C.; The Rochester Institute of Technology; IBM Corporation; AT&T Building, Golden, Colorado.

Prices are available upon request. There is a 10% retainer for sketches. Supervision of installation by artist is available on request.

(Top) Kansas City Southern Railway, K.C., MO. 4′ × 15′ fiber relief
(Bottom Left and Right) Esson Residence, St. Joseph, MO. 8′ × 17′

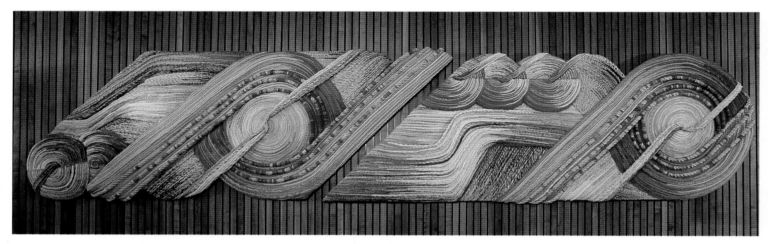

236

# Janet Kuemmerlein

Kuemmerlein Fiber Art Inc.
7701 Canterbury
Prairie Village, KS 66208
(816) 842-7049 (studio)
(913) 649-8292 (home)

(Top) "Free Float" 4' × 12'
(Bottom) "Four Part River" 4' × 30'

# Peggy Clark Lumpkins

Masterweaver
R.R.1 Box 113
Brownville, ME 04414
(207) 965-8526

Peggy Clark Lumpkins' pieces are distinctive for their colors, that illuminate and change with the time of day; for their designs, that stem from nature; and for their consistent fine craftsmanship. Her Transparent Tapestries are handwoven inlay of colorfast linens and wools, they are durable and lightweight. They are often hung in open space, solitary or dangling groups in mobile form; suspended a few inches in front of walls; and in windows. Her pieces are in corporate and private collections across the United States.

Prices range from $50-$150 per sq. ft. retail, depending on complexity of design.

A portfolio is available upon request. Commissions are accepted, including collaborations. Average turnaround, from first contact to installation, is 1½ months.

(Top) "Night Wings" 35"w. × 25"h.
(Bottom) "Amaryllis I" 14½"w. × 24½"h.

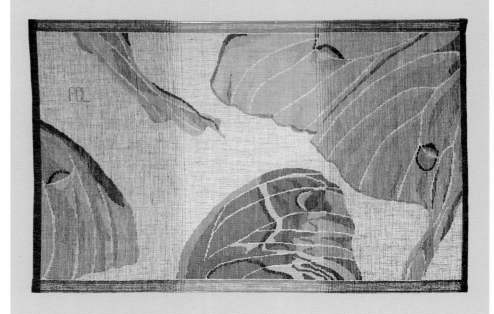

# Nancy Lyon

102 Shaker Street
New London, NH 03257
603-526-6754

Nancy Lyon creates impressionistic landscapes in fiber. Her weaving techniques and compositions explore the many ways in which color, form and texture interact.

Wall hangings are available in different handwoven fabrics with surface decorations including brushed mohair, lustrous cotton and reflective metallic yarns.

Pieces are available in limited editions and by commission. Work ranges from $60–$90 per square foot, retail.

Recent commissions include: IBM; Dupont; Honeywell; New England Telephone; Price-Waterhouse, Pizza Hut Nat.Hdq.; Hyatt Hotels; General Motors; Holiday Inn.

"Sunny Morning Landscape" 52"w × 40"h $866 (retail)

"Copper Fields and Cummulus Sky" 50"w × 56"h $1166 (retail)

# Cynthia Nixon-Hudson

**Cynthia Nixon-Hudson/Images in Fabric**
**P.O. Box 89**
**Pine Grove Mills, PA 16868**
**(814) 238-7251**

Cynthia Nixon-Hudson has designed quilt installations, known for their detailed imagery and rich colors, for public, corporate, and residential settings since 1978. Painted with permanent textile pigments on fine cottons, each multi-layered piece is meticulously machine-quilted for strength and texture. The quilts are displayed behind plexiglas inside enameled frames.

Exhibited nationally, Nixon-Hudson's work is published in five books on contemporary quilting. Commissions include the Baltimore Hilton and Dickinson College.

Prices for site-specific pieces begin at $100 per sq. ft.

"Harrisburg Skyline and Historic Bridges", Polyclinic Medical Center, Harrisburg, PA, 52" × 180"

# Elizabeth Nordgren

**6 Ryan Way**
**Durham, NH 03824**
**(603) 868-2873**

Elizabeth Nordgren designs and weaves contemporary wall pieces. She uses textile inks to
create separate layers of colored warp which
are woven into a single warp-face piece. This
technique allows a play of contrasts of the
basic geometric structure of the weaving
against the organic flow of colors. The heavy
parallels of weft allow for shimmer and an
optical shift as the viewer's position changes.
Each piece is one of a kind and may be developed into multiple images both horizontal
and vertical.

Retail prices range from $60-$70 per square
foot. Please contact the artist for information
about commissions and slides of available
work.

(Top Right) 'Smooth Stones' 31½"w × 50½"h,
(Bottom Right) 'Swoosh' 29"w × 50"h. Both
pieces are woven of viscose with acrylic rods.

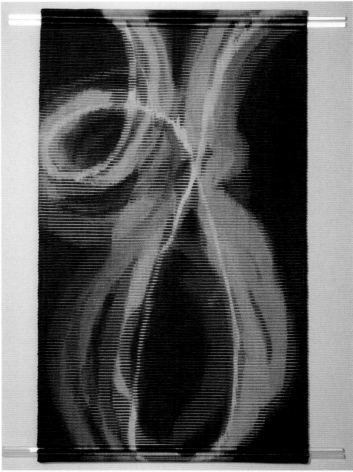

# Irene K. Pittman

**Artist Studio**
**115 South Lincoln**
**Tampa, FL 33609**
**(813) 870-0527**

Irene Pittman hand-paints silk in abstract or realistic designs for various methods of display. Silk panels can be framed for wall installation, or sandwiched between two pieces of acrylic and used as room dividers or aerial mobiles. Painted silk can also be stretched over wooden or aluminum armatures to create flying kites, birds or umbrellas, as shown below.

She also weaves tapestries which range from lightweight, ethereal gauze-weaves to three-dimensional constructions containing textured wool, steel and acrylic.

The silk paintings are priced from $500 for a 40″ × 36″ piece, and the large works are priced according to size and design specifications. Delivery, installation and fireproofing services are available.

Clients include hotels, hospitals, state and county governments, national and international corporations.

(Below) Two of fourteen painted silk umbrellas, which were created for the atrium lobby space of a major hotel.

# Amanda Richardson

Richardson Kirby
P.O. Box 2147
Friday Harbor, WA 98250
(206) 378-3224

Amanda Richardson developed the technique 'Porphyry Tapestry' in which fabrics are bonded together to form a single textile. These fabrics are hand dyed, cut into intricate forms and pieced together, layer on layer, to build up a rich and complex final image. These images give the impression of great spatial depth, with a visual impact few art mediums can equal.

Richardson graduated from Goldsmiths' College, London University. A professional artist for twelve years she has had numerous shows both in America and Europe. The artist works to commission including large tapestries for public places.

Price is $250 per square foot plus installation if desired. Design fee is 10%. Colour brochure: $6.00.

Sandstone Cliff 10½' × 15½' - Rouse Co./Koelher McFadyen
East Anglian Urn 6' × 12' - Carr Co./Washington, D.C.

# Martha Roediger

15 Cloyster Road
South Portland, ME 04106
(207) 799-7548

Working with wool, pearl cotton, rayon, linen, and a striking spectrum of colors, Martha Roediger incorporates movement and light into her designs. Works include transparent linen banners and room dividers.

Roediger earned a B.S. in Art from Skidmore College in Saratoga Springs, New York and completed graduate studies in textiles in Helsinki, Finland. She has more than 20 years experience in creating commissioned work and her pieces have been included in numerous gallery exhibitions.

Prices begin at $90 per sq. ft. (includes design fee). Completion of working drawings and weaving of commissioned works requires minimum of two months.

Slides and a resume are available upon request.

(Top) "Swift Currents", linen, cotton, gold metallic fiber, 12½"w. × 108"h.
(Below) "Currents III", wool and cotton, 96"w. × 74"h.

244

# Koryn Rolstad

**Bannerworks Inc.**
558 1st Avenue South
Seattle, WA 98104
(206) 622-8734

Bannerworks Inc. is a 14-year-old design firm specializing in architectural textiles. Working in collaboration with architects, interior designers and real estate developers, their projects are showcased in shopping malls, museums, airports and corporate art collections.

Koryn Rolstad, whose background is in architecture and industrial design, has developed the firm's scope of services to include working drawings through installation specifications. Drawing from a wide range of resources, Rolstad addressed lighting, acoustic and aesthetic concerns while maintaining the architectural integrity of a space.

Bannerworks, Inc. is pleased to include the Walt Disney Corp., The Smithsonian Institution and the Denver Museum of Natural History as collectors of its work.

Pictured below are commissions for the Doubletree Suite Hotels, Seattle, WA; Jonah's Restaurant, Holiday Inn, Bellevue, WA; Myrtle Square Mall, Myrtle Beach, SC; Architypes, pieced felt. Same image front and back. Collection of the artist, Seattle, WA.

# Jude Russell

4149 S.W. 43rd Ave.
Portland, OR 97221
(503) 297-3546

Jude Russell challenges and expands the traditional concepts of textile arts in a rich and diverse body of work which includes fabric collage, multiple layered transparencies, painted and layered fabric pieces and three-dimensional aerial sculptures and banners.

Russell works in collaboration with architects and design firms on a regular basis and maintains professional standards from preliminary design to execution of all commissions.

Collectors include The Smithsonian Institution, NIKE, Inc., Nordstrom, and Kaiser Hospitals.

Prices range from $100.00–$150.00/sq. ft. retail. A preliminary design fee of $350.00 is required. Completion time after contract approval is 6–12 weeks. Brochure available on request.

(Top left) "Hibiscus" Kress Building, Portland, OR 3' × ll'w.
(Top right) "Hibiscus" detail
(Middle right) "Fandango" 39"h. × 44"w.
(Bottom right) "Mirrored Columns" 40"h. × 50"w.
(Bottom left) "Heavy Showers, Mixed with Rain" 28"h. × 44"w.

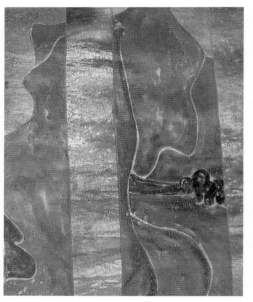

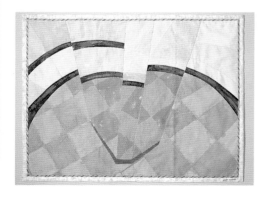

# Joy Saville

**244 Dodds Lane**
**Princeton, NJ 08540**
**(609)924-6824**

Joy Saville's work is informed by color. Cotton, linen, silk, and wool fabrics are used in a unique process of piecing which results in a subtle but densely textured painterly surface. Each abstract, non-objective concept is developed as a personal expression or a response to a specific site. Work is mounted on a hidden frame and size is unlimited. Hanging instructions and care procedures are provided.

Ms. Saville has received two New Jersey Council on the Arts Fellowships. Her work has been exhibited internationally and is included in the collections of the Newark Museum, H.J. Heinz, Pepsico and Colorado Mountain Bell. She works with individual collectors, architects and consultants on site specific commissions.

Please contact the artist for information about commissions, current schedule and slides of available work.

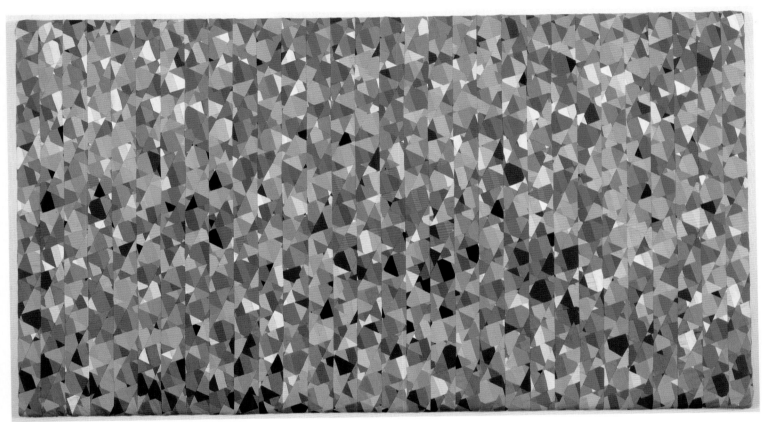

"Nymphaea" ©1989, 41"h. × 73"l., Commissioned by Schaff, Motiuk, Gladstone, Moeller & Reed, Flemington, NJ

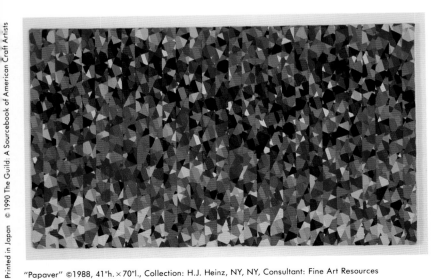

"Papaver" ©1988, 41"h. × 70"l., Collection: H.J. Heinz, NY, NY, Consultant: Fine Art Resources

"Nymphaea", Installation: Conference Room, Flemington, NJ

# Sissi Siska

**154 Second Street**
**Hoboken, NJ 07030**
**(201) 963-9673**

Inspired by the contrast of city life and tropical utopias, Sissi creates paintings on silk. Her unique creations combine ancient batik and modern resist methods. This perfect blend of artistic tradition and contemporary sensibility adds drama to any environment.

An award winning artist, Sissi has twenty years experience designing textiles and has been shown world-wide. Her work was exhibited at Artpark in Lewiston, N.Y. during a recent residency, where a large environmental painting was produced on-site.

Sissi designs large-scale pieces and wall hangings on commission to meet the specifications of private, corporate or architectural settings. Smaller paintings feature museum quality framing.

Further information and current exhibition schedules available upon request; work may also be viewed by appointment.

(top) "Leland's Garden" 30" × 32"
(bottom) "Butterflies" detail, 20" × 20"

248

# Susan Starr

1580 Jones Road
Roswell, GA 30075
(404) 993-3980

Tapestry and wall and free hanging constructions by Susan Starr are rich in color and texture. A wide variety of materials are used, including hand-dyed wools, silk, cotton, rayon, plexiglass, wooden rods and handmade papers. Starr's work has been featured in publications such as *USA Today, Interior Design* and *Contract*. AT&T, Bank of America and Marriott and Hyatt Hotels are among her many corporate clients.

Works are available in a range of sizes; the largest to date measures 50' × 27". Designed for specific sites in consultation with architects, interior designers, galleries and individuals, her wall pieces hang in hospitals, office lobbies, hotels, residences and restaurants.

Types of work available include: flat and dimensional tapestries, stick constructions, kite forms, and handmade paper constructions.

# Janice M. Sullivan

4166 A 20th St.
San Francisco, CA 94114
(415) 431-6835

By exploring reflective material in conjunction with woven structures and painted surfaces, Janice Sullivan creates one of a kind "Woven Paintings". Textural effects are developed by layering, pleating, and handpainting multi-patterned woven fabric. The interaction of light with metallic and rayon fibers, and manipulated surfaces enhance the dramatic effect of these wallpieces.

Sullivan exhibits nationally, and is represented in many corporate and private collections. The wallpieces range in size and are priced per square foot. Commissioned work is accepted with a $300 design fee which includes consultation, drawings, and marquette woven to scale. Average delivery time is 6-8 weeks. Portfolio and prices are available upon request.

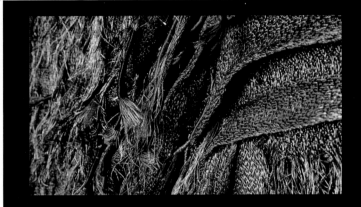

(top) "On Edge", 1988, 36" × 48" × 2"
(middle) Detail
(Bottom) "Hot Tips", 1987, 48" × 48" × 4", Collection: Kaiser Health Organization of Northern CA.

# Cameron Taylor-Brown

418 South Mansfield Avenue
Los Angeles, CA 90036
(213) 938-0088

Cameron Taylor-Brown creates dimensional woven reliefs composed of intricate patterns and colorfields. Her work reflects a sophisticated manipulation of structure and color and a rich attention to detail.

Direct purchase and commissions are available. Taylor-Brown works directly with the interior designer to develop the most appropriate piece for the site.

Prices range from $100 to $150 per square foot, based on size, materials, and technique. Commissions include a sketch or model, with a woven sample, and take from two to six months to complete.

Cameron Taylor-Brown exhibits nationally. Her work has been published in American Craft, Designers West, Interior Design, and Fiberarts. Clients include the Sheraton Hotels, Daon Corporation, William Feldman Associates, and Palmcrest House.

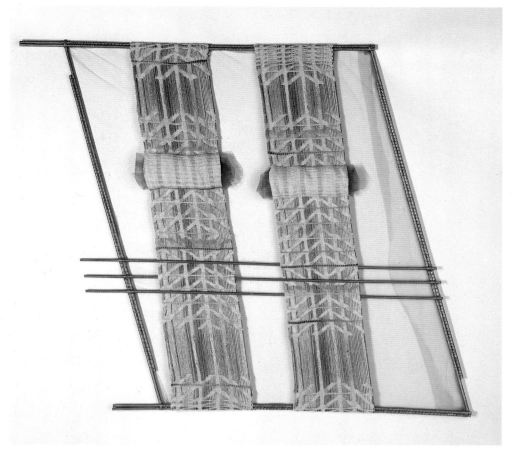

All That Glitters/Diamonds on the Move 45" × 39"

Suspended Animation 50" × 84" × 14"

No More Tangles 36" × 36"

# Vincent Tolpo
# Carolyn Lee Tolpo

55918 U.S. Highway 285 P.O. Box 134
Shawnee, CO 80475
(303)670-1733

Since 1981, Vincent and Carolyn Lee Tolpo have created site-specific wrapped fiberart for public, corporate, and residential spaces. Working with clients, designers, consultants, and architects, their collaborative fibers consider color, concept, space, and budget. Project art can be commissioned direct by phone and correspondence beginning with pre-approved color drawings and material samples.

The Tolpo's fiberwrapped art provides a lightweight, durable, cleanable, high-tech/high-touch, sound-absorbant, textural form for today's contemporary setting. Imagery ranges from landscape to abstract. Surfaces may be flat, bas-relief, three-dimensional, or combined structurally with metal, metallic mylar, acrylic prisms, or stoneware.

Prices, video, photo/slide catalogue including other media available. Prices: $80-$200 square foot. Delivery and installation available.

Collections: Digital Corporation, U.S. West, Rosewood Development.

(Clockwise) Irides, Zona Moonset, Equilibrant, Scrolls.

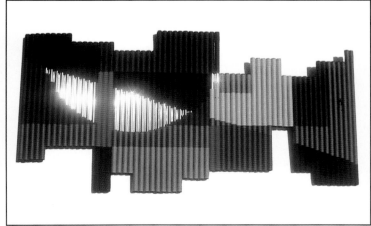

# Pamela Twycross-Reed

117 Lamarck Drive
Snyder, NY 14226
(716) 839-2691

Weaver Pamela Twycross-Reed creates three-dimensional wall-hung or free-standing works featuring abstract landscape tapestries. After completion of the weaving process her tapestries are stretched on wood-laminated convex forms and framed in plexiglass and wood.

Working with designers and architects the artist has completed over 100 commissions for private and corporate installations.

Prices range from $85 - $100 per sq. ft. plus cost of frame and shipping or installation.

(Top left) 5 piece tapestry 8'w. × 6'h. "Tideless Gardens."
(Top right) Installation, Civic Center, Saratoga Springs, NY 15'w. × 5'h.
(Bottom) 4 piece tapestry 8'w. × 5'h. "Fiesta"

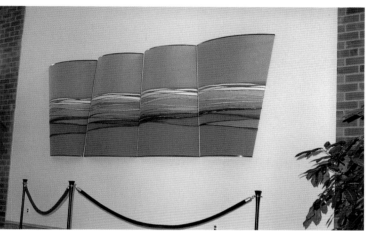

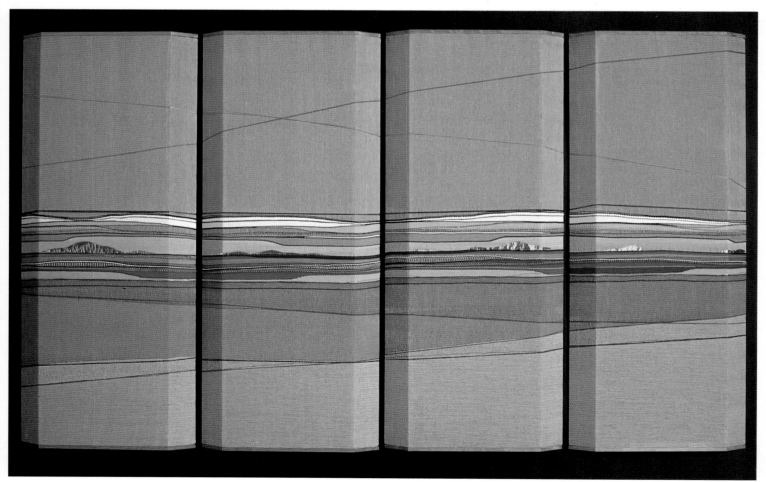

# Joen Wolfrom

**104 Bon Bluff**
**Fox Island, WA 98333**
**(206) 549-2395**

Joen Wolfrom specializes in creating art for site-specific residential and contractual interiors, having over 15 years of experience in the field. The diversity of the artist allows her to create scenic or abstract art, depending upon the client's desires.

The artist's works are in numerous national and international collections, including museums, hospitals, medical, business and law offices, and manufacturing headquarters.

Ms. Wolfrom uses both hand-dyed and commercially-dyed textiles of the highest quality. Her work may be framed, placed in Plexiglass boxes, hung loosely, or suspended from the ceiling. She welcomes innovative design placement.

Delivery time depends upon the scope of the commission and the artist's current schedule. Price range: $100–$250 per square foot.

Photos: Artwork commissioned by Ulster Folk and Transport Museum; Belfast, Northern Ireland

# Paper and
# Mixed Media

# Karen Adachi

**702 Monarch Way**
**Santa Cruz, CA 95060**
**(408) 429-6192**

Karen Adachi creates her three-dimensional handmade paper pieces by using layers of irregularly shaped vacuum-cast paper. She makes free-standing two-sided sculptures and wall-pieces for corporate, private and residential interiors. Her work is shown nationally through major galleries and representatives.

The pieces are richly-textured and embellished with dyes, acrylics, metallics and pearlescents. Painted bamboo and sticks are used to create a dramatic statement of pattern and line. Three-dimensional sculptures are mounted on painted metal bases for stability and strength.

Retail prices range from $250-$5,000 depending on size. Custom work in any size, shape, and color is available.

Contact artist for further information and slides.

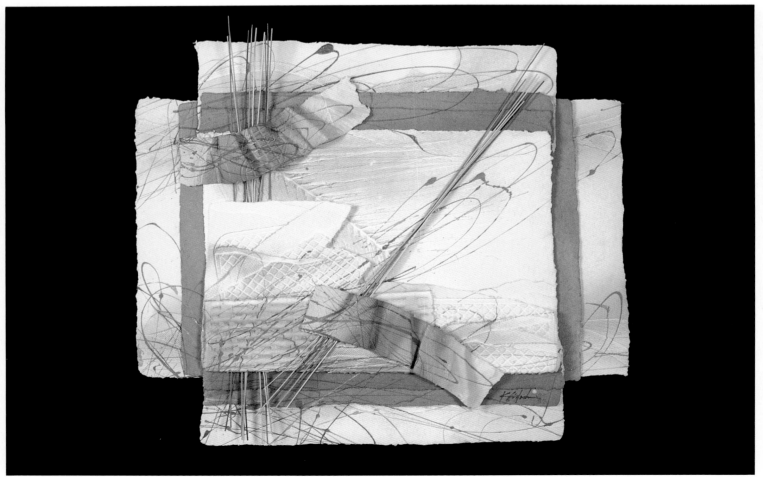

# Blake Alexander

**1306 Hollywood**
**Dallas, TX 75208**
**(214) 333-4561**

Blake Alexander's three-dimensional "structures" combine her handmade, handdyed paper with other media such as balsa wood, reeds, quills, beads, and linen fibers. Her handpainted designs are based on architectural concepts. The two pieces shown are titled "Rooftop" and "Bridge."

Framed prices range from $275.00 to $2000.00. Commissioned work, collaborations and installations available. Production time depends on intricacy of piece and artist's schedule.

Portfolio and additional slides available upon request.

Blake Alexander also designs a two dimensional line of artwork combining her handmade paper with other materials.

She creates both abstract and representational images. Prices range from $40.00 to $350.00. Portfolio and additional information available.

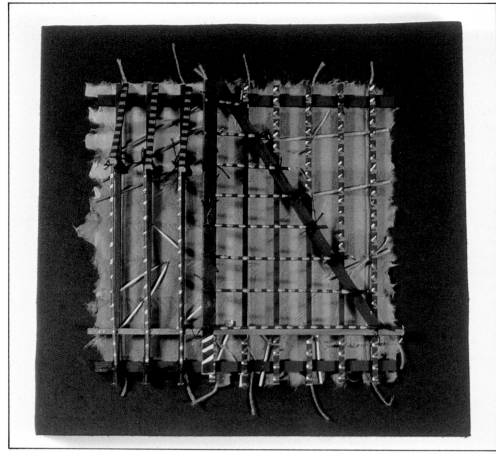

"Rooftop"—Handmade paper with structure 10"w. × 10"h. × 4"d.

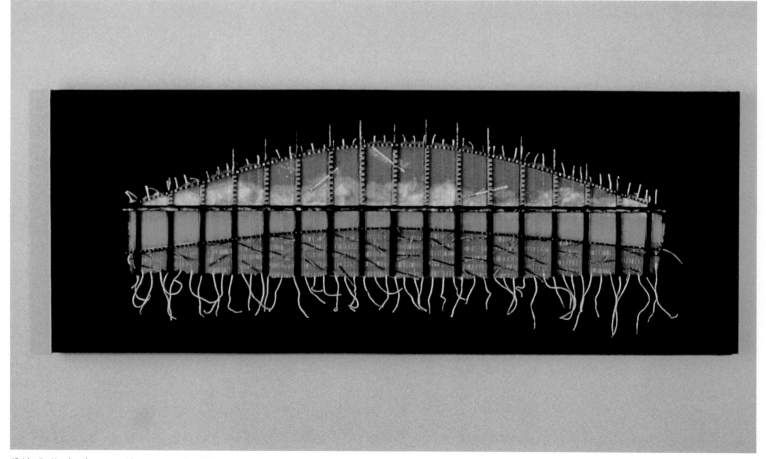

"Bridge"—Handmade paper with structure 46"w. × 18"h. × 6"d.

# Dona Anderson

1913 13th W.
Seattle, WA 98119
(206) 284-8333
(206) 283-4951

Dona Anderson works in a multitude of innovative materials from foamcore and aluminum to colored nail polish and plastic, creating 3-D wall pieces in which surfaces are composed by layering until the design depth comes through.

Works are usually large, meant as focal points of special rooms. They can be shipped F.O.B. Seattle, framed in custom plexiglass boxes or unframed. Prices range from $700-3,000 at retail.
Andersons mixed media pieces are included in many corporate and private collections including: Charles Russell Museum, Great Falls, MT, Nora Eccles Harrison Museum of Art, Logan, UT, Westin Hotels, Great Western Savings Bank, Ben Bridge Jeweler, Washington State 1% for art.

(Top) Contemporary Landscape 50"h × 40"w.
(Bottom) Downtown Traffic 40inh × 60"w.

# Therese Bisceglia

Rt. 9, Box 90-KS
Santa Fe, NM 87505
(505) 982-5914

Therese Bisceglia's new work in handmade paper is influenced by her move from Boston to Santa Fe. Each piece is a brief narration of a glimpse of life as seen through the artist's eyes and sense of humor. Non-narrative work which focus on color and texture is also available. Portfolio is available upon request. Commissions are welcome. Prices range from $75.00 to $200.00 per sq. ft. depending on complexity.

(Top) "New Beginnings-Far from Home", 36" × 39" × 1"
(Bottom) "New Beginnings-Time Change", 57" × 30" × 3"

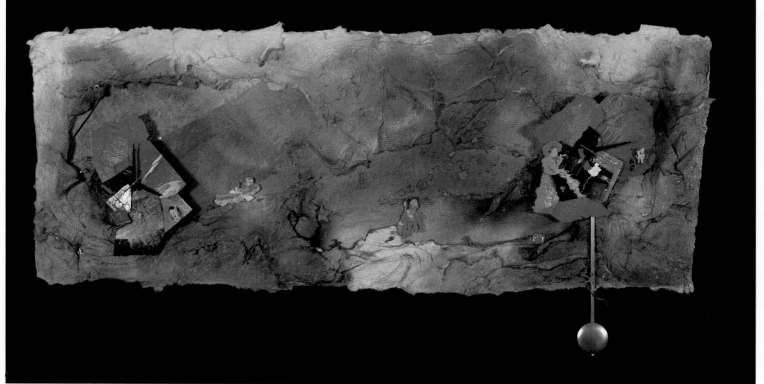

# Martha Chatelain

**Artfocus, Ltd.**
833 "G" Street
P.O. Box 127238
San Diego, CA 92112
(619) 234-0749

Martha Chatelain creates three-dimensional handmade paper wall sculptures from cotton and abaca fibers. Richly textured and enhanced with fiber reactive dyes, acrylic paints and iridescent mica powders, Chatelain's artwork complements the architectural and design features of the interior spaces for which it is created.

Prices range from $900–$6000 depending on the size and complexity of the work. Allow 6–8 weeks for delivery following design approval and price contract. Works are shipped FOB San Diego unframed or in custom plexiglas box frames.

Selected collections and commissions: Bank of America, The Hahn Company, IBM, Nordstrom; Potlatch Company; Price-Waterhouse; and the Hilton, Radisson and Sheraton hotels. Contact Chatelain to discuss design specifications and client environment, corporate or residential.

(Top) "Virtuoso", 28″×89″×4″
(Bottom left) "Windrow", 35″×21″×3″
(Bottom right) "Shikuramen", 56″×75″×4″

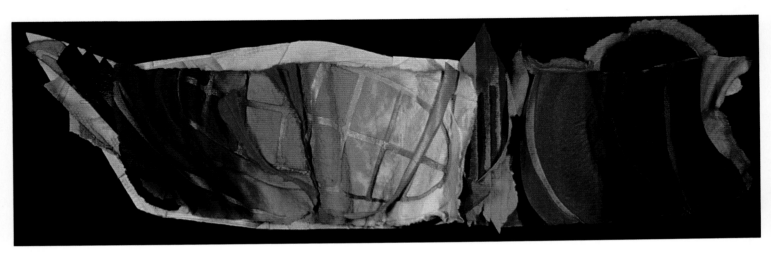

# Susanne Clawson

**5093 Velda Dairy Rd.**
**Tallahassee, FL 32308**
**(904) 893-5656**

The handmade paper and fiber works by Susanne Clawson are vibrant with color, texture, and depth. Fiber-reactive dyes and pigments are used in the handmade papers to ensure bright, fade-resistant color. The fiber pieces are created from wool, rayon, silk, and metallic yarns.

Her works have been exhibited nationally and have won awards. Recent corporate purchases include IBM and the State of Florida.

The artist custom designs her work to fit corporate and residential specifications. Prices range from $500 to $10,000. Average time for completion of commissions is 6–8 weeks, after design approval and deposit. Please contact the artist for additional information and slides.

Left: "Starport: Rigel," mixed media on handmade paper
Right: "Firebird" (detail), handmade paper with dyed sisal fibers
Bottom: "The Jewelled Forest" (detail), fiber

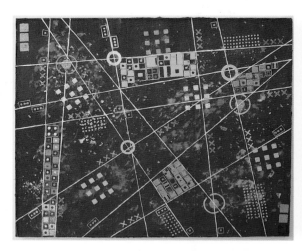
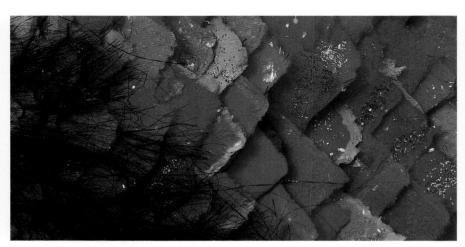

# Beth Cunningham

32 Sweetcake Mountain Road
New Fairfield, CT 06812
(203) 746-5160

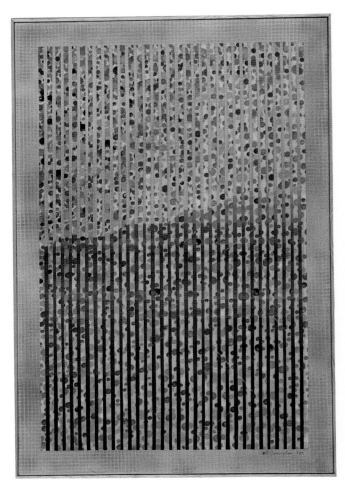

Through the use of unprimed canvas, muslin, silk tissue paper, acrylic paint and polymer and a collage technique, Beth Cunningham creates a product which trancends both fine art and fine craft. Recent abstractions vary in color from the subtly pastel to the sensationally vivid. Her goal is to produce a durable product for the corporate and residential sectors. Her most recent acquisition was by the Heinz Corporation, NYC.

All wall pieces are designed and executed by the artist, with collaborative work considered. Commissions: 125-$150 per sq. ft. retail depending on surface texture selected. Average delivery time is 6 to 8 weeks after contract approval and receipt of deposit. Completed works are also available. Information available upon request.

These featured works are representative of the color gradation and graphic layout found in her constructions.

(Top) Strata, 36" × 24"
(Bottom) Future Tense Melody, 26" × 38"

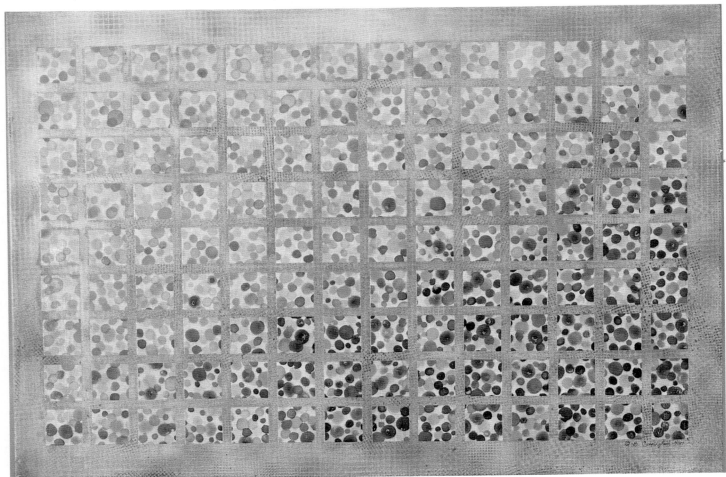

# Eileen Custer

**E. Custer Paperworks**
**870 Red Oak Lane**
**Minnetrista, MN 55364**
**(612) 472-3189**

Eileen Custer has been creating artwork for residential and corporate collections since 1977. She has presented her work through invitational and juried shows internationally.

Eileen works with clients to create site-specific pieces for contemporary and traditional interiors.

Her paper is made from natural material including cotton, linen, cattail, and abaca. Dyes are not used. Colors and textures are derived from a combination of fabrics, resulting in fade resistant colors from pastels to deep rich tones. These dimensional pieces may incorporate found objects, surface embossing, painting, pearlescent crystals, and sculptural forms.

Prices range from $90 to $200 per square foot. Works shipped ready for framing. Please contact the artist for further information and catalog.

# Pamela Dalton

Scherenschnitte
RD 2 Box 226A
Harlemville
Ghent, NY 12075
(518) 672-4841

Pamela Dalton's Scherenschnitte are created in the tradition of early nineteenth century American paper cutting. Biblical motifs and themes focusing on rural life are frequently used. Each piece is cut from a single sheet of paper and then water colored. Pieces cut from solid black silhouette paper and antiqued white paper are also available. Work is framed in wood which is false grained in the traditional vinegar/pigment method by the artist.

Prices for standard designs range from $60 to $1,000. Custom and personalized work is also available. Prices on commissions are determined by size and intricacy of the piece. Inquiries are welcome.

(Below) "Anniversary" 26"h. × 32"w.

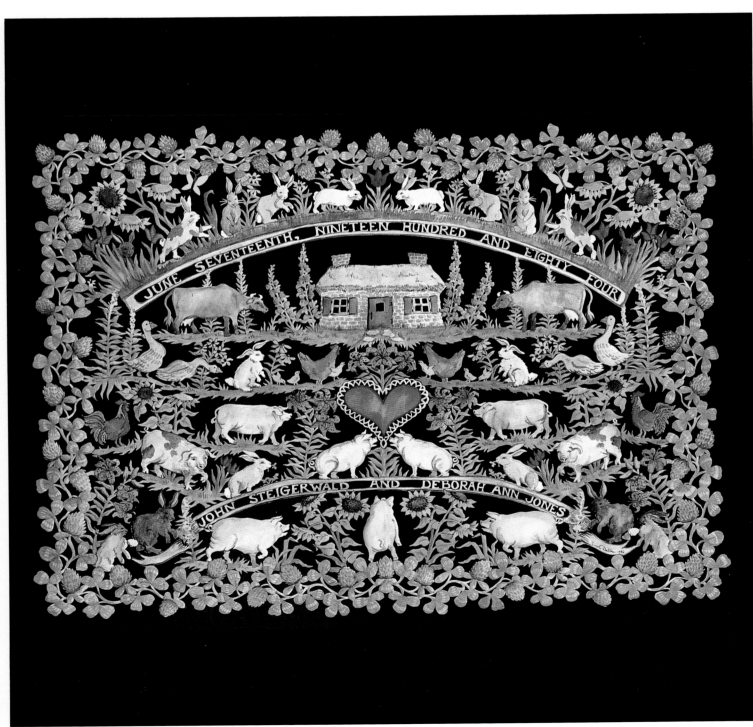

# Crafts in the Office Environment

As the complex technology of the office environment increases, there is a trend to surround the employee with items and objects that recall familiar and more human aspects of life. The new phrase "high tech/soft touch" has real meaning as human beings deal with the lack of free form inspiration in rather sterile office spaces. The typical employee stares at a computerscreen for an average of eight hours a day. There is need for relief from the regimented information that data bases usually produce. For a break from that form of visual order, we will always want a sense of excitement, color, and joy through our material expressions, even in the office.

In my former association with an architectural firm, it was always interesting to walk through a completed office installation at the end of the project and before the client moved in. We wanted every element to be perfect and visually correct for the photographer and to fulfill our own sense of design order. However, six months later, the new employees had put their own version of aesthetics into place. There were exhibits of the kids' first art experiences, the ill-placed vase and plant, and the inevitable softball trophy. These things made the office more livable and home like. These expressions are natural human tendencies towards softening the hard edges of contemporary design.

We would never advise against the "melding" of pure architecture and everyday office experience. They are going to occur anyway. However, the advantage of using crafts in commercial design anticipates the user's demand for a human connection that can be enjoyed by all. Crafts add warmth, color, texture, and a sense of comfort away from the home. They also enhance and expand upon corporate art collections. Good craft pieces can ultimately contribute to the value of a corporation's investment as the value of certain artists' work appreciates with time.

It is important to think of the integration of crafts in the office in the early phases of conceptual design. One must educate and inform the client of the process of selection and what the appropriate mix of elements in the ultimate design should be. The more successful spaces incorporate special craft images early on rather than placing work later in a careless way or as an afterthought.

As we move into the 1990's, we are fortunate that the craft movement has spent the last decade becoming organized and professional. The good artists have really come to the fore front of the American arts scene and are recognized through THE GUILD and in their own right. We can take advantage of their exciting artistic work, not only in our personal collections, but in the workaday world. We can make the office a special place to enjoy the cultural expressions that crafts bring to our lives.

**Diane Barnes**
**Principal, Barnes and Brandt, Inc.**
**New York, New York**

# Barbara F. Fletcher

**88 Beals Street**
**Brookline, MA 02146**
**(617) 277-3019**

Barbara Fletcher creates cast paper wall and pedestal pieces. Wet paper pulp is air dried in plaster casts which are made from clay forms. One of a kinds or multiples can be made with this process. The pieces are painted with procion dyes to give a wonderful luminosity. The paper is made in many layers for durability and then coated with a protective acrylic making it appropriate for commercial as well as residential space. Fletcher's pieces are unique for their intense color, texture and whimsicality. Her work has been exhibited nationally and is included in many private collections including writer Stephen King.

Prices range from $200-1000. Slides are available upon request. Commissions are accepted.

(Right) Fish Aquarium and Sculptures on plexiglass stands(Below) Flying Fish and Bird

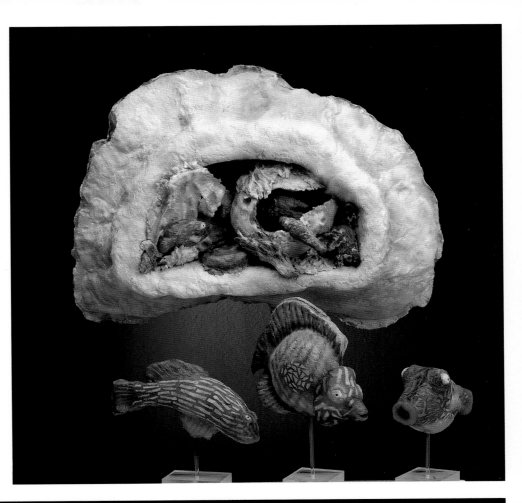

# F.B. Fogg

3208 Burlington Drive
Muncie, IN 47302
(317) 289-7464

F.B. Fogg has been making paper by hand for the last twenty-five years using cotton, lint and a multitude of other materials. The sculptural forms are cast from life and then manipulated, forming provocative statements. The sculptures command a neo-classical presence appearing massive, bold and dramatic, when in fact they are weightless and airy. The colors are limitless and pulps may be dyed to match. Coarse beatings, triple sizing and foam give stability and insulation against shock.

Albright-Knox, Renwick, Indianapolis, Milwaukee, Museum of Contemporary Art, Chicago, Illinois number among the galleries displaying F.B. Fogg's work. Leading shows for this year's season are OB Art Atelier d'Art, Paris, France and the ACC Craftfair in Baltimore, Maryland.

All sculptures are life-size. Columns are made in any height. Figurative and other compositions range from $45.00-$1,800.00 Catalogues available upon request—$2.00

# Kelly A. Harney

150 Weetamoe Street
Fall River, MA 02720
(508) 675-2041

Kelly Harney creates one-of-a-kind wall pieces combining handcast paper, hand-painted fiber and found objects. A variety of techniques and materials are used to develop the glowing color and rich textures evident in her work. Pieces are designed for single or multiple installation and are available custom-framed and ready for display in private residences, corporate environments and public spaces. Prices range from $600-$1200. Commissions are accepted.

(Right) Handmade paper and mixed media on dyed, painted cotton. 16"w. × 26"h. × 4"d.
(Below) Handmade paper and mixed media on dyed, painted cotton. 30"w. × 15"h. × 4"d.

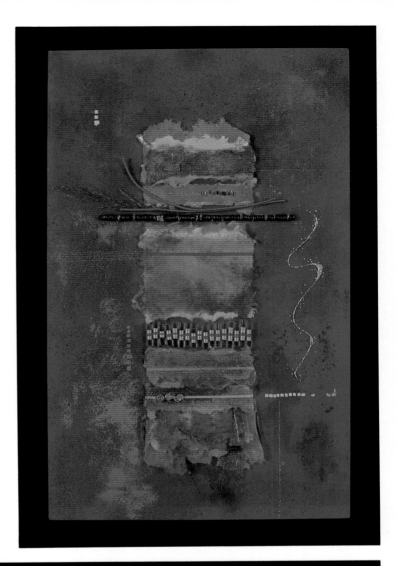

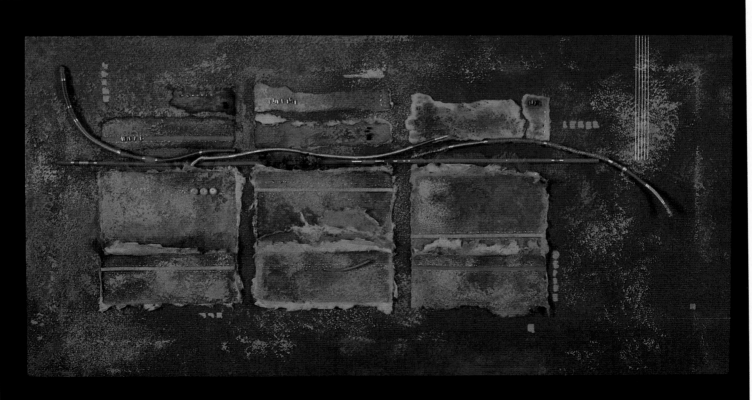

# Carol Herd

**1101 North High Cross**
**Urbana, IL 61801**
**(217) 328-0118 (Studio)**
**(217) 328-4864 (Fax)**

Carol Herd's mastery of paper as a material of personal expression transcends the boundaries of craft. In her work she builds up many subtle washes of pigmented pulp to develop the image. Each work is a single isostatic sheet of fine handmade paper.

The techniques exercised by Herd allow very direct expression of her experience in nature. Each work shares with the viewer a spontaneous influence of mood and season, representing a unique moment and character.

Herd began working in hand made paper in 1980. She received both her baccalaureate and masters degrees for her work in paper. She currently teaches paper at the University of Illinois. Herd is internationally active in papermaking, giving workshops, lectures, and presentations of her work.

Please contact the artist regarding portfolio and pricing. Commissions are accepted. Companion works available.

"Forest Series #62B, C". 38″×26″ each © 1989 Cotton fiber–pigment.

"Forest Series #46". 38″×26″ © 1989 Cotton fiber–pigment.

"Forest Series #31". 35″×31″ © 1989 Cotton fiber–pigment.

"Forest Series #68". 38″×26″ © 1989 Cotton fiber– pigment.

# Annette M. Kearney

**67 Highland Street**
**Portland, ME 04103**
**(207) 772-0802**

Boldly positioned colors, like three-dimensional brush strokes, characterize the sculptural wall pieces of Annette Kearney. Constructed of heavy canvas and nonwoven fabric, the layers of juxtaposed materials glow with the subtle use of iridescent and metallic paints and the rich coloration of acrylics.

Whether using a subdued palette or an intense combination of colors, Kearney's three dimensional forms have earned her national recognition in books and exhibitions. Her work is strikingly used in both public and residential spaces. Prices range from $500—$4000.

(Top) "An Exceeding Sun" 37"w. × 34"h. × 11'd.
(Bottom) "Untitled" 40"w. × 32"h. × 8"d.

271

# Bonny Lhotka

**5011 Ellsworth Place**
**Boulder, CO 80303**
**(303) 442-7163**

Lhotka's work is created on cast paper using acrylic paint to create vibrant images unique in the art world. Her distinctive work is coated with a polymer that enables it to be exhibited without additional protection.

Her ability to finish pieces in 3-4 weeks, while following the client's colors and architectural concepts, has made her one of the most sought after artists in the nation. She is able to work with the designer from concept to installation.

A professional for over 17 years, Her work is in the collections of AT&T, Coca-Cola Foods, Hilton Hotel, Houston Conference Center, IBM, Johnson Space Center, Marriott Hotel, McDonnell Douglas, Prudential Life, Shell Oil, United Airlines, and many others.

A 4×8 foot work retails for around $4400 unframed.

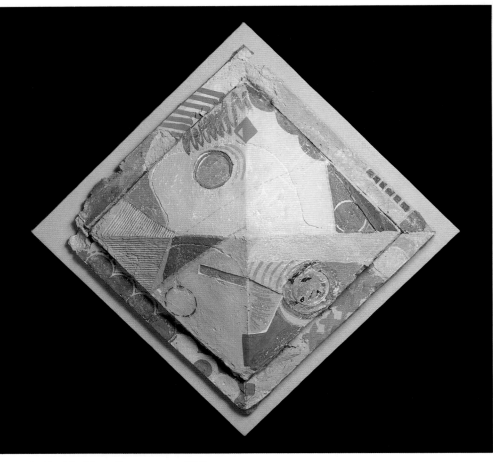

"Pyramid," 27"×27"×10", acrylic on cast paper, $1100

"Recycled," 48"×48"×1.5", acrylic on cast paper, $2200

# Kathy Littel

**Tide Lines Studio**
P.O. Box 406
Harvey Cedars, NJ 08008
609-494-4727

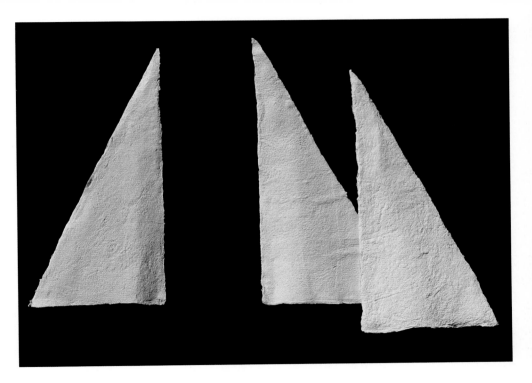

Kathy Littel draws her inspirations from nature, particularly the ocean environment, for her handmade paper works. Her works consist primarily of dimensional wallhangings, pulp paintings, and cast editions. Controlled and freeflowing pigmented pulps, built up in layers, create subtle blends of color. Fields of texture are created using various techniques including pulp spraying, casting, embossing, and embedded objects. The light weight of pulp is ideal for large wallhangings.

Her works are exhibited in galleries throughout the US and have been featured in many exhibitions.

Prices from $10–$35 per sq. ft., depending on complexity.

Corporate, commercial, and residential commissions invited, as is collaboration on site-specific work.
(Top) Sailboats 3½' × 6' Cotton, flax.
(Bottom) Surf Waves 3' × 5½' Abaca.

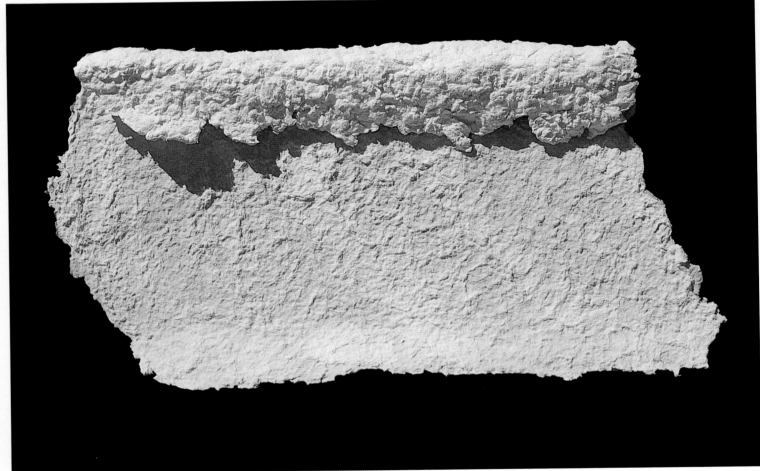

# Peter Nelson

**14116 True Mt. Dr.,**
**Larkspur, CO 80118**
**(719) 481-3293**

From ordinary materials an extraordinary, new medium is born. In Peter Nelson's paintings, warm inviting colors dance across geometrically defined tapestry-like surfaces. To create this effect, Nelson applies airbrushed opaque and metallic acrylics to laminated strips of corrugated board. These unusual works add interest to public spaces and intimate settings alike.

Each painting is sealed with matte acrylic varnish, and a rigid framework is attached to the back. For larger wall areas, paintings are completed in sections and shipped ready to hang.

Prices run about $75 per square foot, plus shipping. Delivery time is 3 to 12 weeks, depending on size and complexity of design. To see a representative portfolio, please contact the artist.

Shown below: (Top) 69″ × 26″
(Lower Left) 39″ × 39″
(Lower Right) 59″ × 38″

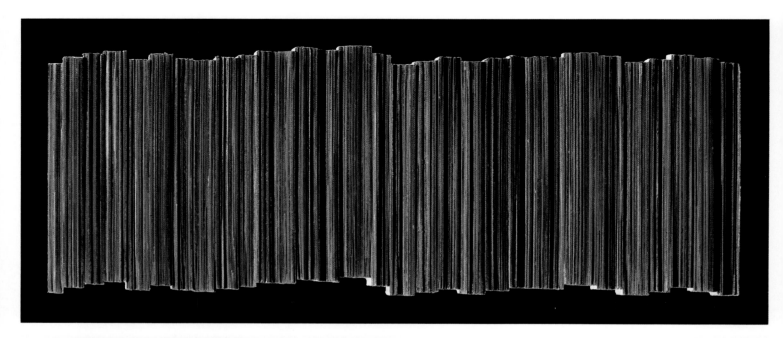

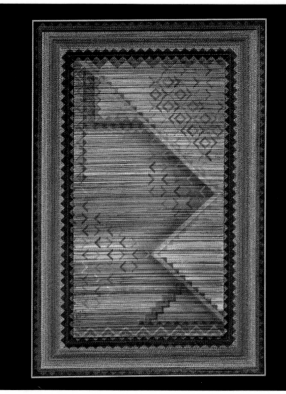

# Nancy Stage Robinson

**Robinson Studio**
**219 West Colorado Avenue, Suite 208**
**Colorado Springs, CO 80903**
**(719) 632-4777**

Nancy Robinson works in a variety of mediums: monotype, hand made paper, and oil on canvas. Her subjects range from abstract to landscapes, florals, and Orientals. Nancy offers a variety of styles and subjects to give interest to large installations.

The artist's work is in corporate, hotel and private collections nationally and internationally—she welcomes site-specific commissions. Prices are determined by complexity, size and type of installation and range from $600 to $10,000.

## Publications, Exhibits and Installations

*Art Business News*
*Springs Magazine*
*Colorado Springs Gazette* - Feature 1985 and 1989
Business of Art Center
Colorado Springs Fine Art Center
Trump Castle, Atlantic City
Hilton, Las Vegas
Red Lion Inn, Salt Lake City
Marriott Hotels, Providence, RI
       Colorado Springs, CO
       San Diego, CA (Symphony Towers)

Portfolio and video available

"Kimono" - 48 × 40 - oil on canvas

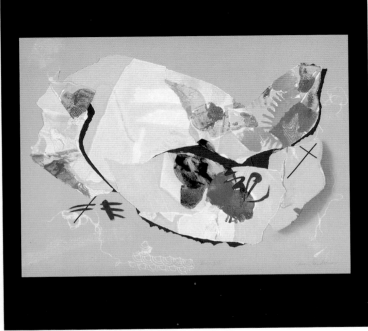

"Collage de la Chine" - monotype - paper

"Floral" - 40" × $15' center of triptych Providence, RI Marriott (lobby) oil and gold leaf on canvas

# Ruth H. Schiffer

**57 Old Rock Lane**
**West Norwalk, CT 06850**
**(203) 966-8330**

Ruth Schiffer's abstract handmade paper pieces are rich in color, texture and sensibility. She has explored many techniques and offers a wide variety of styles. Each work is original and adheres to current archival standards.

Schiffer welcomes commissions from both corporate and private clients. She will work to particular size and color specifications. Pieces can be grouped or used as multiples to accommodate large spaces. Prices fluctuate depending upon size and complexity. Works start at 12" × 18" for $250 retail and range currently to 6' × 7' for $6,000. Some can be shipped unframed while others need the protection of plexiglass boxes.

Selected collections include: Xerox, Great Northern Nekoosa, Indianapolis Breast Center, Champion International, Weatherspoon Art Gallery, University of North Carolina, Royal Orleans Hotel and The Pyramid Companies.

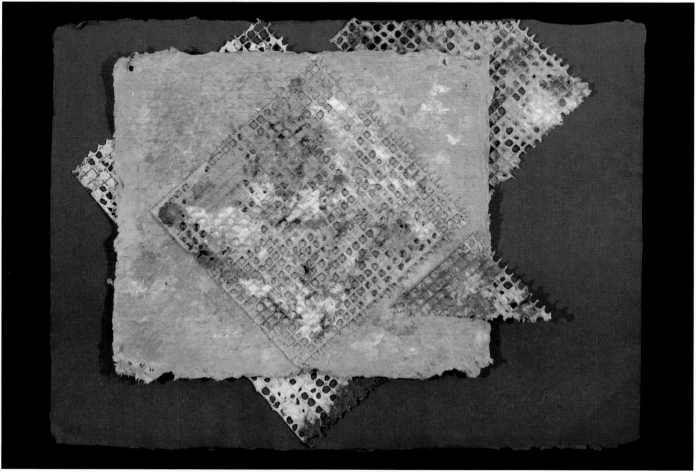

Opposite Page:

(top left) "Camouflage." (Detail)
(top right) "Camouflage." 1988. 20 × 24 × 2¼".
(bottom) "Squared Away." 1989.
23½ × 31½ × 2".

This Page:

(top) "Sunset." 25 × 63 × 2¼"
(bottom) "Sunset." (Detail)

Photography by Craig B. Allen

# Pamela Shore

**71 Park Street**
**Brookline, MA 02146**
**617-734-0409**
**513-522-8674**

Pamela Shore is currently working in collaboration with Rug Road Handmade paper in Summerville, Massachusetts. The pieces shown here are original paintings made from multiple layers of colored paper pulp. Her pieces are primarily still lives rich in color and texture.

Her pieces have been used in corporate and private spaces. Prices slides and resume are available upon request.

# Wayne Fuerst

(508) 881-2525

# Pamela Shore

(617) 734-0409

Pam and Wayne have been working for three years on this project. A collaboration of Handcrafted Plates and Bowls filled with bright color.

The forms are thrown with Terracotta clay by Wayne and slipped with a porcelain clay. Pam Shore designs and paints the surface with under glazes. The pieces are then finished with a gloss glaze.

Vases, tiles and dinnerware are other products available by Fuerst and Shore.

Slides, Resume and Prices are available upon request.

Photos: Marc Malin

# Patricia Spark

**Spark Fiber Art**
**1032 Washington St. S.W.**
**Albany, OR 97321**
**(503) 926-1095**

Patricia Spark creates mixed media wall pieces using wrapped willow sticks with handmade wool felt and/or silk paper. She obtains the rich hues in her pieces by using colorfast dyes. The fibers are then blended so that intricate color transitions are created. The finished, one-of-a-kind works are attached to an archival linen ground and then framed for pest and dust protection.

Spark's award-winning art work has been exhibited widely in the United States and Europe. She is represented in public and private collections throughout the United States.

Prices range from $200–$1,000 depending upon size and intricacy. Contact the artist for commissions and slides of available work.

(Above) "Wings" 30"w. × 36"h.
(Below) "Night's Falling II" 28"w. × 30"h.

# Emily Standley and Peggy Vanbianchi

**7035 Crawford Drive**
**Kingston, WA 98346**
**(206) 297-3068/(206) 842-8795**

Hauntingly beautiful, award-winning artwork. Mysterious pieces that recall distant cultures with a contemporary interpretation.

Emily Standley and Peggy Vanbianchi are collaborative artists who are willing to work closely with designers to meet budget and space requirements. The art works are constructed from translucent materials, then encased in plexiglass for easy care, convenient installation, and durability. Restaurants, hotels and corporate offices have commissioned their pieces for the unique way they define space and allow light to filter through.

Standley and Vanbianchi have their pieces in public and private collections, galleries, museums, and publications. Please write for further information.

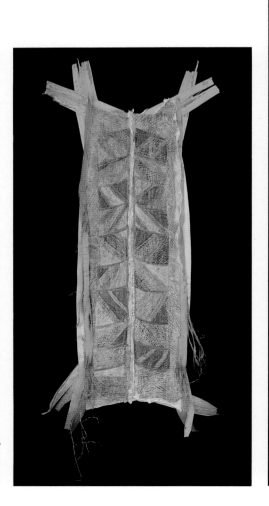

# Beth Ames Swartz

5346 East Sapphire Lane
Scottsdale, Arizona 85253
(602) 948-6112

MEDIA; mixed media on layered paper; collage on canvas; stained-glass. Public and Private commissions, stained glass windows, contemplative environments; will collaborate and install; price range $5,000 — 15,000

Twenty five solo exhibitions nationally; three traveling museum exhibitions; Inquiry into Fire (1978-1980); Israel Revisited (1981-1983) premiered at the Jewish Museum, New York; A Moving Point of Balance (1985-1992).

Selected Public and Corporate Collections: National Museum of American Art, Smithsonian Institution, Washington, D.C.; San Francisco Museum of Modern Art, San Francisco, CA; The Jewish Museum, New York, NY; The Brooklyn Museum, New York, NY; IBM Corporation, Prudential Life Insurance Company; Phoenix Sky Harbor International Airport; Doubletree Inns; Performing Arts Theatre, Calgary, Canada.

# Raymond D. Tomasso

Inter-Ocean Curiosity Studio
2998 South Bannock
Englewood, CO 80110
(303) 789-0282

Using his own 100% rag handmade paper, etched gold, silver or copper leaf and various mediums of color, Raymond D. Tomasso creates rich and timeless images that belie the eye and mind. What appear to be remnants of archaeological collages are three-dimensional handcast paper pieces which are given a clear coat of flat lacquer to insure both intrinsic and extrinsic durability.

Tomasso has specialized in this medium for over 15 years and is recognized both nationally and internationally, in private, public and corporate interests. Selected commissions and collections include: IBM, AT&T, Coca Cola Company, American Bell, US West, Prudential-Bache Securities, Sheraton Hotels, Hyatt Regency, University of Arizona, Emory University and Knoxville Museum of Art.

The artist will design this work to custom fit architectural specifications.

Bronze Tile Game (Copper Version) 17" × 20½"

Notes From The Last Auction of Dreams 36" × 24"

The Memory of the Dream was Sunburned by the Light of Day and Started to Peel 37" × 25"

# Marjorie Tomchuk

44 Horton Lane
New Canaan, CT 06840
203-972-0137

As a professional artist for 27 years, Marjorie Tomchuk has art in more than 50 major corporations, including: IBM; Xerox; Citicorp, AT&T, General Electric. She specializes in limited edition embossed prints on artist-made paper also, paintings on cast paper. Style is semi-abstract.

The embossings are editions of 100, retail 600.00, available immediately. They can be sent out for client approval, shipped COD— check held 30 days. A 12 page color brochure packet can be obtained for reference, price: 4.00 ppd. Commissioned art: sizes up to 4′×6′, retail: 2000.00–3200.00. Maquette fee 150.00, delivery: 6–8 weeks. Also available: a hard cover book "M. Tomchuk, Graphic Work 1962–1989", 143 pages, 32.00 ppd.

Top right: "Red Hills," mural 3′×16′, painting on cast paper, commissioned by Northern Telecom. Below: "After the Storm" original print, 26″×36″, edition 100, 600.00

# S. M. Warren

**Box 7, Middletown Road**
**Grafton, VT 05146**
**(802) 843-2369**

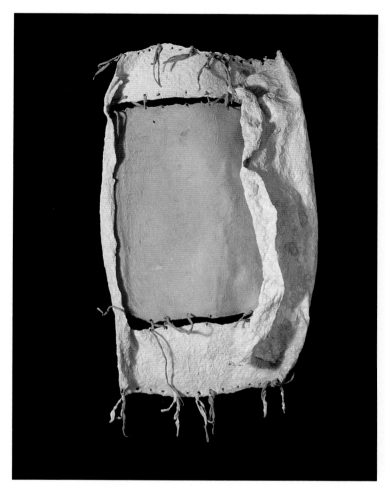

These seductively textured, organically shaped handmade paper pieces are suitable as wallhangings, atrium mobiles, pedestal or desktop pieces. Sizes range from 6"H. sculptures to 15-foot wall-pieces and mobiles. The work has been exhibited across the country in juried shows as well as private galleries.

Warren's 13 years of experience as a paper-maker insures excellent workmanship. All colors (custom tailored) are lightfast. An occasional dusting is the only maintenance required.

Prices range from $400–$4,000 for commissioned works.

A price list, resume, and slides of sample work are available upon request. Allow 6–8 weeks for delivery after the contract is signed. Custom plexiglass cases available.

(Top) "Ancient Book", handmade paper, 10½"W × 18"H × 5"D
(Bottom) "Blue Bowl in Ruined Basket", handmade paper, 8"W × 6"H × 9"D

# Leanne Weissler

50 Webster Ave.
New Rochelle, NY 10801
(914)235-7632

A strong sense of transparency and space is the first impression when viewing Leanne Weissler's elegant, durable paper relief paintings of linen and oriental fibers.

Overlays of painted fabric, airbrushed, drawn, and stitched additions create a richness of detail and color that can be appreciated in both large public spaces and intimate settings. These abstract images are available framed and unframed, and can be used singly, in multiples, free-standing or as paneled screens.

The collages are more personal, and can be interpreted using the client's photographs and memorabilia. Commissions and custom coloring are accepted and each design is one-of-a-kind, signed, dated and copyrighted.

The artist has taught and exhibited nationally, is a member of Pindar Gallery in Soho, and is featured in Fiberarts Design Book 111, and Interiors Magazine '88. Corporate collections include; IBM, Coffee and Sugar Exchange, Touche-Ross Co., Zales Jewelers, R.P.I.-Rochester, Great Northern Nekoosa Corp. and Apple Computer.

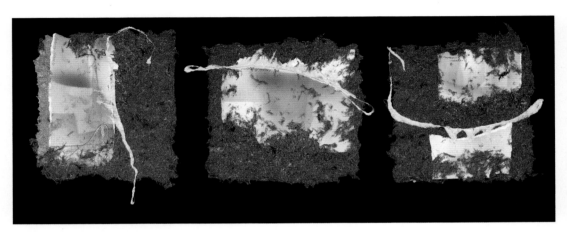

"Blue-Skies" tryptich, Linen paper, airbrush and pencil drawing 42"×12", $450.00 retail

"Panels 1", Linen paper and pencil drawing, 21"×28", $550.00 retail

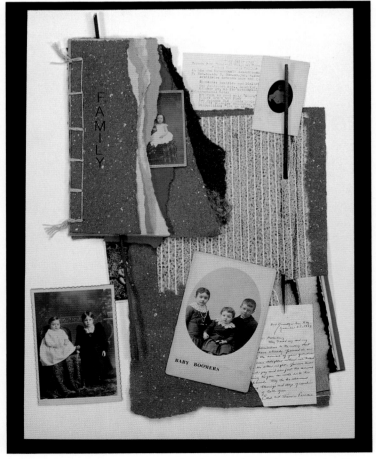

Family series - "Baby Boomers" collage, Hand-made paper, photographs and mixed media,

# Nancy J. Young

11416 Brussels Avenue, N.E.
Albuquerque, NM 87111
(505)299-6108

Nancy J. Young designs and produces unique two-and three-dimensional works in hand-made paper. These durable works are available in a variety of sizes, textures and colors. They are composed of 100% rag museum quality fibers.

Commissions can be custom designed and site-specific, based on corporate or residential client consultation.

Prices range from $200–$2,000, depending on size and complexity. Allow 3–6 weeks from design approval and contract. Work is shipped FOB Albuquerque.

Selected collection include: Burlington Northern; Hallmark, Inc.; IBM; American Express; AT&T; Alaska 1% for the Arts Program

(Top right) "Desert Serenade" shallow vessel 30" diameter × 4" deep; "Anasazi" vessel, 10½" diameter × 9½" high; "Petroglyph Canyon" 23" high × 8" deep. All cast paper.
(Top left) "Dreamweaver" 29"h. × 18"w.; "Red Sky" 8"high × 9"diameter; "Plum Dawn", 6"high × 7"diameter. All cast paper.
(Bottom) "de Chelly" 4"h. × 20"w., handcast paper.

# Ellen Zahorec

**Island Ford Studio**
**1418 Country Club Rd.**
**Brevard, NC 28712**
**(704) 883-2254**
**Southern Highland Handicraft Guild**
**P.O. Box 9545**
**Asheville, NC 28815**
**(704) 298-7928**

Ellen Zahorec creates one-of-a-kind contemporary mixed-media canvas constructions and handmade paper collages. The fusing of fine art media and craft process is Zahorec's trademark. Structural elements and materials are combined with symbolic patterning and color forming a complex system of dialogue and magic.

Zahorec is holds an M.F.A. from the University of Tennessee and has shown internationally. Her work is included in the collections of T.V.A., I.B.M., Fez Museum, Mint Museum, and Malt Beach Art Center, Finland. Artwork is available for private and corporate commissions and are designed to any dimension and color range.

Prices are $150 per sq. ft. for canvas constructions and $200-$3000 and up for framed handmade paper collages.

(Top right) "Dog Diptych," mixed media paper collage.
(Top left) "Parallelogram," detail.
(Bottom) "Parallelogram," 42"×78".

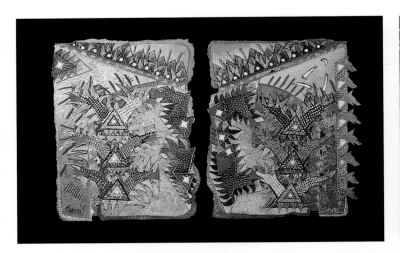

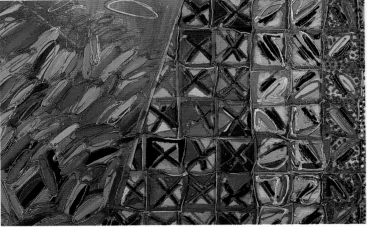

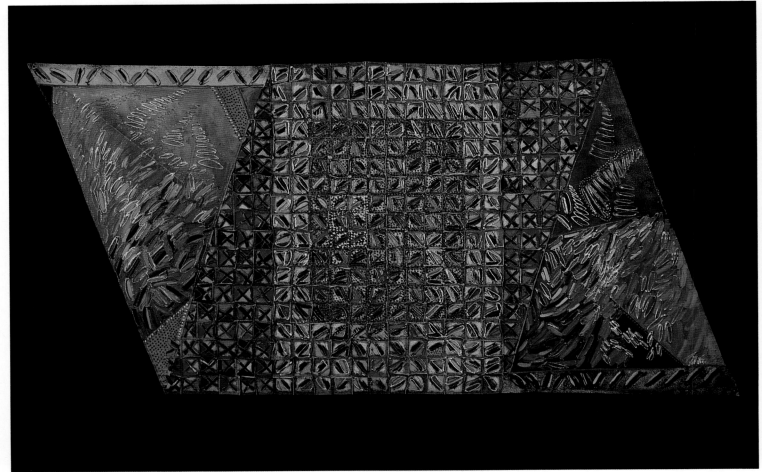

# Wall Installations

# Carol Adams

2355 Main Street
Peninsula, OH 44264
(216) 657–2681

To enhance the interior of a building, office, or home, Carol Adams' designs create rich visual textures which unite a space.

Adams will collaborate on projects to unify the mood, texture, and feel transforming any area into a showplace! Her commissions add an exciting focal point.

Adams' artwork reflects the landscapes and images experienced in her extensive travels and theatrical influences. They can incorporate weaving, handmade felt, metals, enamels, stitchery, carved wood, neon, or stage lighting.

As art consultant, she can arrange a variety of art for a projects environment. A recent commission was awarded first prize for public building interiors by ASID, Ohio.

(Top) "Crator I: Clavius," handmade felt, enamels on copper, chrome and neon, 60"×30"×18", and installation view.
(Bottom) "Fairway I & II: Doral," enamel on copper, handmade felt, and stitchery, 33"×18"×3" and detail

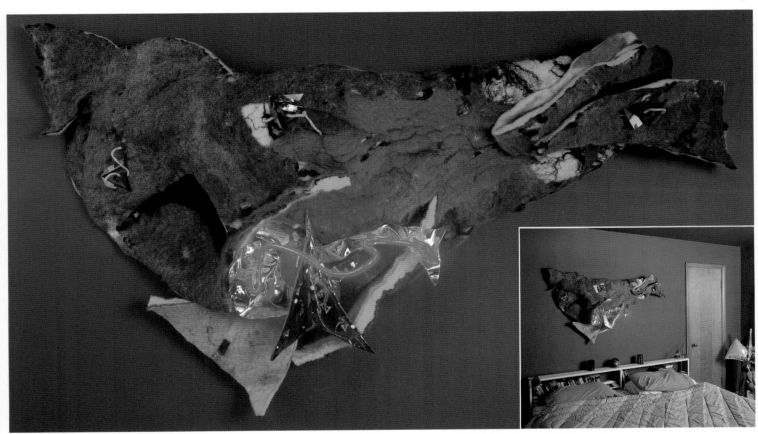

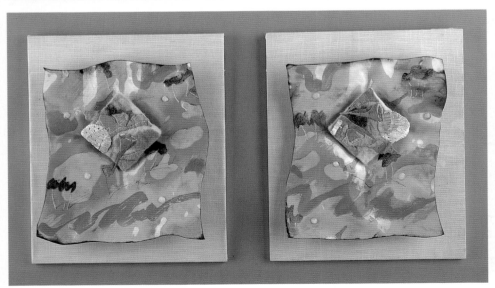

# Azo Inc.

**Susan Singleton**
**1101 E. Pike Street**
**Seattle, WA 98122**
**(800) 344-0390 or (206) 322-0390**

Susan Singleton has placed many site-specific commissions for architectural spaces. Lobby and atrium sculptures of bamboo and paper, metal, plexiglass, and handpainted fabrics. range in price from $5,000-$120,000. In 1986 Susan began the AZO Atelier inviting other artists to make limited edition prints and monotypes. The Singleton and AZO prints retail from $250–$650. The Atelier produces special editions for clients and galleries. Please call for more specific information on pricing, photos of installations and available print work. The list of corporate clients is extensive.

Susan Singleton in the AZO Atelier          Dick Luria

'Alihtan' 7'×16'×3' varnished okawara paper on bamboo Washington Federal Savings and Loan Bank Seattle, WA          Chris Eden

# Sandra C.Q. Bergér

**Quintal Unlimited**
**100 El Camino Real #202**
**Burlingame, CA 94010**
**(415) 348-0310**

"Crystal Sheer" (4'w. × 3'h. × 9"d.), natural light

Internationally exhibited and published designer, Sandra Bergér has a long history of laudable collaborations with interior designers, architects, developers and private clients. Her studio, Quintal Unltd. enhances environments with wall reliefs, atrium sculptures, leaded and laminated glass panels, glass block, window treatments, room-dividers, and entrances.

Depicted here, "Crystal Sheer" continues a series exploring Glass Halos. Using luminous glass tubes, light and color emerge from behind this multi-dimensional wall sculpture (bottom). The same piece is shown (top right) in natural light.

Prices of custom work begin at $1,500. Worldwide service.

"Crystal Sheer" (4'w. × 3'h. × 9"d.), neon illumination "Vectors II" (11"w. × 13"h.) small vessel sculpture on console.

# Therese Bimka

1685 East 5th Street #1G
Brooklyn, NY 11230
(718) 998-5869

Therese Bimka's colorful and dramatic ceramic wall sculptures depict mythical and symbolic imagery reminiscent of ancient cultures. Bimka's low relief ceramic installations are durable, require virtually no maintenance, are easy to install, and can be modified for interior or exterior use. Bimka accepts site-specific commissions as well as offers private works for sale.

Therese Bimka has a Masters Degree in Architectural Ceramics and has been working professionally in clay for ten years. Her work is on display in various New York City public and private locations.

Portfolio and pricing information available upon request.

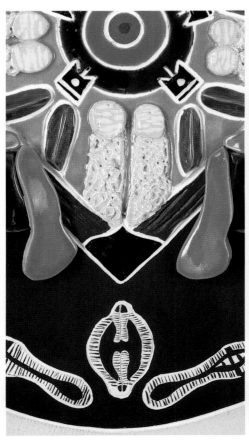

# George M. Blackman

**114 E. Crescent Lane
Stelle, IL 60919
(815) 256-2281**

George Blackman, a ceramic artist for over 13 years, works in Raku using a copper matt finish and the traditional crackle glaze. Sprayed metallic oxides, precisely fired, make for vibrant colors on intriguing accent pieces.

Vessels are available in a variety of styles and sizes, incorporating contemporary and ancient themes from Egypt and the Orient. Some have sculptural additions. Raku wall tiles may be grouped together creating options for endless designs.

Commissions are welcome. Raku tiles may be grouped for a framed wall hanging (assembly, matt and framing included), or lager tile murals may be commissioned. Prices begin at $100; a price list and order form are available upon request. Orders are generally filled within two months.

Blackman's work may be seen in various galleries around the United States. Write or call for further information.

Single wall piece, 25"h × 18"w, Tall banded vessel, 22"h × 14"w, Round vessel, 17"h × 17"w
Three-piece wall unit, 53"h × 15"w, Gold banded vessel, 19"h × 16"w, Shell vessel, 21"h × 12"w

# Irene Bos Studio

11744 Moorpark #F
Studio City, CA 91604
(818) 985-2448

Irene is internationally known for her very exclusive leather artwork. Whether the location for her art is a private home, bank lobby, office or hospital, Irene is open to collaborating with consultants, designers or architects to create the most successful result.

Her work has been featured in *Interior Design*, *Art in America*, *Designers West* and other magazines.

Prices begin at $135 per sq. ft.
Delivery time ranges from 4–6 weeks.

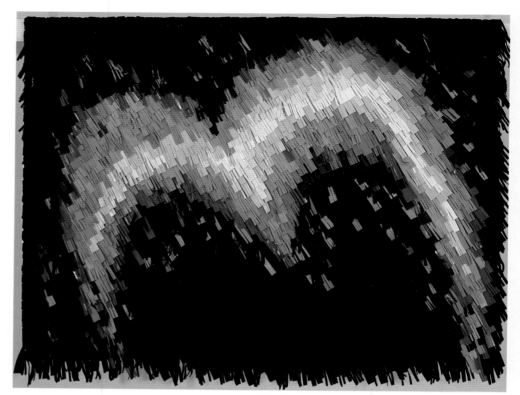

'Sweet Desire' — leather — 30" × 40"

'Field of Change I' — leather — One of a series of three — 48" × 144"

Printed in Japan © 1990 The Guild: A Sourcebook of American Craft Artists

# Frank Colson

1666 Hillview Street
Sarasota, FL 34230
(813) 953-5892

Frank Colson opened the Colson School of Art in 1963. The school today is used as a professional studio for the construction of handmade freestanding and modular sculptures in clay and bronze. Many of Mr. Colson's works are individual one of a kind pieces which are sold through gallery representation. On site commissions have been a normal endeavor of the Studio for some twenty-five years.

A portfolio and price list are available upon request.

(right) Winged Face Fountain modular relief for residential entryway (7'6" high × 46" wide). Slow flowing water highlights and reflects surfaces.
(bottom) Close-up detail of Winged Face Fountain.

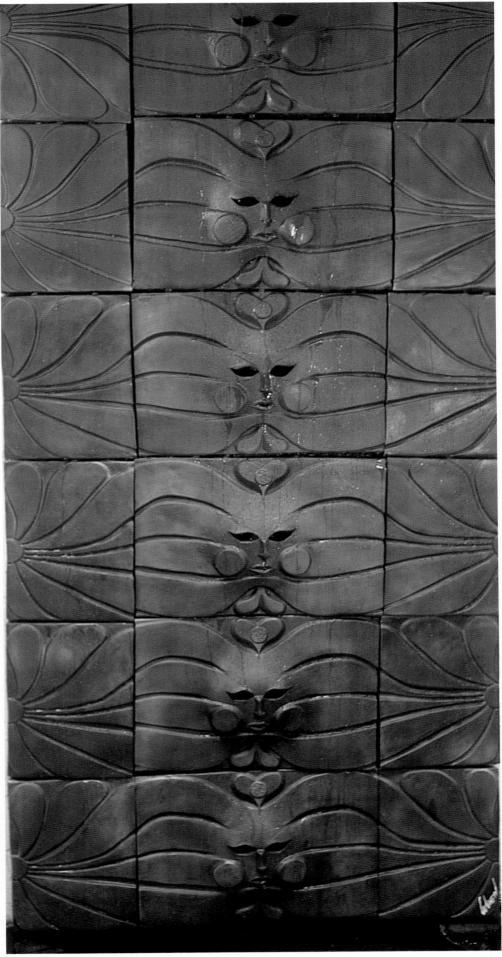

# Phillip ! Danzig

**Architect**
**86 Edgemont Road**
**Upper Montclair, NJ 07043**
**(201) 746-0709**

Phillip Danzig practices architecture
(Columbia University, Master of Architecture)
and is a mural artist. He has completed
nearly 50 commissions in a variety of media
(ceramic-paint-fabric) with an emphasis on
mosaic-tile. His work has been featured in
architectural magazines and numerous
articles and has received several awards.

Danzig is noted for the compatibility of his
work with the architectural setting for which it
is specifically designed. This results from his
versatility of approach and his sensitivity to
style.

The tile works are truly permanent, and may
include hand-cast, industrial and found
materials, according to the needs of the
image at hand. The works have been installed
indoors and outdoors, in commercial,
institutional and residential settings.

Prices are available upon request.

The work illustrated was commissioned for the Essex County Visitors Center, Newark, New Jersey.

# Patricia J. Fay

45A N. Maple Street
Hadley, MA 01035
(413) 586-2848

Patricia Fay is a versatile artist capable of working with a variety of materials and approaches. Existing works range from the wraparound marine environment of "Ocean View" (below), to more conventionally scaled free hanging pieces and tile murals. The combination of diverse media—tile, wood, marble, metal, glass—provides an unlimited range of color and design possibilities. The artist also produces one-of-a-kind narrative wall pieces incorporating vintage photographs and found objects. Prices start at $1000, and vary according to the size and complexity of the project. All pieces are site-specific and client-specific, and are planned, executed, and installed in collaboration with the architect/designer. A full portfolio is available on request.

(Top left & bottom) "Ocean View", 11½' × 25' × 10', permanent installation, University of Massachusetts
(Top right) "House/Two Views", 4' × 4'6", tile/marble wall piece

# Penelope Fleming

**7740 Washington Lane**
**Elkins Park, PA 19117**
**(215) 576-6830**

Penelope Fleming designs wall pieces for public spaces, corporate collections and residential environments. The primary material is clay with some additions of slate, anodized aluminum, bronze and collective other materials. Color and scale is unlimited. Pieces are easily shipped and installed.

Fleming has worked with many art consultants, galleries and designers to meet the criteria of design integrity, budget and completion deadlines. Recent lobby wall pieces have been hung for Ragu' Food, Inc., Connecticut; Smith Kline Beckman, Pennsylvania; and Tuverson & Hillyard, California. Price quotes and visuals are available upon request.

(Right) "NYC", 31"×32"×4"
Private collection, NYC, NY
(Bottom) "On Edge", 26"×39"×2"
Private collection, Baltimore, MD

# Mark W. Forman

121 Sandringham Road
Cherry Hill, NJ 08003
(609) 424-3086

Mark Forman creates raku-fired wall forms detailed in paint, pencil and paper collage. These pieces may be hung as a painting or permanently adhered to a wall surface.

Having been awarded fellowship grants from the New Jersey State Council on the Arts for "Evidence of Man" series, work has continued and progressed. The wall forms have been exhibited nationally and are being collected by individuals and corporations.

Forman is a highly experienced ceramic artist with a strong background in painting. This combination of skills makes possible a wealth of experience from which to draw.

Working with designers and architects is a "specialty of the studio," and works may be commissioned in most sizes, shapes and colors.

Slides and information are available upon request.

# Donna Getsinger

5039 Dominick Spur
Minnetonka, MN 55343
(612) 933-8705

Donna Getsinger's porcelain wall reliefs evolve from the visual imagery she has developed during years of work as a painter, printmaker and sculptor.

The artist works with a complex palette: Underglazes and stains, pastels and other permanent pigments are applied throughout the production process. The surfaces are durable; the results yield rich and subtle patterns of coloration.

Her wall reliefs are comprised of multiple modular forms which permit flexibility in the original design and installation. Each element is lightweight and as easy to install as a painting.

All are adaptable to residential, corporate or public spaces. Prices begin at $250 wholesale. Site-specific commissions accepted.

"Winter Garden", 40"w. × 30"h. × 3"d. Porcelain. Above—detail.

# Robert Harding

413 East 70th Street. Apt. 11
New York, NY 10021
(212) 744-8243

painter, sculptor

Focus:
Relief
Free Standing Sculpture
Environmental Sculpture
Park and Playground Design
Wall Hangings
Private Collections USA, Europe
Everson Museum
Safad Museum, Israel
Johnson Museum, Cornell University
INA Collection, Philadelphia
University of Iowa Museum

Detail.

"Cobatlyr," Painted wood wall relief 8' × 6'6". 1989, private collection.

# Deborah Hecht

**Custom Design on Tile**
**6285 Thurber Road**
**Birmingham, MI 48010**
**(313) 855-2475**

Deborah Hecht, painting with overglaze fired onto commercial ceramic tile, produces work of uncommon richness of color and detail. Her award-winning art has been exhibited in New York and the Midwest. She has recently been showing large-scale tile paintings of people.

Because of the medium's durability, the work is suitable for public spaces as well as homes. The art can be mounted and hung as paintings or permanently installed as murals and border patterns for kitchens, baths, and fireplaces. Most jobs are custom designed and collaborations are welcome.

Price range $150–$250 per sq. ft.

(Above) "Window", 37"×75", tiles hung separately on wall (Photo © Glen Calvin Moon) (Below) "Interior", 42"×59", mounted and grouted on wood (Photo Mary Onifer/Merzy Photographic)

# Katherine Holzknecht

22828 57th Ave. SE
Woodinville, WA 98072
(206) 481-7788

Katherine Holzknecht creates one-of-a-kind mixed-media artworks for interior spaces. Constructed with dyed or painted wood, wire, metal, fabric and paper, the artworks are ideally suited for architectural sites because of their durability and lightfastness.

Prices start at $100 per square foot retail. Commissions accepted with a $200 design fee. Installations are additional. Please contact the artist for resume, slides of available work or information about commissions.

Holzknecht's work has been exhibited extensively in the Northwest and nationally, and is included in the collections of IBM, the Hyatt Regency Hotel, the Westin Hotel and the Seattle and Washington State Art Commissions.

(Top) "Into the Unknown", collection of Pacific First Federal Bank in Tacoma, Washington. (Bottom) "Data Capsule", commissioned for Westlake Center Office Tower Lobby in Seattle, Washington.

# Margie Hughto

**6970 Henderson Road**
**Jamesville, NY 13078**
**(315) 469-8775**

Margie Hughto is nationally recognized for her ceramic paintings and collages. These elegant wall reliefs are made of stoneware clays, slips and glazes, and are constructed of beautifully colored and textured elements. The works range in size from small intimate pieces up to installations of architectural scale. Commissions are welcome and existing works are available. Prices, slides and further information are furnished upon request.

Works are represented in numerous museum, corporate and private collections including: Museum of Fine Arts, Boston; Everson Museum, Syracuse, NY; IBM, Kodak, NYNEX, Mayo Clinic, Port Authority, NYC; NFTA, Buffalo; Connecticut State University.

(Top) "Lake Reflections," 1989, 41″H × 96″W, ceramic with gold leaf, commissioned by Kodak, Rochester, NY
(Bottom left) "Hidden Treasure," 1988, 42″H × 34″W, private collection.
(Bottom right) "Lakeside," 1988, 42″H × 60″W, corporate collection.

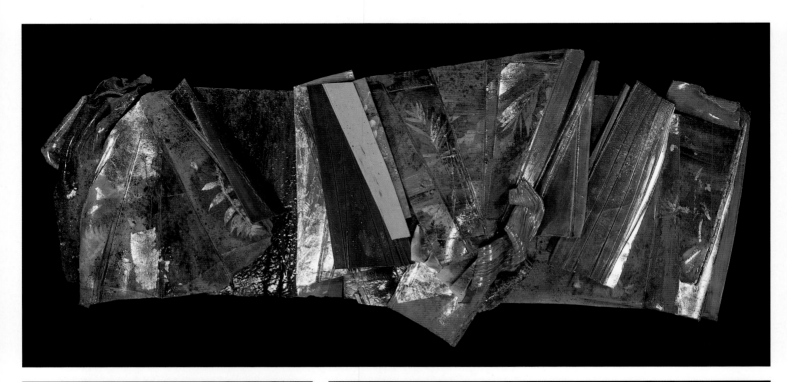

# June Jasen

36 East 10 Street
New York, NY 10003
(212) 674-6113

June Jasen specializes in cloisonné enameling. She takes this traditional multiple firing process a step further by integrating pigmented silicas with low fire ceramic materials to achieve a rich patterned effect in the enamel. The modification of the enamel enriches the surface and depth of Jasen's work, paying particular attention to the reflective and refractive qualities of the fired glass enamel.

Her wall pieces incorporate over-scale cloisonné pieces with drawings.

Prices begin at $500 for jewelry (not pictured here) and wall pieces. The artist is willing to collaborate with architects and designers on special projects from inception of design through final installation. Commissions are also available.

Please contact the artist for more information.

"Queuing Up" #2 framed: 20"h. × 40"w. Enameled Sections: 12"h. × 9"w.

Photo by D. James Dee

# Pamela Joseph

**Metal Paintings, Inc.**
**RR#3 Box 140**
**Pound Ridge, NY 10576**
**(914) 764-5732 (home); (914) 764-8208 (studio)**

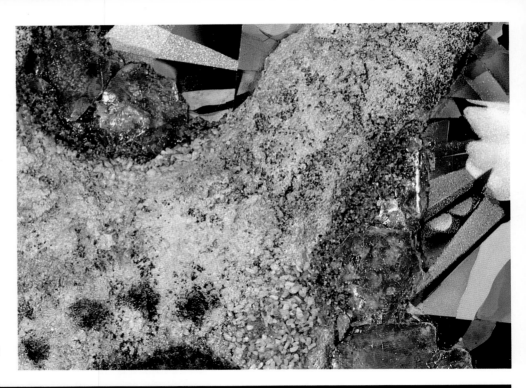

Pamela Joseph, working with experts in the field, has evolved a system that layers traditional materials such as oils and acrylics with contemporary mediums such as airbrushed lacquers, urethane, pearl powders and metalflake, all on aluminum. This 1989 bas-relief, "Homage to Pech-Merle", 5′ × 5½′ × 10″, also incorporates mica (detail) embedded in a stone aggregate matrix, and is a prototype for site-specific wall installations.

The resulting artworks are dynamic under changing light conditions, while providing state of the art durability for public display. Prices range from $8500 for a construction such as "Pech-Merle" to $35,000 for multi-unit 10′ sculptures.

# Rip Kastaris

Kastaris Studio
3301-A South Jefferson
St. Louis, MO 63118
(314) 773-2600

Euripides "Rip" Kastaris combines spontaneous, expressionistic paint applications with precisely controlled gradations of airbrushed color and lights (including neon) to create bold, arresting images.

He is a conceptual thinker who collaborates well to render one-of-a-kind results. Preliminary color sketches, specific price estimates and completion schedules are given to accommodate individual client needs.

Your inquiries will be answered with enthusiastic consideration and follow-up.

Prices range from $750.00 and up.

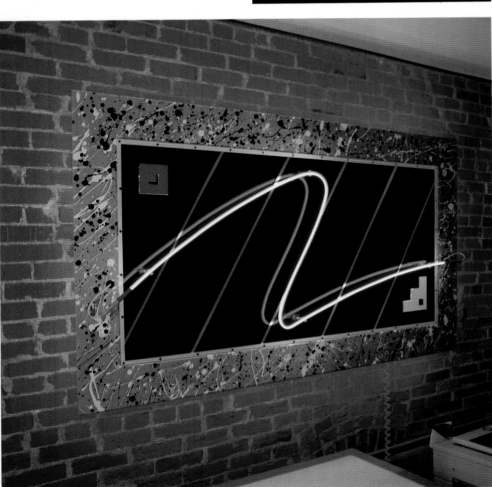

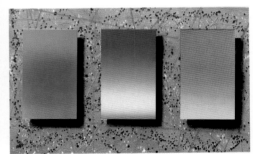

# Cynthia Laymon

P.O. Box 5147
Greensboro, NC 27435
919-230-0254 (studio) 919-668-7388 (home)

Cynthia Laymon's mixed media wall reliefs possess distinctive silhouettes, rhythmic movement and pattern, and rich, vibrant surfaces. Superb craftsmanship is evident in the construction. Great care is taken in the selection of the most permanent papers, pigments, and support materials. The two series currently in progress are executed in various sizes. Collaboration with architects is possible to produce portal images integrated into doorways of buildings and homes.

The artist's work, exhibited nationally and internationally, is represented in numerous permanent collections including IBM Corporation, Delta Airlines, McCann Erickson Inc., the U.S. Embassy in Madrid, USA TODAY— Gannett Company, Deloitte, Haskins, & Sells, Cincinnati Bell Information Systems, Eastman Pharmaceuticals.

Inquiries and commissions are invited. Portfolios and price list are available upon request.

(Top) PORTAL: DECO 03, 47½"h × 26"w × 2"d
(Bottom) SHADOW ARCHES,
30½"h × 126"w × 2"d

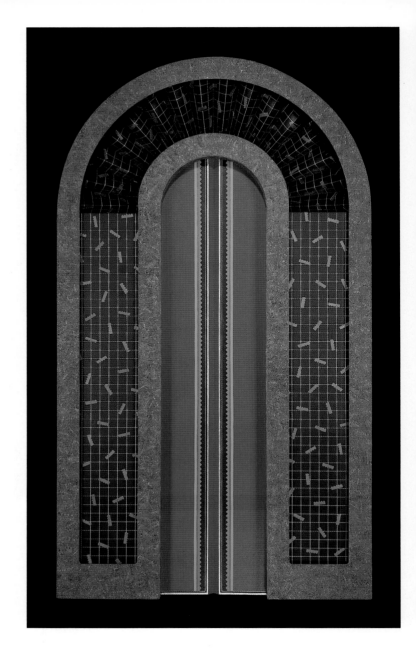

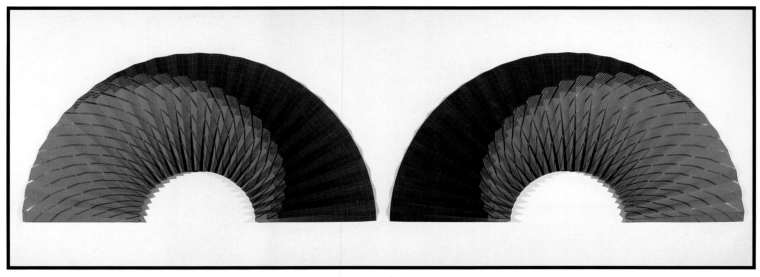

# Washington Ledesma

Ledesma Designs Studio
P.O.B. 1712  Beach Street Extension
Vineyard Haven, MA 02568
(508) 693 -7181

Washington Ledesma's work reflects the vitality of the life force itself. His works in clay have been evolving from plates and large pots to tiles and murals with his unique decorations. Using ancient techniques learned from a confluence of different cultural energies of which he carries the traditions, his art exhibits a wonderful sense of humor, a deep respect for nature in all its manifestations and exhibits a great sense of joyful aliveness.

Washington Ledesma exhibits in galleries across the country and in his own gallery on the Island of Martha's Vineyard. These ceramic murals are used in unique customized decors.

(Top) Rectangular Terracotta Handmade Tile, "Joseph Playing the Violin", 9¾"11" × -¼". Multicolor Underglazes and Sgraffito.
(Bottom) Rectangular Terracotta Handmade Tile, "Claire", 9" × 11¾" × -¼". Multicolor Underglazes and Sgraffito.

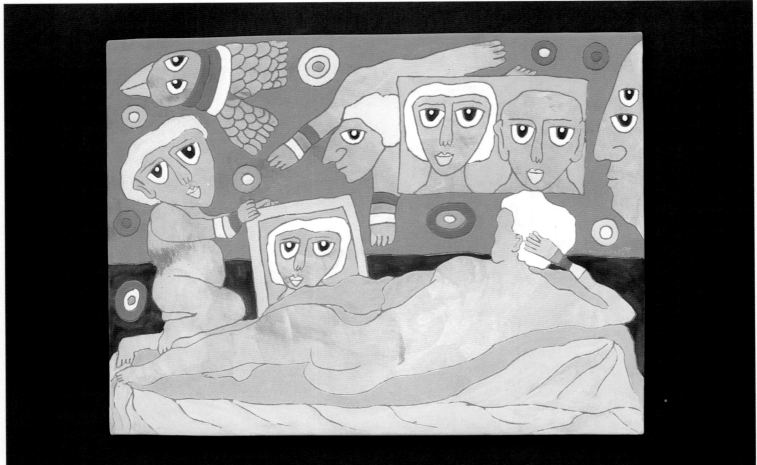

# Joyce P. Lopez

1147 W. Ohio St.
Chicago, IL 60622
(312) 243-5033

Joyce P. Lopez treats all of her commissions as "site specific" works taking into account all the client's needs. She is, therefore, frequently called upon to do commercial, residential, or gallery installations. The uniqueness of this work is what immediately generates excitement drawing a large clientele of collectors both in the private as well as corporate sector.

Where a painting/fiber sculpture combination commission is not desired, Lopez does fiber sculptures or paintings alone. All art work is easily maintained.

Please write or call for additional information on this much in demand, exciting work. The artist's work ranges from small works to large scale installations in the areas of fiber, painting, sculpture and drawings. Prices start at $800 retail for drawings and from $4000 retail for fiber sculptures.

Artist holds the copyright on all work.

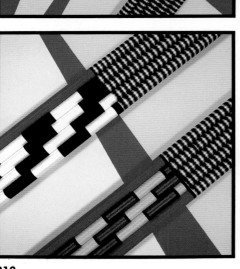

K.U. Corp., Milwaukee, Wis. commission ©, — latex paint, thread, chrome, ink.

# Joyce P. Lopez

**1147 W. Ohio St.**
**Chicago, IL 60622**
**(312) 243-5033**

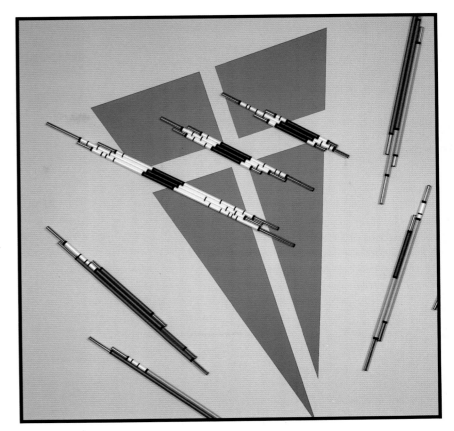

St. Lukes Hospital—Milwaukee, Wis. © — latex paint, chrome steel, thread. 16' × 12' × 1"

# Merri Pattinian

**Pattinian Art & Design**
**3119 Hollow Creek Court**
**Houston, TX 77082**
**(713) 497-0745**

Specializing in mixing as many unusual materials together as possible. Ms. Pattinian creates unique one-of-a-kind pieces of art. Whether it be a large site-specific installation, or a collaged painting, her use of materials is unique and creative.

Her background as a graphic designer enables her to approach each commission with a well designed eye and the patience to deal with clients, deadlines and budgets.

Her achievements include several one-person shows and inclusion in many group exhibits. She has been published in the *First Compendium of Women in Design* and been reviewed by the *L.A. Times*. Her work can be found in numerous private and corporate collections.

Corporate and residential commissions are welcomed.

Slides available on request!

# Michael Rocco Pinciotti

**Neon Art**
**29 John Street #1108**
**New York, NY 10038**
**(212) 285-0959**

Rocky Pinciotti uses neon with mixed media to create thought provoking, humorous and illuminating works of art for gallery, public and private spaces. An innovator in neon art, his work reflects the poetry of place by using architectural elements, house icons and temple references. The integrated neon adds depth, energy and intensity to each piece. The multi-layered panel constructions are lightweight and hung as any framed artwork.

As an artist exhibiting extensively and internationally, Rocky creates one of a kind pieces as well as limited editions. He has a masters degree from Pratt Art Institute and has been creating with neon since 1979. His work is featured in both *The Magic of Neon* and *The New Let There Be Neon*.

A slide portfolio and prices are available upon request.

(top left) "The Call from Afar" 36″×28″×2″
(bottom left) "The Pillar of Strength" 36″×28″×2″
(top right) "Neonized Column" 22″×36″×6″
(bottom right) "Neonized Alphabet-N" 28″×36″×5″

# Siglinda Scarpa
# Lisa Derosby

**Scarpa Design Studio**
**Box 710**
**Peekskill, NY 10566**
**(914) 424-3254**
**(207) 766-2143**

Under the artistic and technical direction of Siglinda Scarpa, the studio created distinctive architectural ceramics for interior and exterior spaces. Shown here are examples of tile assemblages (mosaics), clay paintings that can also be installed permanently as an entire wall or floor or as an element—a surround for a window, door, or fireplace, for example—in a larger scheme. These designs are the result of ancient Italian techniques in the service of an altogether contemporary imagination.

Scarpa Design Studio will collaborate with architects, designers, and other clients on custom and site-specific installations of any scale for corporate, public, or residential environments. Prices are competitive and vary with the size and complexity of the project. Please write or call Lisa Derosby, Co-Director of the Studio, for more information and a slide portfolio, (207) 766-2143.

Siglinda Scarpa's European commissions include Feldpausch, Inc., Locarno, Switzerland; Genevay, Inc., Geneva, Switzerland; the estate of Arthur Rankin, Jr., Bermuda and New York; and the residences of the Garofalo family, Rome, Italy.

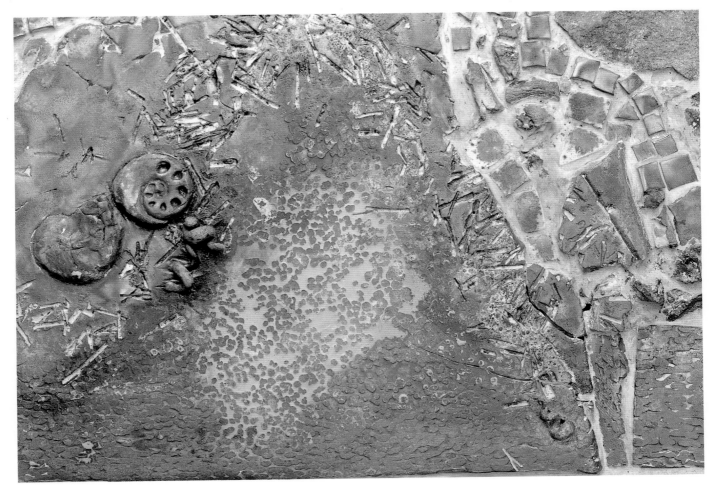

# Barbara Schaff

RD #3, Box 232
Stockton, NJ 08559
(201) 782-7742

The paintings of Barbara Schaff are recognized for their bold use of color and vigorous brushwork. They are at home in both residential and corporate environments. Because these paintings are on clay, unique effects specific to the ceramic process create a richness of surface and translucency of color that cannot be achieved with conventional painting materials. The works are especially suited to highly lit spaces as the color is not affected by sunlight.

Selected collections include: Chubb Corporation, Warren, NJ; Boston Consulting Group, Boston, MA; Bell Communications Research, Red Bank, NJ; Boca Rio Golf Club, Boca Raton, FL; Meldisco Corporation, Mahwah, NJ; Squibb United States, Princeton, NJ; NJ Natural Gas, Wall, NJ; Lakeshore National Bank, Chicago, IL; New Jersey State Museum, Trenton, NJ; Brockton Art Museum, Brockton, MA.

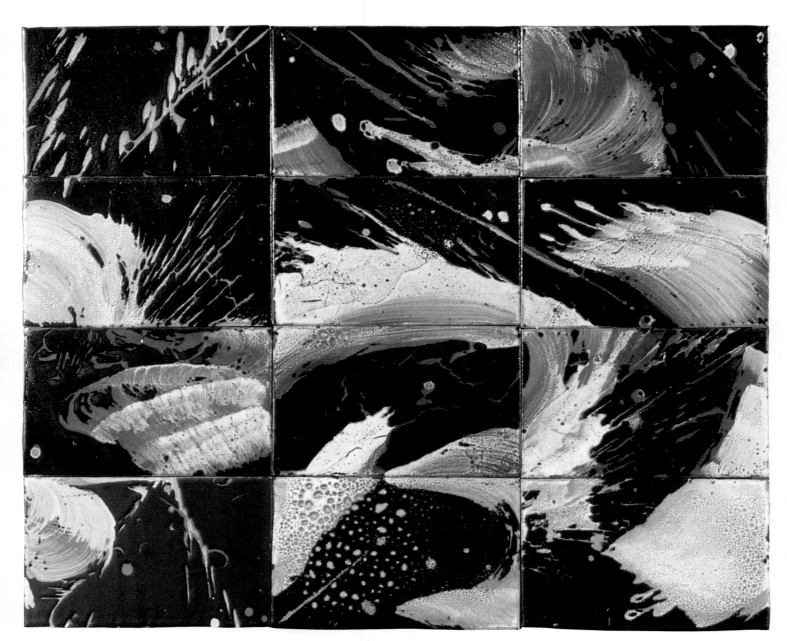

"Tao" glaze on porcelain 30" × 36"

# Linda Schneiderman

**Schneiderman Studio**
**57 Judson Ave.**
**Dobbs Ferry, NY 10522**
**(914) 693-0236**

Linda Schneiderman creates sculptured paintings using acrylic paint and wood. The subject matter is predominantly whimsical in feeling, whether it be figurative or an interpretation of an interior locale. In order to intensify the gesture of the figure or the contour of an object, each piece is separated from the surrounding surface by cutting them out, in relief or completely isolating them from the background. The retail price of a piece is approximately $500–$2,500, depending on the intricacy of the design and the size. Work can be prepared for outdoors. Linda Schneiderman has been exhibited nationally, her commissions include private and corporate spaces.

# Learning Crafts from a Master

The first time I visited Jack Lenor Larsen's loft in New York City was to join him for lunch on a chilly winter day. Any invitation to Jack's is a treat but if it involves a meal that's even better. In the French tradition, meals are served in various parts of the loft. It makes it quite interesting for frequent guests because you never have any preconceived ideas about either the food, what it will be served on (Jack has quite a beautiful collection of table top accoutrements, some of which he has designed but also including the work of Dale Chihuly, Nils Landsberg, Brad Miller and Dona Look) or where it will be served.

This particular day we were actually dining in the dining room and during a light refreshment, he brought me into his studio, which also serves as an office, bedroom (up two stairs) and bath. Behind large, fabric-covered sliding doors he revealed what was probably one of the most significant collection of crafts in the country, all beautifully displayed. What a treat this was to be taken through the collection one by one by the master himself. Jack will never admit this but he probably is one of the most eloquent men I have ever had the pleasure to be "craft educated" by. The conversation continued through lunch, and when it was over I was very sorry to have to catch a cab to my next appointment. Certainly I had known about crafts from my visits to Rhinebeck and local Westport, Connecticut fairs, but I never realized what a truly beautiful craft could be or what an addition to any home these artifacts made, both to the decor and to the conversation.

It is so much a part of the American ethic, the growth of artisans in various parts of the country and the support of their efforts. Jack Lenor Larsen certainly is one of the most famous among modern craftspeople who have supported the efforts of craftsmen. But he is also a man who is more a teacher of fine style.

A few years have passed since my lunch with Jack, but as I become more and more exposed to things decorative in my daily job of editing for an audience of hungry home enthusiasts, I always remember Jack and our discussion of his crafts collection. It's his genius that brought me to appreciate this truly sensational art form.

**Joseph Ruggiero**
**Editor-in-Chief, HOME Magazine**
**Los Angeles, California**

# Nick Starr

116 Mildred Avenue
Syracuse, NY 13206
(315) 463-5507

Nick Starr, Syracuse ceramist, has developed a series of wall installations reflecting both contemporary and classical structures and forms. The rigid geometric format contrasted with a highly textured and rich painterly surface creates an exciting hybrid. His modular system of construction, comprimising individually installed panels eliminates stress on walls and allows for freedom in design and the possibility of large scale commissions.

Starr is recipient of the National Endowment of the Arts Fellowship Award in ceramics. His works are included in private and corporate collections, including the Prudential Insurance Company, IBM and Omni Hotels.

(Top) "Mood Bleu" Ceramic Wall installation 4'8" × 3'6"
(Bottom) "Horizon," 6' × 3'6"

# Robert Sullivan

**Fused Glass Studio**
**14715 Goodrich Drive, N.W.**
**Gig Harbor, WA 98335**
**(206) 857-4605**

Known for his imagery and rich colors, Robert Sullivan is commissioned for large paintings of high-fire fused glass wall reliefs and architectural installations. Sullivan custom designs individual works for the public, corporate, and residential settings. He is exhibited nationally and internationally and is in numerous collections.

Prices start at $150.00 per sq. foot. Proposal fee is 10 percent of final cost. Allow 6-8 weeks for delivery. Commissions and collaborations are welcome. Further information available upon request.

Exhibited regularly are his highly decorative, stylized portraits of contemporary women titled the 'Urban Women Series'.

(top left) "Glacial Movement", 6.5' × 6.5'
(middle left) "Fizzures", 7' × 5'
(bottom left) "Erica, Urban Women Series", 18" × 18"
(top right) "Passage", 14' × 4'
(bottom right) "Bayeta", 6' × 4'

Photo: Philip Amdal

# Dale Zheutlin

**55 Webster Avenue**
**New Rochelle, NY 10801**
**(914) 576-0082**

Unique ceramic wall reliefs, hand built in a wide range of dimensions and color palettes, provide art for public, corporate and residential spaces. Prices vary depending on the size and complexity of the project.

Selected commissions and collections include: Wang Laboratories Inc., New York City; IBM, Armonk, NY; Chase Manhattan Bank, New York City; Bankers Trust Company, New York City; Peat, Marwick and Main, Indianapolis, IN.

Slides and price list are available upon request.

(Top) "Images", 1988, ceramic construction, porcelain, 13'w.×3'h.×6".
(Bottom left) "Images", installed at Wang Laboratories, Inc., New York City.
(Bottom right) "Images", detail.

# Barbara Zinkel

**333 Pilgrim**
**Birmingham, MI 48009**
**(313) 642-9789**

Barbara Zinkel is internationally recognized for her serigraphs which are included in many corporate and private collections. The silk-screen prints are published in limited editions of 200–250 and are priced from $200–$500. Many of the pieces are large in scale, approximately 3½'–5', and have over 50 colors.

Zinkel's silkscreens are in collections of Steelcase, Inc., Grand Rapids, Michigan; Shearson Lehman Brothers, New York; Vialle Autogas Systems, Son, the Netherlands; Villa Palmera Town Houses, Chula Vista, California; Texas Instruments, Dallas, Texas.

(Top) Serigraphs in limited editions of 250: "Imperial Red," 30"×30", "A San Francisco Night," 40"×60". "Burgundy Blue," 30"×30", Dean Medical Center, Madison, Wisconsin, designed and built by Marshall Erdman and Associates, Inc.
(Bottom) Serigraph: "New York At Noon," 40"×60", edition size 250, $500

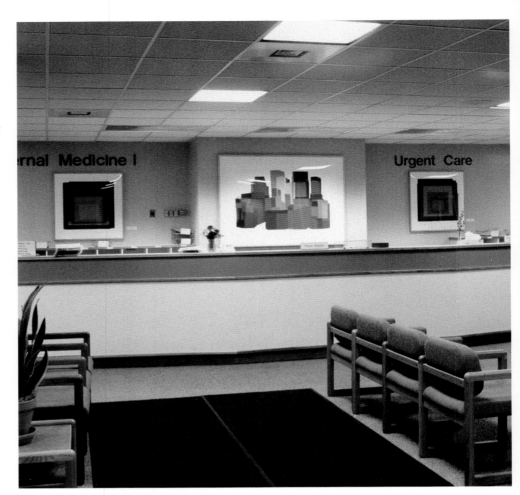

# Tiles and Mosaics

# Architectural Ceramics

**Elle Terry Leonard**
**P.O. Box 49645**
**Sarasota, FL 34230**
**(813) 951-0947**

Architectural Ceramics specializes in large scale, site-specific commissions in clay for corporate and residential clients.

Elle Terry Leonard produces handbuilt, originally designed ceramics for architectural application. Specialities include relief murals, fountains and custom treatment for fireplaces, walls and floors.

Complete studio services range from concept and consultation through production, shipping and installation.

Commissions include: Arvida Corporation, Longboat Key, FL; Barnett Bank of Southeast Florida; Chamber of Commerce, Sarasota, FL; Trotter's Restaurant, Springfield, MO; The Polo Grille Restaurant, Palm Beach Gardens, FL; The Worldgate Marriott Hotel, Reston, VA.

Prices range from $36-150 per sq. ft.

A portfolio is available upon request.

(Below) "Polo", 40' × 5½', The Polo Grille Restaurant, Palm Beach Gardens, FL

# Beagle Tiles

**Marcy Pesner**
**135 Plymouth Street**
**Brooklyn, NY 11201**
**(718) 797-0262**

Beagle Tiles is a small friendly firm that has invented and manufactures decorative wooden wall tiles that come in a variety of shapes & sizes.

They can be tinted dyed, stained and pickled and even left natural.

Beagle Tiles also manufacturers handcrafted cabinets with a hint of Santa Fe, Cape Cod and the Adirondacks.

Please write or call for more information.

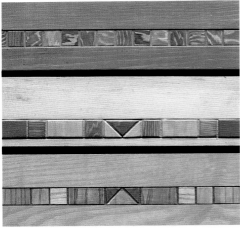

(Bottom) Brooklyn Brownstone  (Upper Left) Inlay Samples  (Middle) Santa Fe Stenciled Tiles  (Upper Right) Handcraft Cabinet w/Tiles

# Design Works, Inc.

**David Wright**
**P.O. Box 163**
**Murfreesboro, TN 37133**
**615-895-1645**
**615-890-0934**

Design Works, Inc. has specialized in hand-made vitreous porcelain and stoneware tile for interior and exterior use for over ten years. Working from his own design or in collaboration, David creates kitchen and bath tile as well as tabletops and exterior signs. His work has been featured in designer show-case houses, commercial installations, and homes across the country.

Design Works provides custom colors, designs, and installation. Each project is approached with the client's needs in mind. Prices start at $65 per square foot, excluding installation. The usual project takes no longer than ninety days. Photos and prices are available upon request.

Top: Bathroom wall relief 96″ × 96″
Bottom: Kitchen backsplash 18″ × 124″

# Kyle's Tile

**Kyle Evans**
**4516 Lovers Lane**
**Suite 158**
**Dallas, Texas 75225**
**(214) 827-2822**
**FAX (214) 739-3330**

Kyle's Tile produces commissioned silk-screened designs on standard size tile. Studio glaze colors are specifically matched to your color schemes, then permanently fired into the surface of the commercially available field tile. This hand silk-screening process encourages diverse designs at an economical price, suitable for commercial spaces. Kyle's modern expertise of tile use has gained her a reputation producing high quality wallpaper facsimiles in tilework.

More than a decade of experience and collaborations with designers, architects, and private clientele has presented new dimensions, intimate environments and creative design alternatives using tile.

Nationwide commissions include the Sheraton Hotel, Broadmoor Hotel, Jack Tar Village in Puerto Plata, and many fine homes and estates.

Bids are quoted on a per job basis. Resume and photographs available. Inquiries welcomed and technical questions invited.

Tabletop relief design

Nondirectional floor tile

Casino wall tile, Dominican Republic

French curve botanical wall tile

330

# Paul Lewing

**Paul Lewing Custom Tile**
**4315 Burke Avenue North**
**Seattle, WA 98103**
**(206) 547-6591**

Paul Lewing specializes in one-of-a-kind tile murals for interior or exterior use in both commercial and residential settings.

Paul employs numerous glazing and graphic techniques, at two different firing temperatures, to produce murals of his original design or to execute the designs of architects and designers. He can paint on hand-made, unglazed tile, or on most commercial field tiles and has matched wallpaper, fabric, and dinnerware. While he specializes in landscapes and Oriental florals, Paul's repertoire includes Art Deco, Art Nouveau, cartoons, signs, animals, and religious subjects.

The 3' × 6' sign at right is painted on commercial tile, while the 18" × 10' backsplash below uses high-fire glazes on unglazed porcelain tile.

Prices range from $75 to $125 per square foot. Call or write for price and schedule estimates.

# Elizabeth MacDonald

Box 186
Bridgewater, CT 06752
(203) 354-0594

Elizabeth MacDonald produces tile paintings by layering color onto thin, textured stoneware, achieving a surface that combines the subtlety of nature with the formality of a grid. These compositions are suitable for either in or out-of-doors and take the form of free standing columns, wall panels or architectural installations. Attached to ¼" luan with silicone, the tiles (often 3½" square) weigh approximately 1¾ lbs per sq ft, are durable and require a minimum of maintenance. Imagery can vary from formal patterning to reflections of the sky and land. Ms. MacDonald is experienced in working with the requirements of clients and can produce either small or large scale work. Terms and prices are available upon request.

Recent commissions: New London Courthouse, CT; Shands Hospital, Gainesville, FL both are % for Art; Red Mountain Ranch (for Mobil), Mesa, AZ; Prudential-Bache, NY; Marriott in Palm Desert; Sheraton Grande in Tokyo. Collections of Chubb, Pitney Bowes, AETNA and IBM include her work.

(Below) detail
(Right) private commission

# E. Joseph McCarthy

**Custom Tile Studio**
**12 Solon Street**
**Greenfield, MA 01301**
**(413) 773-5719**

E. Joseph McCarthy and his staff have been designing and executing fine ceramic tile environments for over a decade. Specializing in large-scale murals, each piece is custom-designed to fit into the decor and configurations of each individual location.

He has worked closely with professional designers, developers and architects, and is deadline conscious.

Prices range from $50 to $150/sq. ft.

(Top) 26'w. × 4'h. (104) sq. ft.) 6" × 6" tiles, New England Meat Market
(Bottom) 30'w. × 4'h. (120 sq. ft.), 8" × 8" tiles, Koehler Products Showroom, Peabody, MA

# Kathryn L. McCleery

1517 University Avenue
Grand Forks, ND 58201
(701) 775-0807

Kathryn McCleery produces works using the raku technique which takes full advantage of the translucent and reflective qualities possible with glazes over an undulating surface. They interact with the position of the viewer and varying lighting conditions to produce a sense of movement and change. Lightweight for their size, they can be moved. Integrating art and architecture, she also produces bas-relief carvings in face brick suitable for both interior or exterior areas where durability is a concern.

This brickwork can be glazed, lustered, or slip decorated for a wide range of color. Working in clay for 20 years, McCleery is a versatile artist who has studied Moroccan architectural tile work and is experienced in most ceramic techniques. Her work is collected nationally and internationally.

Please write for further information.

"Golden Delicious", brick 2' × 3' 1989.                Photo: Randy Haight

"Mu", photo by Dana Sherman

# Jim Piercey

**J. Piercey Studios, Inc.**
**1714 Acme Street**
**Orlando, FL 32805**
**(407) 841-7594**

J. Piercey Studios, Inc. designs, executes and installs stained glass and stone mosaic for exterior and interior surfaces. Most work is commissioned, usually through close collaboration with the architect or interior designer. Inquiries are welcomed.

(Top) Detail.

(Bottom) 96" × 24" signage of slate, various marbles, black glass.

# Post Ceramics

Sara and Tom Post
2405 Regis Drive
Davis, CA 95616
(916) 758-9365

**represented by:**
Zona, New York, NY
The Artful Hand, Boston, MA
Orleans, MA
Virginia Breier, San Francisco, CA

Post Ceramics majolica tile is hand made and painted in over one hundred color and pattern variations. Lively animals, fruit, floral and geometric patterns may be used in repeat sequences or mixed randomly.

Tile may be cut to individual specifications for custom installations or to combine with commercial tile as accents. Higher firing temperatures create a majolica tile that is strong and durable for home and commercial installations. Priced from $40. to $90. per sq. ft. Catalog available.

336

# Karen Singer

72 West Washington Lane
Philadelphia, PA 19144
215-844-1767

Karen Singer is a sculptor and ceramic tile maker whose training includes an MFA in Sculpture from the University of Pennsylvania, and an apprenticeship at the Moravian Pottery and Tileworks. She has worked with ceramic tile for over six years. Her work is exhibited frequently, most recently at the American Clay Artists exhibition in Philadelphia.

Singer uses ceramic tile in a wide range of applications that can be incorporated in residential and commercial spaces, both exterior and interior. Her work is characterized by the broad use of textures, from high relief to incised linear patterns.

Singer approaches a commission as an opportunity to work with the unique characteristics of a site. She is an effective collaborator, who likes to incorporate imagery that has meaning to the client or that relates to the character or history of the site.

Resume, price quotes and photos are available upon request.

# Beth Starbuck and Steven Goldner

**Starbuck Goldner Tile**
**315 W. Fourth Street**
**Bethlehem, PA 18015**
**(215) 866-6321**

Beth Starbuck and Steven Goldner specialize in the design and production of handmade ceramic tile. Using flat or embossed tile, they design for specific sites or spaces to both fulfill functional needs and satisfy aesthetic criteria. Collaborations are welcome. Their tiles are appropriate for interior or exterior settings. Regardless of clay color or glaze type, they meet strict standards for strength, freeze-thaw requirements and glaze fit.

Prices range from $25–350 per sq. ft. Prices do not include installation. With few exceptions, installation can be handled by any competent tile setter. Starbuck Goldner will install when practical. Manufacturing requires a minimum of two months depending on the size and complexity of a project. Lead time should be allowed for the design phase.

Entry, PEI-Genesis corporate headquarters, frost-proof glazed tile, 60'w.×15'h.×15'd. 1988

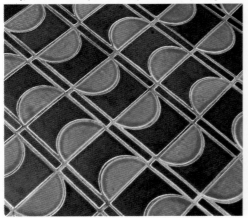

"Half-round Jig," © 1984

"Pinwheel Pentagon," © 1985

"Petal Wave," © 1980

**338**

# Nick Starr

116 Mildred Avenue
Syracuse, NY 13206
(315) 463-5507

Nick Starr, Syracuse ceramist, has developed a series of wall installations reflecting both contemporary and classical structures and forms. The rigid geometric format contrasted with a highly textured and rich painterly surface creates an exciting hybrid. His modular system of construction, comprimising individually installed panels eliminates stress on walls and allows for freedom in design and the possibility of large scale commissions.

Starr is recipient of the National Endowment of the Arts Fellowship Award in ceramics. His works are included in private and corporate collections, including the Prudential Insurance Company, IBM and Omni Hotels.

(Bottom) "Only the Pharoahs" Ceramic Tile Doors 8' × 7'6"

# Elaine Sayoko Yoneoka

**Yoneoka Studio**
**65 Brookside Avenue**
**Jamaica Plain, MA 02130**
**(617) 524-4673**

Elaine Yoneoka creates three dimensional wall pieces using hand made textured raku tile, glass and pastel. Her work is distinctive in conveying the dynamic sense of water with refractive properties of light on iridescent glazes and glass. She has exhibited her work in galleries and museums across the United States and in Europe for the past ten years.

She works with stained glass artist Emanuel Genovese to produce standing screens for office and home interiors. The colors and dimensions can be altered to fit different needs. They are durable, strong and easy to maintain.

Commissions take two to three months to complete. Prices range from $600-1600 for wall hangings, $200/square foot for screens with a $250 design fee.

Please contact the artist for more information.

(Top) "Avril: Paris" raku tile, paper, pastel, glass 19"w. × 25"h. × 2½"d. © 1989
(Bottom right) Folding screen, raku tile and stained glass, 6'h. × 6'w. © Genovese & Yoneoka
(Bottom left) Detail of folding screen

Photography by Rogier Grégoire

340

# Painted Finishes and Murals

# Ahrens & Czopek

**Roberta Ahrens, Bruce Czopek**
**73 Paul Dr.**
**San Rafael, CA 94903**
**(415) 479-1820**

The art of the Painted Finish has been promi-nent in the world of Decoration, Architecture, and Design throughout history.

Ahrens & Czopek continue in this tradition. Working in cooperation with clients to con-ceive and realize their ideas, Ahrens & Czopek have achieved landmark successes in the Bay Area.

Recognized for their skills, from the duplica-tion of an intricate Red Bravura Marble, to the development of new techniques and finishes, the team of Ahrens and Czopek bring sound professional experience and creativity to each project.

(Top Left) Floor section, Intarsia inlay, copper verdi, Black Breche faux marble.
(Bottom Left) Detail-5 panel screen, private commission, San Francisco, CA.
(Top right) Exterior accent wall, private resi-dence, Piedmont, CA.
(Bottom Right) Faux marble columns, Fairmont Hotel, San Jose, CA.

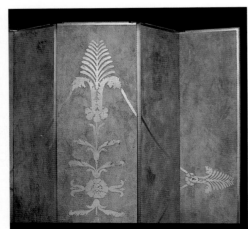

# Judith Aiello

**2390 S.W. Cedar Street**
**Portland, OR 97205**
**(503) 222-2103**

Judy has designed and executed site-specific wall graphics and murals professionally for 15 years. The scope of her work includes custom designed concepts and graphic ensembles for a wide range of interior spaces including banks, restaurants, schools, hospitals, offices and private residences.

She has received recognition for Outstanding Achievement in Graphic Design by Women in Design International and has been awarded two "1% for Art" mural commissions.

The artist welcomes collaborations with architects and interior designers on commissioned projects. Work is priced by the job. Slides are available upon request. Please contact the artist for further information.

Stairwell mural for Intel Corporation Hillsboro, OR 7½'h. × 13'w.

Troy's Seafood Market Gresham, OR 5'h. × 16'w.

# Andrea M. Biggs
# Timothy G. Biggs

**792 Eastern Parkway**
**Brooklyn, NY 11213**
**(718) 771-4221**

Andrea and Timothy Biggs collaborate to create mural paintings and specialized painted finishes. Recent projects include Paloma Picasso's new showroom suite; a *trompe l'oeil* wall mural for the Royal Oak Designers showhouse in Manhattan, which was published in England; painted backdrops for Tiffany & Co. catalog photographs; and a wall mural for a new restaurant in New York's Rockefeller Center. Much of their work is in private residences.

Andrea Biggs holds the MFA degree from Bard College and has exhibited widely; Timothy studied at Parsons School of Design. The Biggses welcome opportunities to collaborate with clients in designing site-specific art works. Prices range from $4000 to $10000 and up, depending on size and complexity of the project.

Wall mural painted on curved sheetrock wall; *trompe l'oeil* windows, *faux bois* mahogany, glazed walls.

*Trompe l'oeil* mural with *faux* ashlar stonework.

Wall mural painted in *grisaille* on canvas.

# Design:
# A National Priority

Excellence in design and craftsmanship is a vital national issue.

Until recently the world's largest creditor, the United States, is now the largest debtor. Despite significant devaluation of the dollar, the U.S. balance of trade remains unacceptably high and out of control. Our products do not compete adequately in sophisticated world markets. In 1989, the 50 largest West German corporations sold abroad 40 percent of what they produced. In France the figure is 28 percent—this compares to only about 6 percent in America.

For several years, blame was laid on the high value of the dollar, trade policy deficiencies, and perceived weaknesses of management techniques and our labor force. The actual design and quality of our products were hardly, if ever, mentioned. This is now changing. The importance of design is becoming increasingly evident to American business.

What does this have to do with crafts and craftsmanship? Or with architecture and design? I believe that architects, craft artists, and designers can—in fact, must—play a major role in re-energizing American production. It's not only in large nations such as Japan and Germany that high quality design can be seen to make a major quality of life difference, but in other less well-endowed nations as well. For example, the architects, craftsmen, and designers of Finland have made an extraordinary contribution in that small nation. Much Finnish trade is based upon exceptionally well designed textiles, glassware, ceramics, furniture, cruise ships, prefabricated houses, and other products. With the Finnish standard of living in some ways exceeding the American standard, Finland's designers have transformed their country since World War II.

As a society, much can be done. Unlike most major industrial nations, the United States has no national policy on design. America could honor and support design excellence in numerous important ways, but does not. We need to improve the quality of design education dramatically—not so much in the rudiments of design itself, but in educating designers to be culturally and historically aware professionals who recognize the social, moral, and ethical issues of their craft. As members of professional societies, presumably dedicated to the improvement of our products, we can and should work to promote our vision of design excellence in our councils, institutes, and craft organizations.

During my year as chairman of the American Institute of Architects Committee on Design, we conducted a series of conferences to discuss these issues. In Washington the focus was on design as a national issue; in Minneapolis we discussed educational, moral, and ethical issues; in Helsinki, Finland, at an international conference co-hosted with the Finnish Society of Architects, we examined the design achievements of the Finns as a case study. In all this, it has become apparent that design excellence is rooted in processes more fundamental than those within the individual disciplines of architecture, design, and the crafts. What is most obviously lacking in America is a successful integration of vision among the design arts. Given a sufficient degree of concern, this synthesis will come in time—as it did in the arts and crafts movement in England, at the Bauhaus, and at Cranbrook.

Still, what we can achieve as individual architects, craftsmen, and designers is the most important single issue. Art and craft have been historically the fountainhead of manufacturing, trade, and economic development. It would, I believe, be wise and highly rewarding if more of us paid more attention to the development and production of products carefully targeted to regional and even international markets.

William Morris admonished us to have in our homes only things which we know to be useful or believe to be beautiful. It is clear from his work that he meant them to be both. We, too, should dedicate our efforts to improve the quality or *all* that we see and use in our daily lives.

**Boone Powell, FAIA**
**Chairman, 1989,**
**Committee on Design**
**The American Institute of Architects**

# Evans & Brown Co., Inc.

**Mark Evans, Charley Brown**
**2119 Bush Street**
**San Francisco, CA 94115**
**(415) 255-2735**

Evans & Brown is a firm that is a modern day atelier designing and painting a vast array of murals, trompe l'oeil and special effects. Best known for their Renaissance and baroque murals Evans & Brown's work can be seen in residential and commercial spaces all over the world.

Grounded in classical technique, they have a command of all styles and periods. Their projects range from the belle epoque murals at the Casino de Deauville, the art-decco "Normandie" paintings at the Grand Hyatt-Hong Kong, to the baroque splendors of the Monadnock Building in San Francisco.

Pricing varies according to size and complexity of the project. Minimum: $5,000.

Information package is available.

Bank of the West, San Jose, CA, acrylic on canvas. 400 sq. ft.

Casino de Deauville, tryptich panel, oil on canvas. 540 sq. ft.

Monadnock Building, San Francisco, acrylic on canvas. 800 sq. ft.

# EverGreene Paint Studios

635 West 23rd Street
New York, NY 10011
(212) 727-9500

EverGreene Studios offers a wide range of architectural painting skills including mural painting, faux finishes, trompe l'oeil, stencilling and restoration. Working in a variety of styles from modern to traditional with a constant emphasis on lasting quality. EverGreene has developed a reputation for fine craftsmanship throughout the United States.

EverGreene will collaborate with architects, designers or artists, providing services ranging from an original idea to complete execution and installation. Projects can be executed on site anywhere in the U.S.A. or on canvas in the studio for installation later.

EverGreene has completed projects for governments, corporations and individuals. Recent projects include work for the Library of Congress, the state capitols of Tennessee, Michigan and Indiana. Cartier, Bergdorf Goodman, Saks Fifth Avenue, The Limited, the Ritz Carlton, the Plaza Hotel, Donald Trump, Richard Haas and residences.

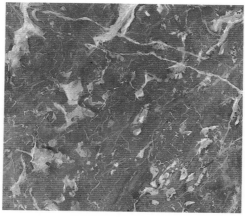

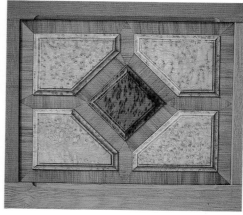

(Top) 1879 stencil design (Above) Faux Marble (Right) Faux Bois and trompe l'oeil panel

Trompe l'oeil mural, Jean Paul Gauttier Shop, Bergdorf Goodman, New York

348

Crown building lobby: Architectural trompe l'oeil, (Inset) Detail of pictorial panel

# Nancy B. Frank

P.O. Box 844
162 Park Lane
Telluride, CO 81435
1-303-728-6544

If it's made of wood, Nancy B. Frank can paint it. Whether it is custom-designed by the artist and built by a woodworker or "found", each piece is uniquely painted with acrylic and finished in high-gloss polyurethane.

Color and mood can be suggested by sending photographs or color samples. Prices depend upon size and surface area, ranging from $500–$5000, retail. For an estimate, send dimensions and a photograph.

Delivery time for commissioned pieces is approximately 3 months. Slides, resume and P.R. information are available upon request, and the artist will gladly work on location.

# Yoshi Hayashi

**351 Ninth Street**
**San Francisco, CA 94103**
**(415) 552-0755**
**(415) 924-9224**

Yoshi Hayashi creates twentieth century interpretations of traditional Japanese lacquer art, with a keen awareness of the finest details. He produces a wide variety of original designs, which range from traditional to modern. His designs on screens, boxes, furniture and decorative objects are contemporary reflections of Hayashi's Japanese heritage.

His work has been exhibited in the V. Brier Gallery, Gump's and Neiman-Marcus in San Francisco, Nikko Hotel and Galleria Design Center's shears & window.

Commissions are accepted.

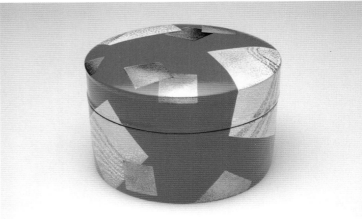

# Thomas Masaryk

515 40th Street
Brooklyn, NY 11232
(718) 853-4940

Old World Craftsmanship is what distinguishes Thomas Masaryk in the field of Trompe L'oeil and painted finishes. He will transform environments and furniture to meet client/designer/decorator/architect needs, whether historic period pieces or showcase, Masaryk specializes in the area of faux marble and wood intarsia and pietre dure. Services include murals, gold leaf, folk glazes (american, european, oriental) and faux architecture. This skilled artisan with years of experience and pride of work ethic accepts commissions to travel and is available for consultations for a fee. The pietre dure tabletop shown here was made for a coffeetable in the florentine baroque style. It is made in a signed/limited addition with changes of faux marbles and semi-precious stones. Folding screens are also available in limited additions representing antiquity to art deco.

# George Middleton

George Middleton Studios
144 Moody Street
Waltham, MA 02154
(617) 899-9230

For nearly a decade, Middleton has worked closely with design professionals. He paints 2 and 3-D trompe l'oeill renditions, specializing in old walls and rock surfaces, and murals—both realistic and fantastic. His work can be viewed in restaurants, public spaces, private residences and in corporate environments.

George works on location and in his studio; carving, texturing and painting on canvas, walls, panels and ceilings. Smaller paintings and textured pieces are also available. Please call or write for additional information, estimates and prices.

(Below) old European wall 10' × 18' painted canvas mounted on interior wall
(Bottom left) carved and painted wall relief depicting crystals embedded in layers of rock 6' × 8' × 9"
(Bottom right) architectural fantasy mural 8' × 12'

# Miller Wagenaar Studios, Ltd.

**1720 N. Marshfield**
**Chicago, IL 60622**
**(312) 276-5300**

William Wagenaar and Rita Miller Wagenaar work with a wide array of physical textures as well as rich metallic and iridescent finishes on moveable walls and screens. Miller Wagenaar produces limited edition designs. They will also collaborate with architects and designers. Information available upon request.

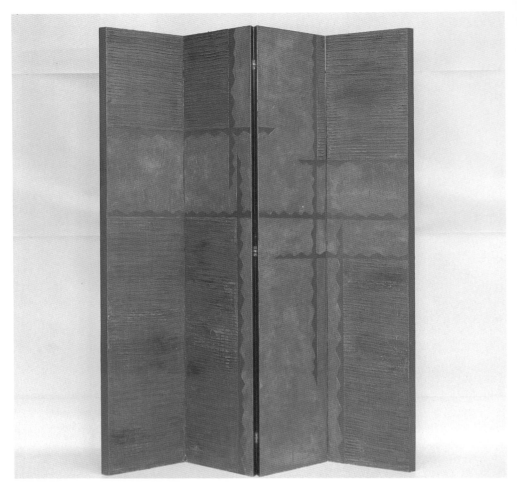

# Miller Wagenaar Studios, Ltd.

1720 N. Marshfield
Chicago, IL 60622
(312) 276-5300

William Wagenaar and Rita Miller Wagenaar specialize in trompe l'oeil, environmental abstract murals and fine painted finishes of the highest quality. Working in a traditional or contemporary format, they offer the designer or architect the option of executing work on site or supervising the installation of a studio-produced piece on any number of materials such as canvas, masonite or metal and shipped anywhere in the world.

Their commissions include Apple Computer, DuPont, Firestone, Kimball, Modern Mode and Herman Miller. They have collaborated with such firms as SOM and Murphy/Jahn.

Please contact Miller Wagenaar Studios for a brochure or to discuss a potential project.

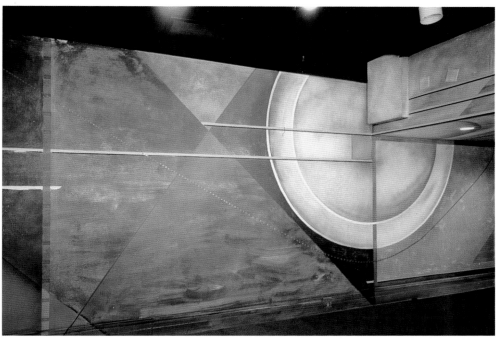

Detail of mural wall 9'–0" × 15'–0"

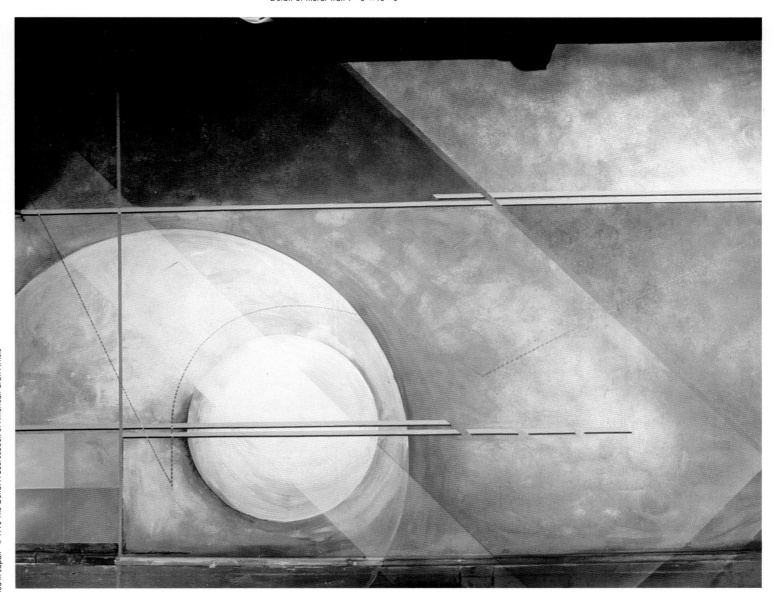

Abstract mural wall. 9'–0" × 20'–0"

# Nolan Studios

**Risë Abramson, President**
**1290 Oak Point Avenue**
**Bronx, NY 10474**
**(212) 842-4077**
**Fax: (212) 991-1180**

Spanning four decades, Nolan Studio's bastion of masterpainters have reigned supreme in the theatrical world of painted scenery. Increasing design demand for one-of-a-kind artistic statements in commercial and luxury residential spaces, has brought about the emergence of a new division of Nolan Studios.

Under the direction of Risë Abramson, the same fecundity of imagination and talent awaits the collaboration of Interior Designers and Architects, Space Planners and Specifiers.

Paint can imitate almost beyond detection, as is evident in the large-scale murals and tromp l'oeil wall canvases created by Nolan Studios. The magic of vision and light is brought to each work by comprehension of color harmonies, knowledge of art history and dedication of integrity to the craft. Nolan Studio's inspired artisans "meet the challenge of the wall."

(Top left) M Butterfly, painted silk show curtain, Eiko Ishioka, designer
(Top right) Restaurant mural rendering, whimsical montage of Venice, Arnold Abramson, designer
(Bottom) Mural adaptation of Gobelin tapestry, Marcel Gromaire: The Earth, 1943

# Gabriel L Romeu

206 Morris Street
Philadelphia, PA 19148
(215) 336-3308

Gabriel Romeu constructs furnishings, accessories and wall murals as a vehicle for his figuratively painted surface design. The form, use and the environment of the installation dictate the appropriate imagery, making his work particularly suitable for commissions and collaborative enterprises. The wide diversity of textural applications, the breadth of pallet, and his interest in a variety of subject matter will present a multitude of options for your client. Each one-of-a-kind piece is designed so all parameters of space requirements, budgetary considerations and scheduled completion arrangements are satisfied.

Acrylic pigments constitute the pallet. The finish is chosen to provide maximum durability.

pillows — $300–$400 per set, floorcloths — $600–$1200, headboards — $800–$1100 screens — $1900–$2200   commissions have been from $3000–$10,000

Slides are available upon request . . .

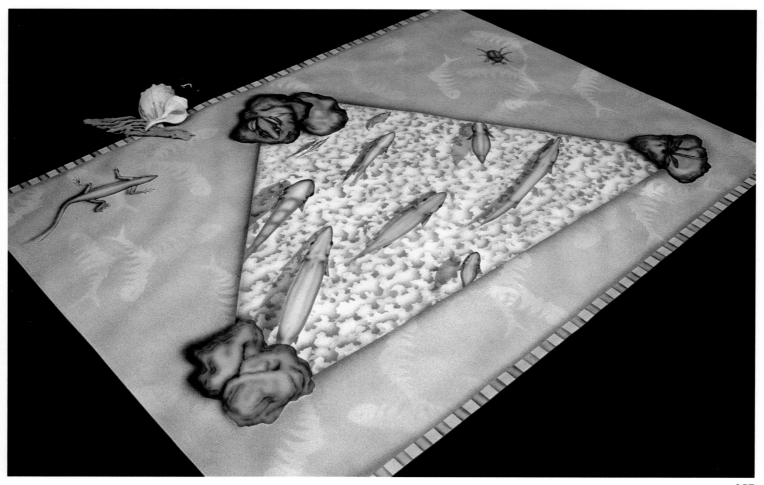

# Separate Dimensions

**Jenifer Tifft and Susan Wren**
**P.O. Box 190**
**West Peru, ME 04290**
**(207) 562-7271**

The artists of Separate Dimensions build and hand paint one-of-a-kind folding screens. Detailed renditions of exotic flora and fauna combined with mottled backgrounds of faux stone, marble, or oxidized metal create a style they call "fantasy realism."

Standard sizes and shapes of the screens vary. Heights range from three to eight feet. General color and subject matter preferences are taken into consideration. Retail prices range from $750 to $2,500.

Commissions are welcomed. Unusual shapes can be made. Special sizes and number of panels can be specified. Write for details and prices.

(Top left) "Lizard and Poppies" (36"h. × 60"w.)
(Bottom left) "Bird of Paradise" (48"h. × 54"w.)
(Top right) "Small Ruin (60"h. × 66"w.)
(Bottom right) "Sandstone Desert" (72"h. × 54"w.)

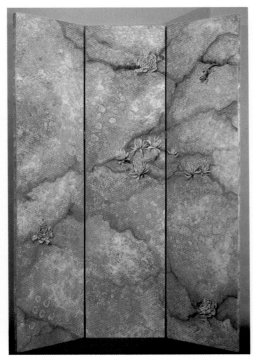

# Split Image Designs

**Lori Sanchez & Kathleen O'Hair**
**2328½ Norwalk Ave.**
**Los Angeles, CA 90041**
**(213) 259-0353 or (213) 463-0394**

Split Image Designs' co-owners, Lori Sanchez and Kathleen O'Hair are graduates of the Art Center College of Design in Pasadena, CA. Together they've compiled a successful five-year career record as scenic artists. Their work is often seen in major, full-length film productions and in nationally televised commercials. With a client portfolio that includes, "Pee Wee's Playhouse," McDonald's Restaurants, Inc., Disney Theme Park, and Pacific Bell. Split Image Designs welcomes all opportunities to collaborate with clients, architects and interior designers to create uniquely conceived murals, a wide variety of paint finishes, and distinctively customized Trompe l'oeil effects. Willing to travel to all locations, Split Image Designs provides price estimates upon request.

# Christian Thee

49 Old Stagecoach Road
Weston, CT 06883
(203) 454-0340

Trained as a theatrical designer and master scenic artist, Christian Thee has been acknowledged as one of the top trompe l'oeil technicians of his time. His deliberate theatrial style has been incorporated into private and corporate commissions which include restaurant and hotel murals and architectural trompe l'oeil.

His work is both mysterious and romantic. It draws the viewer in and invites them to find the intricate surprises that highlight his painterly inventions.

Examples of his artistry have been featured in the store windows of Tiffany & Co. while larger works include the ceilings for Buccellatti in Trump Tower, NYC, and murals in the dining room of the Merridien Hotel in New Orleans. Shown below: Chamber Music backdrop for the Spoleto Festival USA; "Monkey Screen," screen, acrylic on wood; two trompe l'oeil table tops; and a detail from a residential mural. Information on magazine and book publications as well as prices available upon request.

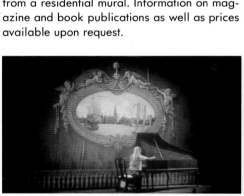

"Felines in Foliage,"

# Tromploy Inc.

**Gary Finkel**
**Clyde Wachsberger**
**400 Lafayette Street**
**New York, NY 10003**
**(212) 420-1639**

**Agent in Japan:**
**Mr. Shi Yu Chen**
**Negishi Bldg, Ground Floor**
**2-23-8, Higashi**
**Shibuya-Ku, Tokyo, Japan**
**(03) 406-3715**

Tromploy Inc. is the partnership of Gary Finkel and Clyde Wachsberger, two artists who combined their backgrounds of archeology, art history, fine art painting, and stage set design to create a studio capable of any type of decorative painting for any environment.

Since 1980, Tromploy has accepted diverse residential and contract commissions throughout the United States and abroad. Tromploy assumes responsibility for the design, execution, and installation of its work. Cost and scheduling are determined by the size and complexity of painting. Simple faux finishes may be accomplished in a week for $10 per square foot; complex architectural murals might cost $100 per square foot and take several months.

Past clients include Hilton, Sheraton, and Marriott Hotels, Chemical Bank, Avon, Steuben Glass, and Estee Lauder Inc.

Telephone or write for a free brochure. Inquiries are welcome.

362

# Architectural Wood and Stone

# Agrell and Thorpe

**BRITISH CLASSICAL CARVERS**
1301 Wazee St.
Denver, CO 80204
(303) 825-6416

British Master Carver, Mr. Ian Agrell and Chief Carver, Adam Thorpe together with their staff create traditional hand carved decoration for architecture and furniture to the highest European standards.

The workshop has undertaken commissions for such major British establishments as Kensington Palace, Ely Cathedral, the new Lloyd's Building in the City of London, and Trinity College of Music.

Their work also graces the residences and palaces of the Sultan of Brunei, the Sultan of Oman, the King of Jordan, and includes commissions for the Saudi Royal family.

For an estimate of cost, send photographs or drawings of your project. Mr. Agrell will collaborate on design and install work anywhere in the world.

# Dimitri Cilione

3725 North Vine Ave.
Tucson, AZ 85719
(602) 323-7858 (office)
(602) 623-2871 (studio)

Dimitri Cilione's longtime devotion to superb craftsmanship and creativity results in works of timeless beauty and quality.

Dimitri works extensively in wood furniture, sculpture, and architectural elements. From an exquisite matching pair of carved mahogany handrails, to bold, sculpted, cedar support columns, he transforms strict functional requirements into beautiful sculptural expressions.

Dimitri's furniture blends traditional and contemporary woodworking disciplines, evoking styles from Southwestern, to Oriental, to painted contemporary, to primitive barbarian, to . . .

Commissions through professional and private contacts are welcome as well as collaborations. Strict attention is always given to function and budget requirements.
Top—Stars 'n' Stripes (low table) (limited edition) $7,500.
Bottom—Puma Head Handrail (1 shown of 2) (commissioned) $5,800/pair.
Photos by—Jeb Zirato

# Fogg Design and Manufacturing Company

**Fred Fogg**
933 Shoreline Drive #201
Alameda, CA 94501
(415) 521-9829

Fred Fogg designs and builds furniture and cabinetry using simple style and flowing lines. His background in product design and mechanical engineering influences his designs toward more functional than furniture-as-art pieces.

Fogg's woodworking ranges from small decorative end tables and formal dining tables, to the semi-circular conference table shown below (20'1"w. × 7'4"d. × 30"h.). Other works include entertainment centers, shelf units, and desks for residential and commercial use.

Each job includes a determination of the requirements of the client, presentation of working drawings and/or renderings, a firm price estimate, and completion date. Most pieces can be available for installation in 8-10 weeks.

Contra Costa County Office of Education, Pleasant Hill, CA

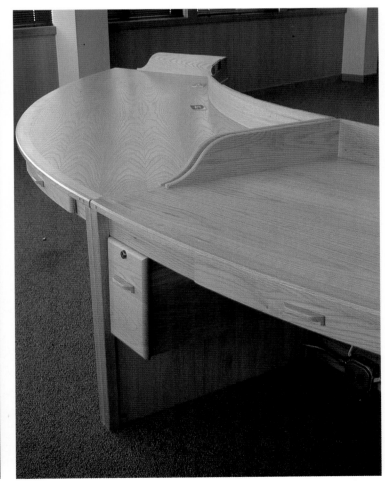

# Dimitrios Klitsas

**705 Union Street**
**West Springfield, MA 01089**
**(413) 732-2661**

For every designer, architect and interior decorator dedicated to exclusive homes and memorable interior appointments, exists Dimitrios Klitsas to fulfill and to surpass their every wood carving vision.

You are cordially invited to discover custom-designed, meticulously hand-carved furnishings of elegance.

Tables, chairs, beds, mirrors, entrances and walls are lovingly crafted for discriminating tastes and opulent surroundings.

Lavish works are created for private, corporate and ecclesiastical circles.

368

Printed in Japan   © 1990 The Guild: A Sourcebook of American Craft Artists

# Juan & Patricia Navarrete

**Navarrete & Associates**
**P.O. Box 2251**
**Taos, NM 87571**
**(505)776-2942**

The Navarretes collaborate with the spirit of the location, the project and their clients. Representing the syntheses of art and architecture, working with accomplished architects, designers, developers, and private collectors, the fresh bas-relief conceptualization and fine craftsmanship of Juan & Patricia Navarrete deem them leaders in their field of functional environmental sculpture. Exploring new uses of stuccos, plasters, cements, adobe, as well as synthetics, this national awarding winning team, fabricate, hand build, cast limited editions, and install site-specific fireplaces, fenestration, passageways, entertainment centers, fountains and walls for both residential and commercial structures, each work unique and signed.

Prices range from $150–$250 per sq. ft. according to number of increments and complexity of design. Portfolio is available upon request, inquiries are welcomed. The Navarretes accept commissions, always completing projects prior to committed schedule.

Sandra Reiner ASID Residence, Master bedroom fireplace, Encino, Ca, plaster

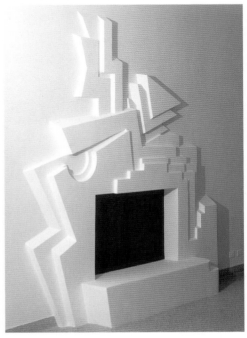

Goldman Residence, livingroom fireplace, Chicago, IL, plaster

Salt River Project, executive lobby reception desk, Phoenix, AZ, hand built plaster

# Robert Sterba Studio

**Robert Sterba**
**12000 Prospect NE**
**Albuquerque, NM 87112**
**(505) 265-6197**

Viewing columns as the ultimate interior element, Robert Sterba delights in adding the crowning touch to an environment. Whether commercial, professional, or residential, wood turning and wood finishing offer creative and unusual alternatives to design situations.

From balusters to columns, the Studio specializes in short runs of 1 to 500 pieces. Projects are often completed in 2 to 8 weeks. Sculptural and larger painted works may require 12 weeks. All works are available finished or unfinished.

Finishes are creative and magical yet low maintenance, usually protected with catalyzed laquer for durability.

Columns start at $400.00. Installations may be quoted and collaborations considered. Specific projects will be quoted on request. Envision a forest of columns on your next special project.

Printed in Japan  © 1990 The Guild: A Sourcebook of American Craft Artists

# Architectural Metal

# Nicholas Brumder

**Liberty Forge**
**40128 Industrial Park No.**
**Georgetown, TX 78626**
**(512) 869-2830**

Nicholas Brumder offers custom designed handwrought forged metalwork using historic European techniques and high-tech tooling in a wide variety of metals. Brumder trained under renowned sculptor Alex Weygers of Carmel, Ca., and master blacksmiths Francis Whitaker of Aspen, Co., Vaclav Jaros of Prague, Czech.

Liberty Forge is well equipped with the tools of the modern blacksmith, and has the capabilities for large commissions. Liberty Forge offers contemporary work, as well as, decorative interpretations of traditional styles.

Design services, including sample and model work, available. Inquiries are welcomed. Brochure and references provided upon request.

Pictures (clockwise from right)—Custom Wine Rack-Forged steel 5'l × 9'h × 5'w. Wine Rack Detail-Hand forged grapes, raised leaves, and heavy vine stock. Baroque Window Grille-Forged steel with raised acanthus leaves-4'6"w × 5'6"h. Wine Display Grille-Forged and pierced round steel. 6'6"h × 5'w. Entry Gate—Forged steel with green patina. 6'w × 8'h.

# Tim Burrows
# Jay Wood

**Burrows-Wood**
**Box 10051 G.S.S.**
**Springfield, MO 65808**
**(417) 866-2612**

Burrows-Wood specializes in one-of-a-kind metal productions designed and handcrafted to meet the individual taste and style of our clientele. Each piece is uniquely crafted from original designs or collaborations. Whether it's a contemporary accent with flowing lines, or an intricate hand-forged relic with rustic charm . . . style and function come together to create a customized theme.

Burrows-Wood crafts are displayed nation-wide . . . and pieces appeared in the 1988 edition of House & Garden magazine. Winners of the craftsmen of the year in 1988 award by the local chapter of the American Institute of Architects.

Price is estimated per project. Guidelines are determined by types of metals and time factor.

Installation available and complete portfolio presented upon request.

# Robert L. Crecelius

St. Francois Forge
Rt. 5 box 5198
Farmington, MO 63640
(314) 756-1201

Robert Crecelius has been forging iron as a blacksmith for over ten years. Specializing in interior pieces Crecelius creates furniture, and lighting in both traditional and contemporary designs, as well as Fireplace accessories and decorative screens and grillwork.

St. Francois Forge is familiar in working with blueprints and can provide scaled working drawings of projects for a retainer fee.

Crecelius is willing to collaborate on specific projects and has done so in the past. Prices vary in range depending on complexity of design and instalation if required. Wrought iron chandelier, above right $650.00 Iron and glass table, lower right $800.00.

Further information is available upon request and welcome.

# Ira DeKoven

**DeKoven Forge**
**5820 Davis Road**
**Walkertown, NC 27051**
**(919) 744-0067**

DeKoven Forge specializes in custom art iron-work. This includes, but is not limited to, firescreens, firetools, grilles, gates, railings, wall pieces, home furnishings, sculpture, hardware, etc. We also do limited production of tables and candleabras.

Although most work is done in forged iron, brass, bronze, copper and aluminum are often employed as visual counterpoint to the iron.

The firedoors pictured are 24"w × 30"h. They are made of forged and fabricated iron, brass and copper. Behind the doors is an iron and brass screen.

# Christian Heckscher

**Sphinx Design Inc.**
**811 Galloway St.**
**Pacific Palisades, CA 90272**
**(213) 459-5438**

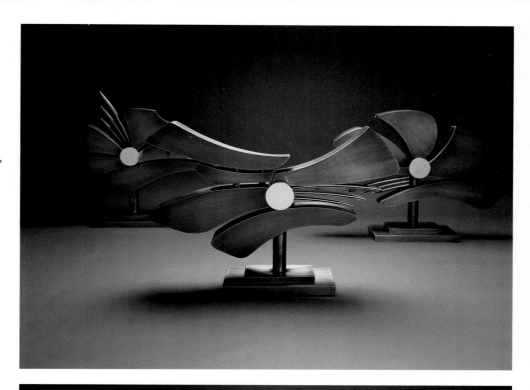

Since 1971, Christian Heckscher has skillfully created and produced a unique range of etched metal artwork (Brass, chrome, copper), combining artistic expression with functional forms. He has specialized in one-of-the-kind pieces or limited series of elevator doors, murals, residence doors, fireplaces and sculptures.

Embracing a variety of styles—traditional, art deco and contemporary—Heckscher's craftsmanship can be adapted to client's budget and specification.

He also welcomes a collaboration with architects or interior designers.

His work has been commissioned by major hotels, restaurants, casinos, office buildings and private homes.

All surfaces are protected by a coat of clear metal lacquer.

Installation available nationwide.

Price and fabrication time is estimate by the project.

(Bottom) Etched brass elevator doors commissioned by "The Mirage" Hotel/casino, Las Vegas 1989

# Chris Hughes/
# James Hughes

**Land Marks**
**RR2 Box 8036**
**Milford, PA 18337**
**(717) 296-8354**

Formerly known as Landmark Restoration, their new name Land Marks reflects a direction towards the fabrication of original design items. They also work on concepts from Architects Designers, and individuals seeking fine ironwork. On the right is an example of a solution to an engineering problem concerning a set of entrance gates opening into an inclined driveway. Below is an overall view of the French Provincial style gates. They measure twenty feet across by fifteen feet high at center. These gates open automatically and were designed and built by Land Marks.

Kerry Stone

378

# Ned James

**65 Canal Street**
**Turners Falls, MA 01376**
**(413) 863-8388**

Ned James has been producing fine hand-wrought metalwork for 14 years. He works in a variety of metals including iron, copper, brass, and bronze, and in a variety of styles, traditional to contemporary.

His products include lanterns, chandeliers, door hardware, iron furniture, grilles, gates, and railings. The capabilities of his well equipped shop range from forging and fabricating to metal spinning, machining, and small castings.

Many notable museums have used his services in reproducing or restoring antique metalwork. He currently specializes in custom work for architects and designers and is comfortable working with blueprints. Ned is happy to collaborate on designing a piece and can add the subtle construction and surface details that make the work stand out.

# Keith Jellum

11535-C S.W. Tonquin Rd.
Sherwood, OR 97140
(503) 692-5803

These wind-activated roof sculptures are mostly one of a kind pieces. The goal is to find a resonance between the spirit of the architecture and its residents, and fuse that with the aesthetics of the artist and the animism of the sculpture.

The pieces pivot on a sophisticated bearing mechanism anchored (where possible) to an under-the-roof support structure. The skin is primarily sheet bronze and stainless steel, heli-arc welded over a stainless steel framework. The bearings are maintenance free and replaceable. The whole unit is designed to withstand the strongest winds and should have a life-span of hundreds of years.

Sizes might vary from four to ten feet and weight from 40 to 230 pounds. Price range from $5,000 to $20,000. Send for brochure.

Monad, 94"L × 37"H × 17"D

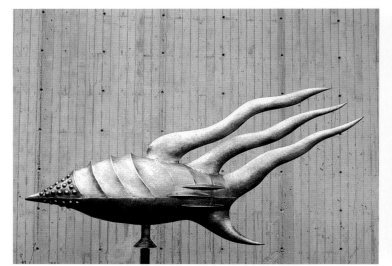

Ichthyornial Probe, 113"L × 52"H × 17"D

Caribe, 85"L × 50"H × 28"D

# David MacDonald

**3515 Springlake Drive**
**Findlay, OH 45840**
**(419) 422-1400, 3131**

David MacDonald, blacksmith, produces functional and ornamental ironwork for residential and corporate environments, using modern hand forged techniques to achieve traditional results.

MacDonald works closely with architects and potential clients for new design development, and for restoration of architectural ironwork. Specially developed coatings give a wide spectrum of durable finishes.

Installation is available nationwide. A 3 month design and production period is required for major commissions.

A representative portfolio is available upon serious inquiry.

(Top right) Hand forged chess set. Graphite and bronze finishes.

# David A. Ponsler

**Wonderland Products Inc.**
5772 Lenox Avenue
P.O. Box 6074
Jacksonville, FL 32236
(904) 786-0144

The forged railing with bronze embellishment represents one of many styles of ironwork we design and fabricate. Our work encompasses architectural pieces, furniture and sculpture of traditional and modern styles.

Wonderland Products Incorporated, founded in 1950, is the recipient of numerous national awards and has international trade affiliations.

We welcome inquiries and will be pleased to provide references.

382

Printed in Japan © 1990 The Guild: A Sourcebook of American Craft Artists

# Dennis J. Proksa

**Blackrock Forge**
**5192 West Old Highway 91**
**Pocatello, ID 83204**
**(208) 775-4975**

The distinctive ironwork of Dennis Proksa at Blackrock Forge is characterized by its vigor and technical virtuosity. He has over a decade of experience creating innovative metalwork fluent in the vocabulary of both traditional and modern forging and fabricating methods, and designs. He has worked in collaboration with architects and developers on a variety of large scale residential and commercial projects in Oklahoma, Texas, Colorado, Idaho, and Washington. Furniture, railings, gates, light fixtures, large and small sculptures have been commissioned and purchased for private residences.

The foundation upon which Blackrock Forge has built its reputation is a background in industrial metalwork and fabrication, a degree in art from Southern Illinois University-Carbondale, collaboration with other blacksmiths, and a shop capable of producing large scale projects.

A brochure and references are available upon request.

(Top) "Frolicsome Fish," stainless steel, 8' × 9' at Simplot Square, Pocatello, Idaho.
(Bottom) "Elk Fence at the EZ Livin' INN," mild steel, 9' × 65', Lava Hot Springs, Idaho.

# Nol Putnam

**White Oak Forge Ltd.**
**P.O. Box 341**
**The Plains, VA 22171**
**(703) 253-5269**

Nol Putnam specializes in designing, creating and installing hot-forged architectural ironwork. Pricing is determined by the complexity of design. The White Oak Forge also restores ironwork, offers consultation and is capable of doing the work. Collaborative work is most welcome.

A portfolio of recent works is available upon request.

(Right) Memorial gate, Washington Cathedral, Washington, DC; forged mild steel, 3'w. × 6½'h., 1988.

Photo: Henry Eastwood

# Joel A. Schwartz

**Schwartz's Forge & Metalworks, Inc.**
P.O. Box 205, Forge Hollow Road
Deansboro, NY 13328
(315) 841-4477

Schwartz's Forge & Metalworks, Inc. designs and produces works that complement and enhance their environments. All projects are treated in a manner deserving of the blacksmith's art. In the tradition of past masters, careful attention is given to every detail during the design, fabrication and installation.

Their work has been recognized by numerous contemporary and restoration architects and designers for its high-quality design and craftsmanship. Care is taken to preserve the architect's and designer's conceptual and visual intent. A representative portfolio is available upon request.

Commissions: Blair House, Washington, DC (balconies); Gracie Mansion, New York City (railings); 222 Central Park South, New York City (entry doors); Del Monte Corporation, Coral Gables, FL (grand stair in association with Rambusch Decorating Company); St. Paul's School Library, Concord, NH (stair, balcony, terrace railings and weathervane)

# Dan Siglar, Blacksmith

315 S. Lawn
Kansas City, MO 64124
(816) 231-6633

Dan Siglar works with ancient and modern tools to create traditional and contemporary designs in iron, copper and brass. Interior and exterior furniture, unique gates, fences, decorative wall pieces and other objects are created as the result of original design or in collaboration with interior decorators, landscape designers, architects, and artists.

Reconstruction and reproduction of hand forged historic ironwork is a unique skill that is offered to individuals and institutions.

Price estimates are available for designs submitted in completed form or original designs can be provided to review for a fee. Firm production prices are given while installation prices are determined by requirements of the project. Projects that require travel to the site for preview and/or installation are welcome.

Lantern: 2'w. × 5'6"h. Gate: 4'6"w. × 4'h.

# Architectural Glass

# Ellen Abbott
# Marc Leva

**Custom Etched Glass**
**1330 Lawrence**
**Houston, Texas 77008**
**(713) 864-4773**

Ellen Abbott has been designing carved and etched glass since 1974 in styles ranging from geometric to representational. She collaborates with designers and architects from conception, providing consulting services as well as site-specific samples.

Marc Leva manages each project and insures a timely schedule from fabrication to delivery and installation. Even the most demanding dealines can be met.

The studio emphasizes quality craftsmanship and service in sandblasting and related techniques. The creative environment allows for the production of large commercial projects as well as the more personal residential work.

Recent commissions include installations in New York City, Orlando, Las Vegas, and Houston. Price varies with each project. Inquiries are welcome.

(Top right) Winter 18" × 18"
(Bottom right) Door panels 12" × 42"

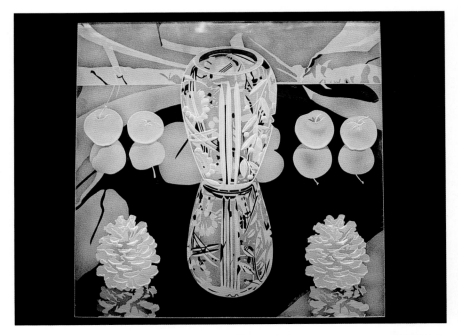

# Kathy Barnard

2000 Grand Avenue
Kansas City, MO 64108
(816) 472-4977

Working with the many possibilities inherent in glass, Kathy Barnard has continuously refined her etched and carved glass art over the years to create works of exceptional beauty. In this edition of the Guild, she introduces that same refinement of artistry in her use of stained glass.

In all her work Kathy's love of nature, distinctive sense of design and emphasis on detail emerge to produce truly fine pieces of art that enhance the environment in which they are incorporated. Be it large or small, her works can range from delicate etched flowers on a goblet to a sensitive interpretation of the "Tree of Life" in a 15-foot diameter stained glass window. Kathy's painstaking craftsmanship and beautiful designs have earned her a national reputation.

(Below) "Tree of Life", Jewish Community Campus Center, Overland Park, Kansas. (Right) detail—"Tree of Life".

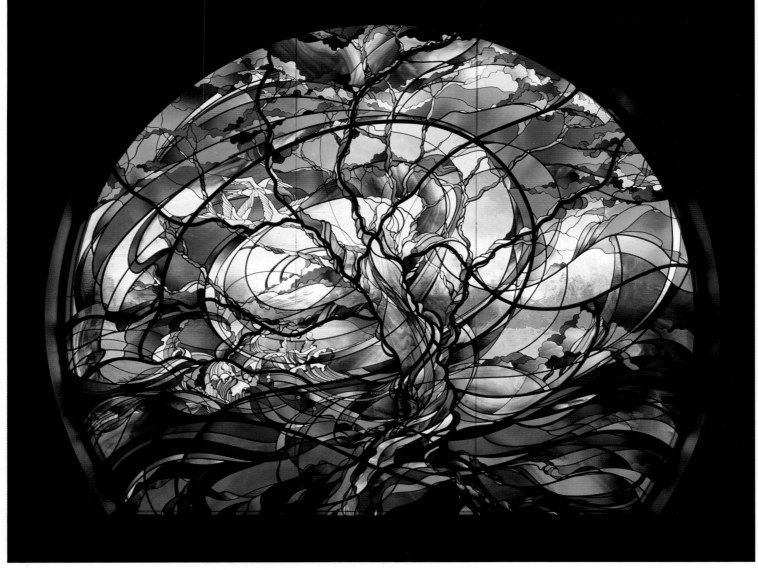

Kathy Barnard—design + color     Larry Etzen—construction     Austin Ironworks—steel framework

# Kathy Barnard

**2000 Grand Avenue**
**Kansas City, MO 64108**
(816) 472-4977

Her designs are signed and numbered limited editions and one-of-a-kind works, commissions installed and exhibited throughout North America. Each piece is carefully designed to reflect the personality of the client and setting. Her work also include unique tableware utilizing handblown glass, tabletops, room dividers, fireplace screens, and door and window panels.

Restoration of the facade of the Midland Theatre for the Performing Arts, Kansas City, Missouri. Built 1927, restored 1987. 20′ × 40′ window with etched-glass arch.

# Barbara Lillian Boeck
# Gene Milo

GB Studio
207 Walker Street
Cliffside Park, NJ 07010
(201) 945-4933

Artist Barbara Boeck and designer/builder Gene Milo offer a limitless array of sculptural carved glass for residential and commercial use. With a combined expertise in the fields of art, glass, lighting and construction, the GB team handles each project from design inception through final installation.

The original designs embrace many styles, creating works of distinction geared specifically to their environment and to client preference. All types of glass are utilized. Sand-etching on stainless steel and brass is also available. Custom installations, both decorative and functional, employ a wide choice of materials that enhance the overall visual image.

Commissioned pieces can be found in such diverse locations as florists, restaurants, car dealerships, and corporate offices, as well as in numerous private residences.

Prices vary according to project requirements. Inquiries welcomed; brochure upon request.

"Tranquility." Wall inset with concealed lighting, 72" diameter.

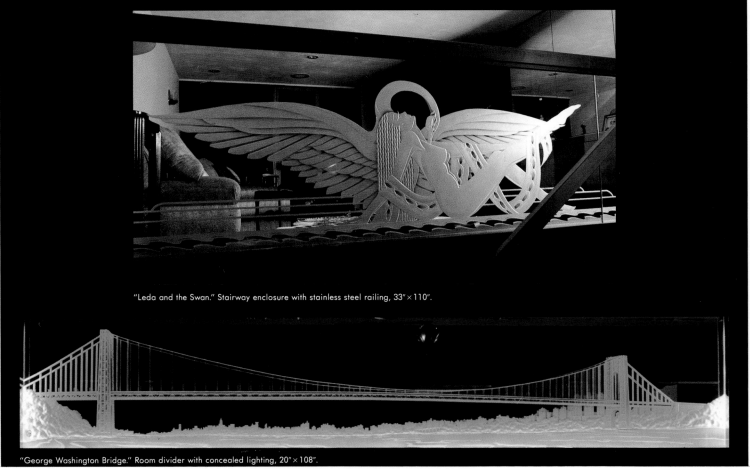

"Leda and the Swan." Stairway enclosure with stainless steel railing, 33" × 110".

"George Washington Bridge." Room divider with concealed lighting, 20" × 108".

Printed in Japan  © 1990 The Guild: A Sourcebook of American Craft Artists

# J. Gorsuch Collins

8283 West Iliff Lane
Lakewood, CO 80227
(303) 985–8081

Originally a graphic designer, J. Gorsuch Collins has been working in glass since 1976. She utilizes stained, beveled, fused and pate de verre glass to create pieces ranging in scale from one to hundreds of sq. ft. Creating works for galleries as well as residential, commercial applications, Collins' greatest assets are her ability to accommodate any architectural setting and to select unusual and subtle color and texture combinations.

Collins' work is in private and corporate collections throughout the United States, has appeared in a wide range of publications and has won many awards.

A brochure and slides are available upon request.

(Top left) Littleton Hospital Chapel, 90 sq. ft., "Tree of Life"
(Bottom right) Private residence, Snowmass, CO "The Actors", 59"h. × 72"w.
(Top right) Littleton Hospital Chapel, exterior view, "Tree of Life"
(Middle right) St. Anne's Episcopal School, Denver. Each of 450 students designed a square which was color orchestrated by the artist and then leaded by the artist
(Bottom left) Private residence, Denver, CO, 23.7 sq. ft.

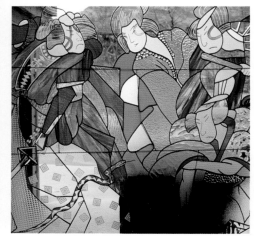

# Barbara E. Cunha

**Flying Colors Stained Glass**
P.O. Box 97
Assonet, MA 02702
(508) 644-2433

(Left) "Spring" 4' × 8'
(Right) "Winter" 4' × 8'

Seasons of Salvation (series of 8)
St. John Neumann Catholic Church
East Freetown, Massachusetts

Nature sings to Barbara.
She translates into glass.
Using the language of color
And broadcasting with light,
She amplifies this music
For the eye.

A professional glass studio, creating
architectural and autonomous artwork of
exceptional quality, that offers:

Timely completion within budget.
Superior craftsmanship.
Professional, personalized attention.
Installation assistance.
Concept development and custom design.
Contemporary and traditional motifs.
Collaborative works.
Limited edition collections.

Additional information on request.

# Jerome R. Durr

**Just Glass Studio**
**202 Marcellus St.**
**Syracuse, NY 13204**
**(315) 428-1322**

Jerome chose glass as his medium in 1973, and began designing and fabricating commissioned architectural stained glass and abrasive carved pieces in 1977. He also joined the exhibiting world in 1981 with free-standing artworks. Both the architectural and freestanding works are directed toward the private residential collector as well as the public and commercial sectors.

The studio is also involved with historically approved restoration and documentation of stained glass, along with Jerome's lectures on various techniques of restoration.

Collaborative efforts are encouraged. Portfolio, slides and project costs are available upon request.

(Top) Residential stained glass entryway
(Bottom) One of nine commercial etched glass entries

# Jean-Jacques Duval

**Duval Studio**
**Gypsy Trail**
**Carmel, NY 10512**
**(914) 225-6077**

Mr. Duval's aim is to aesthetically serve the demands of purpose and environment. Each commission undertaken by him is created with due respect to the nature of the architectural setting and the requirements of the client and architect.

Mr. Duval's commissions can be seen throughout the Country, Japan, West Indies, Europe and Israel.

A slide portfolio is available upon request.

Apartment building, N.Y.C.
Faceted glass detail.
Adams Tower lobby, N.Y.C.
Faceted glass

Printed in Japan  © 1990 The Guild: A Sourcebook of American Craft Artists

# Larry Etzen

**Larry Etzen Studio**
**P.O. Box 22384**
**Kansas City, MO 64113**
**(816) 363-5980**

Larry Etzen has been involved in the production of architectural art glass since 1977. Although versatile, he specializes in the fabrication of light fixtures and leaded glass dome ceilings. Aspects of his work include an innovative use of color and design, quality craftsmanship and durability. His work has been installed throughout the country. Art glass commissions are accepted for public buildings, restaurants, hotels, and private residences. Early planning is recommended. Collaborative efforts are welcome. Inquiries concerning design concepts, cost and installation are encouraged.

Brochure available upon request.

18' grape dome, color shading and color artwork: Larry Etzen. Original design: Kathy Barnard

Harry Starkers Restaurant, Country Club Plaza, K.C. MO.

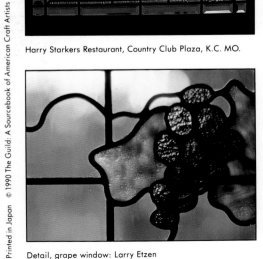

Detail, grape window: Larry Etzen

Photography: Terry Harrison

# Fredrica H. Fields

**Member of the Stained Glass Assoc. of America**
**561 Lake Avenue**
**Greenwich, CT 06830**
**(203) 869-5508**
**By appointment only.**

Fredrica Fields specializes in three-dimensional stained glass. Her work is noted for a unique use of varied glass material. Each work is abstract, original, and one-of-a-kind. Techniques include layering or fitted construction, sometimes in combination with engraving on flashed (2-layer) glass, with extraordinary effects resulting. Construction methods depend on the size, shape, and kind of glass being used. These works must be protected from the elements with thermopane. They will do well in artificial light, though natural light is best.

Installations are in a cathedral, chapel, hospice, meditation/prayer room, and schools, libraries, and private collections.

Commissions are welcomed after a visit by the patron to the studio.

Completed works are also for sale at the studio. Prices begin at $3000. Photographer is Kenneth E. Fields.

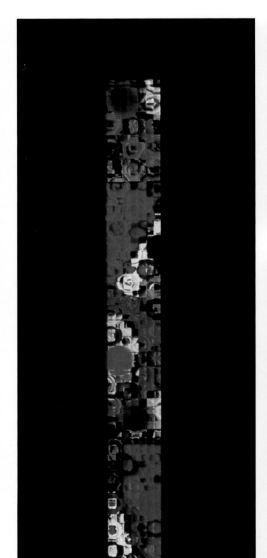

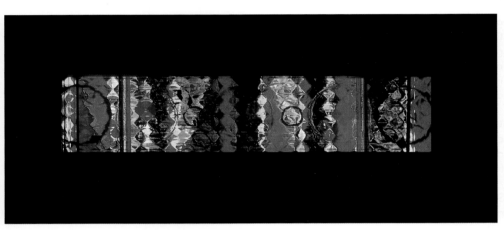

Circus. Exhibition Panel. 5.5"H × 22.5"W × 4"D

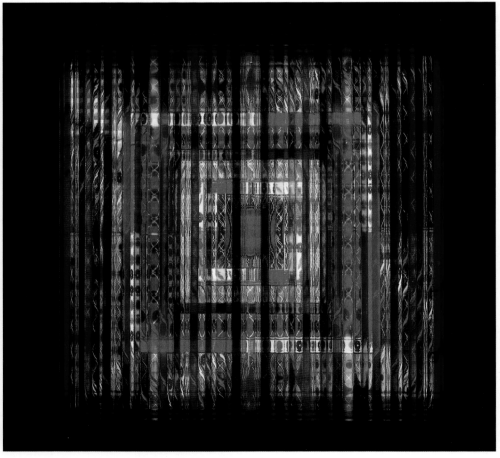

Slim Jim. Exhibition Panel. 37"H × 3.5"W × 4"D

Y.W.C.A., Greenwich, Conn. One of three in the lounge. 30"sq. × 5"D

398

# John Forbes

**Bonny Doon Art Glass**
**7258 Empire Grade**
**Santa Cruz, CA 95060**
**(408) 426-5828**

Bonny Doon Art Glass has completed numerous public and private commissions throughout the U.S.; John Forbes has lectured at professional conferences in the States and abroad. The versatile capabilities of our designers and craftsmen facilitate collaborations with the client, taking the project from concept to installation.

The studio is known for employing conceptual and technical innovations in addressing particular project demands. Expertise in optical grinding and beveling, wheel engraving, acid and sandblast etching, neon, painting and firing, and bending glass allows a broad range of expression.

We are capable of producing large-scale architectural glass including murals, skylights, domes, entryways, lighting fixtures, and furniture.

Slides, resume, and pricing available upon request.

(Top) Residential Window. Design: Jeanne Rosen
(Bottom left) residential dome skylight. Design: John Forbes and Jeanne Rosen
(Bottom right) residential entryway. Design: Jeanne Rosen

# Chuck Franklin

**Chuck Franklin Glass Studio**
**1319 NW Johnson**
**Portland, OR 97209**
**(503) 227-6964**

Chuck Franklin has worked in glass since 1974. His work includes residential and commercial installations, flat window panels, and a wide variety of lampshades and lighting systems.

He specializes in working closely with the client to produce custom work that meets all design and budget parameters. Although skilled at designing, he can also work from drawings and ideas supplied.

His work is found in homes, restaurants, and buildings throughout the United States and Japan.

Chandelier, 5 ft. dia., residence

Harborside Restaurant, Portland Ore.

Printed in Japan  © 1990 The Guild: A Sourcebook of American Craft Artists

# Nancy Gong

**GONG GLASS WORKS**
165 Linden Avenue
P.O. Box 10344
Rochester, NY 14610
(716) 586-1993

Gong Glass Works creates meticulously crafted custom works designed to complement and enhance any private, public, commercial or marine environment or art collection. Collaborating with architects, designers, builders and collectors, the studio offers an almost unlimited range of styles with choices in sandetched, dimensionally sand-carved and leaded glass. This includes decorative detail work in large etched murals, windows, doors, side lites, rails, furniture, wall pieces and distinctive corporate symbols and signage.

Price variables: size, material selection, design detail and fabrication processes. Prices start at $75/sq. ft. for carved glass, $20/sq. ft. for etched glass, $100/sq. ft. for leaded glass.

(Right) "Rhapsody in Lite", (Below) "Whoops". A brochure is available upon request. Glass that reflects your image.

# Wendy Gordon

**Wendy Gordon Glass Studio, Inc.**
P.O. Box 143
Manassas, VA 22110
(703) 791-3287

Wendy Gordon has been creating stained, etched, beveled and fused glass for commercial and residential clients since 1980. She especially enjoys the diversity of styles in her commissions, as well as the excitement and rewards of the collaborative effort. Her work, including a variety of restaurant projects, has been showcased by local and national television programs, newspapers and magazines.

The Wendy Gordon Glass Studio is committed to excellence in design and craftsmanship and to delivering the finished pieces on schedule and within budget.

(Far right) 3-story architectural installation, Washington, DC
(Center) "The Drive-In", may be ordered personalized, 28" × 36"
(Bottom) Private commission, 4-panel room divider.

Photography by Fredde Lieberman

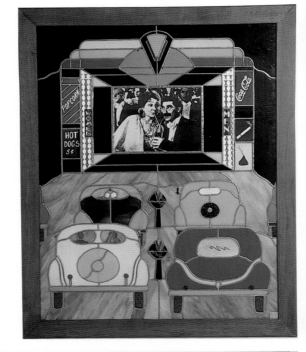

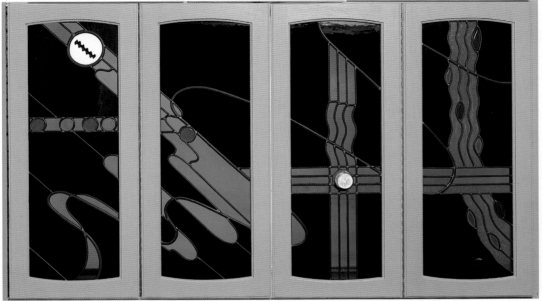

Printed in Japan  © 1990 The Guild: A Sourcebook of American Craft Artists

# Peter Green

**Renaissance Studio**
**25 Saugatuck Avenue**
**Westport, CT 06880**
**(203) 226-9674**

Renaissance Studio specializes in formed, irridized and mirrored three dimensional art glass in either wall mosaic, suspended mobile or traditional window formats. The studio also creates etched sand carved glass doors or room divider screens, beveled leaded glass panels and traditional stained glass windows.

The Westport studio, established in 1970, includes a gallery, and presentation facilities, where artist and clients may view sample artwork or previous commissions in the slide presentation areas.

(Center) Hartford North Bldg., Hartford, CT

# Hall/Zeitlin

**Chatham Glass Works**
**5 Maple St.**
**East Hampton, CT 06424**
**(203) 267-8475**
**\*Inquiries Welcome\***

Collaborating closely with its clientele in the design, fabrication and installation of original design "environmental" glass work, the award winning studio takes into consideration the site specific architectural and budgetary considerations, while designing to meet aesthetic goals.

As a design and fabrication team, Emily Zeitlin and Stuart Hall enjoy the challenges inherent in the creation of such works. Highly versatile in design style and technique, Chatham Glass Works offers lead came fabrication, surface and deep-carved sandblast techniques for interior decor and architectural applications. Limited edition accent pieces available.

Represented nationally, Zeitlin and Hall collaborate with architects, interior and commercial designers, galleries, ecumenical groups and public space foundations. A custom design, firm price estimate and work schedule are presented prior to execution and installation.

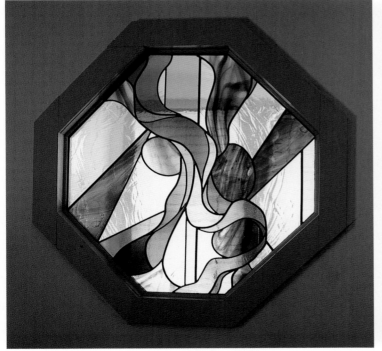

404

# Gene Hester

**Genesis Art Glass Studio**
**2704 Sackett**
**Houston, TX 77098**
**(713) 522-2950**

Gene Hester designs and creates contemporary stained glass windows using various technical skills of beveling, fusing, etching and painting with traditional methods.

Hester's 15 years experience in both commercial and residential work guarantee each commission piece will meet site-specific requirements and budget allotment.

Pricing generally range from $85–175 per sq. ft. Collaborative projects with the architect, interior designer and other artist are welcome. Additional information and color brochure are available upon request.

# Paul Housberg

59 Tingley Street
Providence, RI 02903
(401) 751-7617

Paul Housberg is a graduate of the Rhode Island School of Design (BFA 1975, MFA 1979) and was a Fulbright Scholar (1986–1987) to the Centre International de Recherche sur le Verre et les Arts Plastiques (CIRVA) in Marseille, France for his work in kiln-formed glass. He also studied with prominent English stained glass artist Patrick Reyntiens (1981) with a scholarship from the New York Experimental Glass Workshop. His work has been published in American Craft, Neues Glas and New Work among others. Clients include Nike Inc., Temple Sons of Israel, Allentown, PA and the Hay Group, Washington, DC.

The artist welcomes commissions and collaborations of architectural glass, lighting and wall reliefs for residential, corporate and ecclesiastic settings.

Prices and scheduling vary with the requirements of the project.

Please contact the artist for further information and portfolio.

(Top) Project for wall of cast glass block.
(Bottom right) Leaded glass screen, steel frame, 63"w. × 66"h.
(Bottom left) Platter, kiln-formed glass, 15" dia.

# Lyn Hovey

**Lyn Hovey Studio, Inc.**
**266 Concord Avenue**
**Cambridge, MA 02138**
**(617) 492-6566**

Lyn Hovey is a noted artist/craftsman in stained glass with over a quarter century of accomplishment in the field. Linear architectural works utilizing optically playful transmitted and reflected light effects characterize some of his latest works. His materials often include specialty blown glass, blown mirror, jewels and machine glass. Fabrication of the works is in lead, copper and steel.

Lyn Hovey's award winning stained glass has been exhibited internationally and is represented in corporate, religious and private collections in the United States, Europe and Japan.

Commissions are welcomed. A portfolio is available upon request.

(Bottom) African Dichroic Series exhibited in II International Salon du Vitrail in Chartres, France 1989. Size 31"w. × 29"h.
(Right) African Dichroic Series in corporate reception area. Size 36"w. × 60"h.

# Jurs Architectural Glass

Shelley Jurs
1733 Dwight Way
Berkeley, CA 94703
(415) 549-9648
(415) 763-6796

Jurs Architectural Glass' award-winning designs are part of a collaboration with design professionals, developers and home owners. Recognizing the complexity of building decisions affecting today's construction industry, the company's glass designs are a carefully considered and integrated element in the overall architectural plan.

Founded in Oakland, CA, in 1978, Jurs Architectural Glass is committed to beautiful, simple materials, traditionally handcrafted with a contemporary flair and at home in virtually any decor.

A brochure is available.

(Top) All Saints Chapel, Hayward, CA. 1987. 22'w. × 11'h.
(Bottom) Grand Entrances, Limited Design Series, Standard Door openings.

# Jon Kuhn

**Kuhn Glass Studios**
**705 N. Main**
**Winston-Salem, NC 27101**
**(919) 722-2369**

Communicating a clear integrated image, Jon Kuhn's substantial columns and window installations are elegant compositions of planes of colored glass patterns interacting within a clear matrix of lead crystal.

Depending upon the placement of the viewer and the light source, the imagery within these pieces shift, introducing the element of movement; thus becoming manifestations of continual inner change—a fascinating characteristic found in the smallest of Kuhn's columns to his larger scale architectural commissions.

Price range from $2500–$100,000.

Selected Museum Collections:
  Metropolitan Museum of Art, New York, New York
  Smithsonian Institution, Washington, D.C.
  Musee Des Arts Decoratifs, Lausanne, Switzerland
  Ebeltoft International Glass Museum, Ebeltoft, Denmark
  High Museum, Atlanta, Georgia
  (complete resume on request)

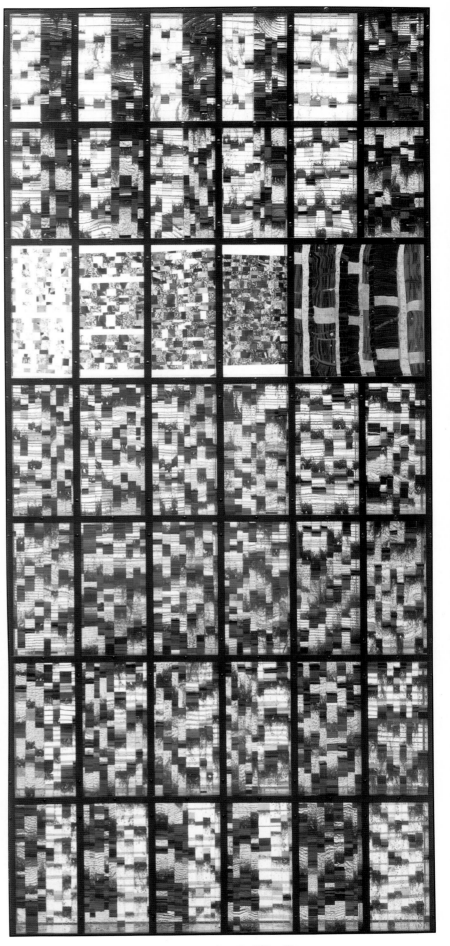

"Tiger Passion," 1989, fused and laminated glass column, 5¾" × 6½" × 25¼"

"Theme of Five," 1988, fused and laminated glass window, 67" × 29¾" × 2⅞"

# Ellen Mandelbaum

**Ellen Mandelbaum, Architectural Glass**
**39-49 46 Street**
**L.I.C. Queens, NY 11104**
**(718) 361-8154**

Architect, client, Brian Percival wrote, "I have greatly enjoyed both process and product! Many thanks. I would not hesitate to suggest your services to an architectural client or anyone desiring artistic glass work."

Mandelbaum is recognized internationally for her painterly architectural glass. She began work in glass in 1975. She is represented in: *Who's Who in American Art, 1990;* "Architectural Glass," Andrew Moor; *Il Salon,* Chartres, France; *Professional Affiliate Member A.I.A., NY Chapter.*

A wide variety of commissions and collaborations accepted. Additional materials and price-guidelines on request. See also *The Guild* 1, 2, 3.

(Top) L. Seiler Hallway, Duluth, Minn.
(Top) R. "Waves×3 for Chartres," (det.)
(Bottom) Dr. William Wedin residence, Southampton NY (det.)

# Bonnie Maresh

42 Carriage Shop Road/P.O. Box 37
Waquoit, Falmouth, MA 02536
(508) 548-6215

Recognized by her graceful design line, Maresh's work has added architectural enhancement to residential and public buildings throughout the Northeast and Midwest. Her leaded glass incorporates detailing techniques such as sandcarving, plating, and fusing.

Brochure available upon request.

Public installations: New England Baptist Hospital, Boston, MA; Otis Air National Guard Base Chapel, Cape Cod, MA; Doreen Grace Brain Research Facility, New Seabury, MA; Canty Recreation Center, Falmouth, MA

(left) "Vineyard Sound" 48"×9", stairway landing, sandcarving and plating detail. Private collection.
(top right) "Five Koi" 24"×44", hot tub window
(bottom) "Moonakis Swan" interior doorway, colorless, textured glass

# Kathy Messman

6422 Casselberry Way
San Diego, CA 92119
(619) 465-6242

Kathy Messman designs and creates unique glass art, specific to its environment. She invites and enjoys collaborative efforts and is proud of her reputation for quality and professionalism. Kathy's work is available by commission for private residences, corporate environs, and public spaces.

Prices for pieces vary and are determined by design selection, with an average price range of $100-$175 per sq. ft. The design fee is $250. Please contact the artist for information regarding commissions and slides of available work.

(Top) "Dawn Solitude", 33"w. × 58"h. etched and painted panel for a San Diego residence. (Bottom) "Pudding at Room Temperature", 33"w. × 25"d. × 18"h., mixed media table. Exhibited "Furniture '88" competition 10/88. (SD, CA)

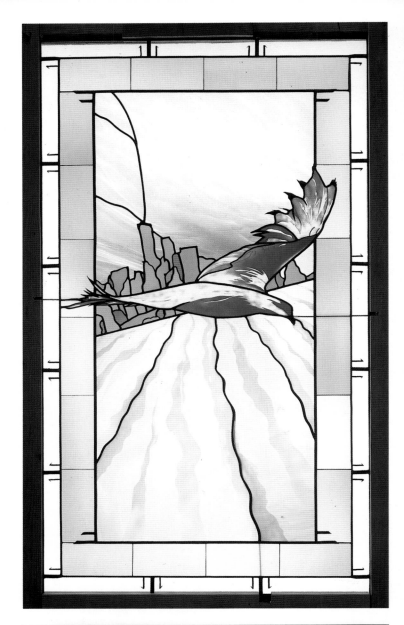

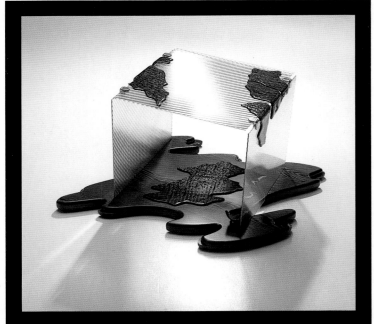

Printed in Japan   © 1990 The Guild: A Sourcebook of American Craft Artists

# William Morris

32609 76th Ave. N.W.
Stanwood, WA 98292
(206) 629-4673

William Morris' superb glass blowing abilities are represented here in two of his series— Standing Stones and Artifact Series. Their mythical beauty, aesthetic spontaneity and lyrical colors have placed his pieces in homes and public places alike. Morris' work is in permanent collections of Corning Museum, American Craft Museum, La County Art Museum and London's Victoria and Albert Museum.

A book about the artist—William Morris/Glass—Artifact&Art, is available in bookstores. Commissions are accepted.

Standing Stone 48"h.×18"w. $6,500.

Standing Stone 40"h.×19'w. $6,500

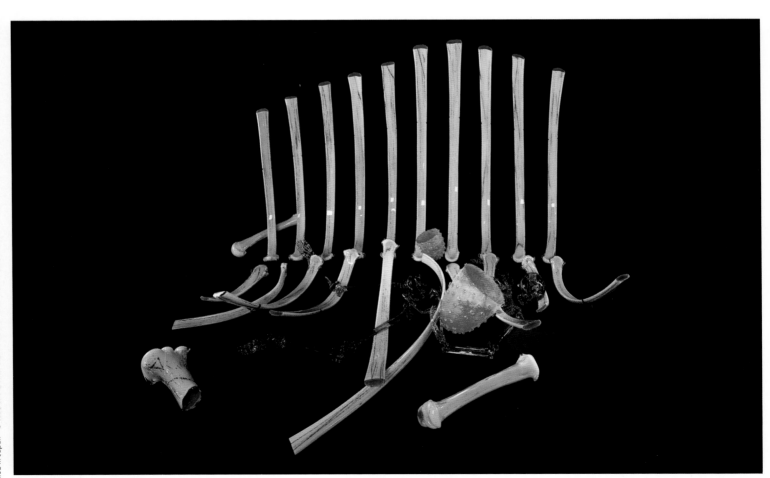

Artifact Series 10'×10'×8' $80,000

# Brigitte Pasternak

301 River Road
Nyack, NY 10960
(914) 359-2004

Brigitte Pasternak designs and, in collaboration with a reputable local studio, builds stained glass installations of any size for private and public buildings. She regards interaction with clients, architects and builders as an integral part of her profession. She welcomes inquiries. She listens. She addresses practical issues such as installation, insulation, cost.

(Top) Residential transom, 3' × 6', Briarcliff Manor, NY. Photo: Harry Goldmark
(Bottom) Residential window, 7' × 6', Riverdale, NY

414

# Brigitte Pasternak

**301 River Road**
**Nyack, NY 10960**
**(914) 359-2884**

Unless intense color and ornate design is required for a given site or concept, Brigitte Pasternak strives rather for clarity and simple elegance in her architectural work, fresh and contemporary, but also timeless and livable.

The simplicity of line and form in turn facilitates sound engineering, affordable pricing, prompt delivery and trouble-free installation. The charges range from $100 to $160 per sq. ft. depending upon complexity. Extremely detailed works cannot, however, be contained within this basic price scale.

(Top) Dental operating room, 2′ × 2.5′.
(Bottom) 'Sun + Glass = Energy,' General Glass International, New Rochelle, NY, 11′ × 10′

# Narcissus Quagliata

**Contact: Brigid Guinan**
**1200 Taylor #30**
**San Francisco, CA 94108**
**(415) 771-5440**

Narcissus Quagliata has created works in glass for residential and commercial spaces around the world for over 17 years. In designing these doors for this modern Mexican residence Quagliata has redefined what decorative glass can be. Using a dynamic combination of custom blown glass, unique bevels and lacquered wood he has designed an entrance that enhances the architecture and maximizes the beauty of glass.

Site-specific works can be viewed at Charles Schwab & Co., Inc., San Francisco, California; Blue Cross Headquarters, Oakland California; Screen Actors Guild Business Arts Plaza Building, Burbank, California; National Advanced Systems, Santa Clara, California.

Museum collections: Corning Museum of Glass, Corning, New York; Oakland Museum, Oakland, California; Yokohama City Museum of Modern Art, Yokohama, Japan

(Below) Private Residence, Xalapa, Veracruz, Mexico. Each door 7'6" × 3'8"

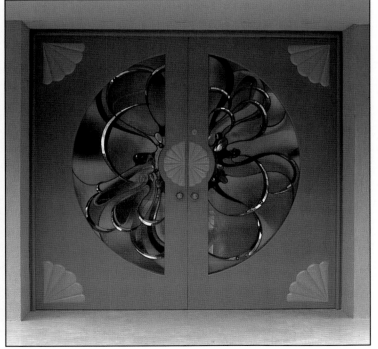

# Narcissus Quagliata

**Contact: Brigid Guinan**
**1200 Taylor #30**
**San Francisco, CA 94108**
**(415) 771-5440**

(Below) Private Residence, Manhattan, New York, 9′ × 12′ custom blown glass and bevels separating dining area from living room in newly renovated Manhattan penthouse.

# Glass:
# A Material With
# A Fourth Dimension

Of all the materials being used with increasing frequency by architects, glass has claimed a very special place. This is a direct result of advances made in the field throughout the past two decades, when few other materials have been explored so intensely and undergone so much change.

At the industrial level the technology of glass as a building material has made possible the creation of environments that redefine the relationship between indoors and outdoors. In the artistic realms, glass has been seized upon by artists as a fresh new material with which to explore the integration of their work in the larger context of an architectural space.

The many talented artists and craftsmen working in this field have achieved so much, so rapidly, that the ensuing explosion of possible new forms and uses of this material have not yet been fully assimilated by the designers that shape our environment. Architects must become more aware of what artists working in glass can do for their space. And the artists themselves must become more capable of functioning creatively and effectively in the team situation which is today's way of shaping an environment.

No material is more suited to this collaborative process than glass. Unlike paintings, which can be added after an environment is complete, glass is structural—structural in the sense that it deals with the very perception of light. Only glass can create a translucent separation between two spaces that both obscures and reveals at the same time. Only glass can take a light source, natural or artificial, and augment it with the use of crystals, or soften it with a screen of soft color. Glass is the architectural material with a fourth dimension, because it adds transparency to the three traditional boundaries of line, plane, and volume.

In the last two decades glass artists have explored many new aspects of this material, from actually fusing imagery into the glass and using the new Dicroic glass developed by Corning to have it change colors as the angle of perception is changed, to assembling and building complex sculptures using high tech glue.

It is my belief that today's renewed interest in decoration, coupled with a fresh approach to interior design, has produced a unique opportunity for architects, designers, and artists to now work together in the creation of completely novel environments of glass and light.

**Narcissus Quagliata**
**Glass Artist**
**Oakland, California**

# Maya Radoczy

**Maya Radoczy Designs**
P.O. Box 31422
Seattle, WA 98103
(206) 527-5022

The studios of Maya Radoczy specialize in site-specific large scale corporate and residential projects. She employs a unique combination of leaded, blown, fused and cast glass to create an original effect for each site. Interior walls, room-dividers, screens, windows and sculpture attest to the variety in her work. She collaborates with the architect or designer from initial concept to installation.

Her work has been published in the *New York Times, Interior Design, American Craft* and the book, *Architectural Ornamentalism*. She is represented nationally: Trump Plaza, NY, Linpro Co., DE, Intrex Inc., NY.

Further examples can be seen in *The Guild*, 1987–1989.

A brochure is available upon request.

(Top) Entry, 7' × 12' – New York Residence
(Bottom) Interior Dividers, 4' × 8' Seattle, WA
Architect Robert Suzuki

Top photo: Robert Perron

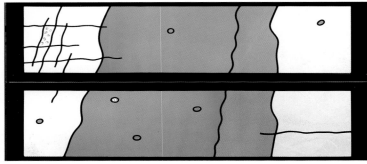
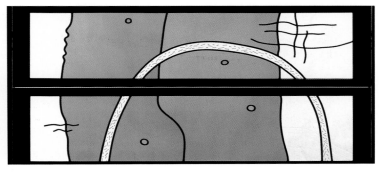

Bottom photos: Stan Shockey

# Jim Robbins

**818 S. Steele**
**Tacoma, WA 98405**
**(206) 383-1315**

Jim Robbins creates glass work of distinctive color combinations and bold imagery. Educated as an architect and with a background in industrial design he is experienced in the presentation skills necessary for the development and execution of large glass installations.

His award winning fused glass is exhibited in galleries and museums throughout the United States as well as being represented in Japan.

Robbins tests the boundaries of what is possible within the discipline of fused glass. He is experienced in a variety of glass working techniques and views his approach to glass as painterly.

Prices for individual pieces begin at $500. Consultation is available for commissioned work.

(Top right) "Espresso Talk"—Electric Geisha Series, 17"w × 14"h
(Bottom right) "Black Madonna," 14"w × 17"h
(Bottom left) "Pilchuck Enamels," 24"w × 36"h

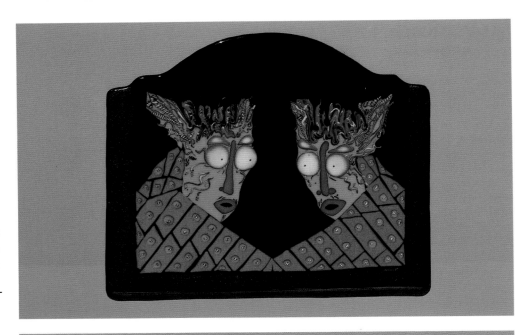

420

# Brian Rowe

**Rowe Studios Art Glass Inc.**
4768 S.W. 72 Ave.
Miami, FL 33155
(305) 666-5164
FAX (305) 666-7212

Brian Rowe has designed and fabricated over 800 art glass commissions in the United States and South America since 1973. He specializes in individual, residential and commercial architectural glass. Commissions include sculptural glass, lamps, wall graphics, floor and partition screens, ceilings, domes, windows and entranceways.

As designer and master craftsman for Rowe Studios Art Glass, Brian is known for his care and attention to detail in each phase of a project. From imaginative and aesthetic design renderings to excellent craftsmanship, Brian's fabrication skills include glass painting, etched, carved, fused, cast and ¼" to 1" thick hand beveled glass.

Additional information, resume and brochures available.

16" dia. Lamp "Desert" series. Bronze base.

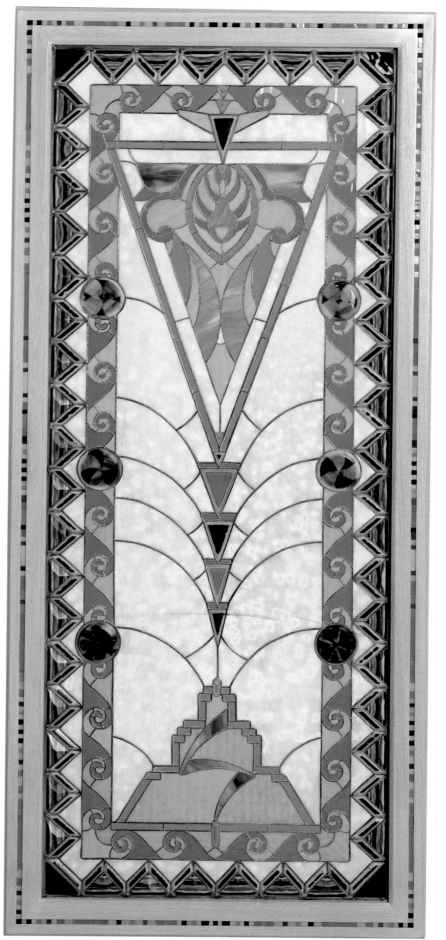

30"×72" "Spirit". Cast and fused glass bevels, copper, mosaic

421

# Wendy Saxon Brown

2410-2 West Saugerties Rd.
Saugerties, NY 12477
(914) 246-4673

Wendy Saxon Brown has the unusual ability to sculpt in glass. She sandblasts incredible depth and detail into her original forms and figures, often combining them with anodized aluminum for color and structure. Her unique free standing and wall pieces range from $1100.00 to $4000.00 and are displayed nationally in museums, galleries, and private collections.

# Skeeter Studios Inc.

**UltraGlas, Inc.**
**18623 Gresham Street**
**Northridge, CA 91324**
**(818) 993-3655**
**(818) 993-1816 (Fax)**

Jane Skeeter and a staff of skilled artists and craftspersons have been creating major glass installations for 15 years. Skeeter masterfullly blends art and function for restaurants, hotels, corporate buildings and exclusive residences in a contemporary or traditional style.

Specializing in all facets of glass, the studio produces beveled, stained, leaded, etched, carved, engraved and painted glass or mirrors and works for windows, full walls, doors and enclosures as well as sculpture and furniture.

Skeeter has now introduced "cast glass" by her new company, UltraGlas, Inc. "Cast glass' is a revolutionary European technique which brings an alluring three-dimensional texture to walls, doors, tables, signage and sculpture; all with a surface which remains clean.

Inquiries are invited.

(Left) Beveled and leaded glass suspended dome — Beverly Hills residence.
(Right) Cast glass — Marie Callender's Restaurant, Thousand Oaks, CA.

# David Stone

**Kensington Glass Arts Inc.**
4213 Howard Avenue
Kensington, MD 20895
(301) 897-0057

Kensington Glass Arts Inc., formerly Victorian Glassworks, specializes in custom designed art glass. For more than 10 years the studio has been producing stained glass and carved glass of the highest quality for the residential client, interior designer and architect.

Its staff is experienced in all aspects of the industry: design development and presentation, specification, fabrication, restoration and installation. In addition to the architectural panels for which the studio is well known, the scope of work now includes furniture and sculpture.

Some recent commissions include a 30-sq.-ft. carved glass topographic map of the state of California for the U.S. Pavilion at the 1988 World's Fair, and carved glass signage for the National Museum for Women in the Arts located in Washington, D.C.

(Right) 6′ × 6′ stained glass panel, private commission.
(Bottom) Carved glass fire screen.

Printed in Japan  © 1990 The Guild: A Sourcebook of American Craft Artists

# Studio Art Glass, Ltd.

**John P. Gilvey and Michael Benzer**
**Route 216**
**Poughquag, NY 12570**
**(914) 724-5088**

John Gilvey and Michael Benzer produce a wide variety of glass combining diverse color menu and mold flexibility. These characteristics allow the architect and designer a unique opportunity in creative freedom. The glass artists create site specific prefab panels or offer raw tile in eleven stock colors. The characteristics of their glass has lent itself to application in lighting, furniture, and decorative accessories allowing for a continuity in design concept.

Left—Glass and Copper Wall Sconce—12"×12"
Center—Echo Cafe—Installations include Rainbow Room, NY, corporate headquarters of Interior Design magazine, and Epcot.
Right—Decorative Accessories and Dinnerware
Bottom—Sapphire—Quartz Table—24"×32", 16" in height

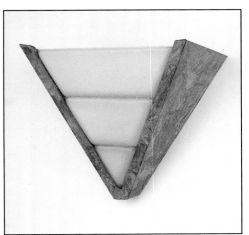

# Angelika Traylor

**100 Poinciana Drive**
**Indian Harbour Beach, FL 32937**
**(407) 773-7640**

Specializing in one-of-a-kind autonomous panels, lamps and architectural designs, Traylor's award-winning work can be recognized by its intricate, jewel-like composition

For panels and architectural work, prices start at $250.00 per square foot, depending on complexity. Lamps start at $2,500.00.

Commissions are accepted on a limited basis.

"Magic Carpet No. IX" 33"h. × 33"w., $6,500.00

426

Printed in Japan  © 1990 The Guild: A Sourcebook of American Craft Artists

# Buz Vaultz

**Exquisite Glass**
**123 Allen Street**
**New York, NY 10002**
**(212) 674-7069/FAX (212) 473-4808**

Buz Vaultz is an artist who, in conjunction with his company Exquisite Glass, Inc. has created numerous beautifully etched and carved glass and mirror projects.

He usually collaborates with designers and architects, bringing their ideas to fruition or, when necessary, he creates a design to complement a particular environment.

Distinctive windows, room dividers, tabletops, folding screens, and decorative artpieces are all a part of his extensive list of corporate, private, commercial, institutional and residential commissions. Exquisite Glass also does outstanding work on tile and stone.

Jobs are priced individually; ranging $30-$500 per square foot. Delivery and installation available. Call, write or FAX for consultation or brochure.

(top) Ralph Lauren Cosmetics 36″×36″
(bottom) Cafe Society, NY 144″×144″

# Kenneth Frederick vonRoenn, Jr.

vonRoenn Studio Group
1110 Baxter Avenue
Louisville, KY 40204
(502) 584-1546

Kenneth vonRoenn is both a practicing architect (Yale University, M.Arch.) and a glass designer. In his almost 20 years in glass design he has designed more than 100 commissions throughout the U.S. and has won numerous major national competitions and several awards. His work has been published in dozens of magazines and numerous books.

VonRoenn is recognized for the sympathetic integration of his work into architecture, which is achieved by his ability to work in a diversity of styles to address the specific esthetic concerns of each project. His work is also noted for subtle use of color and sophisticated application of the natural textures of blown clear glass, as well as the refractive qualities of beveled, engraved and prismatic glasses.

Prices for vonRoenn's work vary with the esthetic requirements of each project.

Private residence in New Jersey

Othello's Restaurant & Jazz Club, Louisville, KY.

428

# Barney Zeitz

R.F.D. 595A Off State Rd.
Vineyard Haven, Martha's Vineyard
MA 02568
508-693-9421

Barney Zeitz has been designing, constructing and installing stained glass windows, panels, and folding screens for 20 years. His techniques include traditional leading, as well as fused and bonded glass using his own kiln-fired tiles. Zeitz fabricates frames in a variety of metals and finishes. He has worked on many public commissions including religious spaces, libraries, hospitals and universities. Zeitz feels it is his responsibility as a public artist to produce work appropriate to each situation, yet true to himself as a contemporary artist. His smaller scale work is included in many private collections. Zeitz is comfortable giving slide presentations, and collaborating with architects, administrators, etc. Prices range from $200 to $1000 per square foot. Slides are available.

(Left) Rodef Shalom Temple. Pittsburgh, PA. National Historic Monument 46″ × 75″.
(Top Right) Private residence, Bermuda 58″ × 58″.
(Bottom Right) Mosaic 15″ × 16″ Model for large scale faceted glass window.

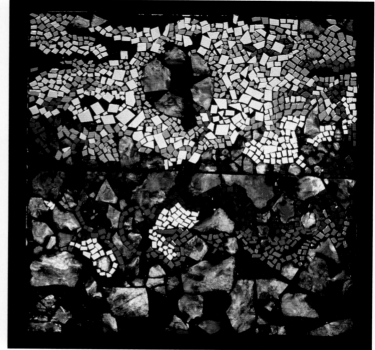

# Larry Zgoda

**Larry Zgoda Stained Glass**
**3447 N. Pulaski Rd.**
**Chicago, IL 60641**
**(312)463-1874**

Larry Zgoda designs and fabricates timeless, original compositions in stained, leaded glass. His clients have included imaginative individuals as well as enlightened design professionals. Larry Zgoda's compositions embrace architectonic, decorative and symbolic genres, and are appropriate for many transparent and translucent architectural applications. Doorlights, skylights, transoms, sidelights, cabinet doors and clerestories are some of the usual applications. Larry Zgoda has a thorough knowledge of the craft and a competent grasp of design. His creative handling of materials and his intuitive approach to composition have produced works that satisfy the most demanding conditions.

(Top) Untitled Stainless Glass, a transom for a Chicago home, 1986, 30"×14".
(Bottom) Untitled clerestory panel for Wesley Jessen Corporation, Chicago, 1988, 150"×26".

430

# Public Art

# Douglas O. Freeman

**Doug Freeman Sculpture Studios**
**310 North Second Street**
**Minneapolis, MN 55401**
**(612) 339-7150**

Douglas Freeman's bronze sculptures enhance public, corporate and private environments with an interactive presence.

Freeman's commissions include: *The Minnesota Fire Service Memorial,* a fourteen foot tall bronze located at the Minneapolis/St. Paul International Airport; a fountain piece for Hilton Hotel's corporation in McLean, Virginia; *Aurora,* a composition located in a fountain outside Marquette Place, luxury apartments in downtown Minneapolis; and *The Cincinnati Flying Pigs,* Sawyer Point Park, Cincinnati.

Freeman invites direct inquiries from clients and welcomes collaboration with architects, designers and other artists.

*Family,* the piece pictured here, was commissioned by the Opus Corporation with BetaWest Properties Inc. 1989. Scale: 1.25 × lifesize/cast bronze.

# Pamela Joseph

**Metal Paintings Inc..**
**RR 3, Box 140**
**Pound Ridge, NY 10576**
**(914) 764-5732 (home)**
**(914) 764-8208 (studio)**

This "Space-Age" formation, a giant crystal of elbaite tourmaline by Pamela Joseph, is "totally unique in its conception, execution and in the utilization of the materials of modern technology."

> —The Katonah Gallery
> *Arts Weekly*, Acorn Press
> December 1987

The 8′ × 9′ × 10′ sculpture, fabricated of aluminum and airbrushed in lacquers and urethane, is the latest work completed by the artist in her continuing fascination with the colors and geometry of minerals. Employing the priming system used on the space shuttle and painting media with ultra-violet screening agents that will not fade or crack when exposed to the elements (not to mention an aggressive general public), the completed constructions are ideally suited to architectural and garden settings.

Prices and brochures are available upon request.

# Elizabeth MacDonald

Box 186
Bridgewater, CT 06752
(203) 354-0594

Elizabeth MacDonald produces tile paintings by layering color onto thin, textured stoneware, achieving a surface that combines the subtlety of nature with the formality of a grid. These compositions are suitable for either in or out-of-doors and take the form of free standing columns, wall panels or architectural installations. Attached to ¼" luan with silicone, the tiles (often 3½" square) weigh approximately 1¾ lbs per sq ft, are durable and require a minimum of maintenance. Imagery can vary from formal patterning to reflections of the sky and land.

Recent commissions: New London Courthouse, CT; Shands Hospital, Gainesville, FL both are % for Art; Red Mountain Ranch (for Mobil), Mesa, AZ; Prudential-Bache, NY; Marriott in Palm Desert; Sheraton Grande in Tokyo. Collections of Chubb, Pitney Bowes, and IBM include her work.

(Right) AETNA Life Insurance Company
(Below) Close-up

# David Stromeyer

**Cold Hollow Iron Works**
**R.D. #2**
**Enosburg Falls, VT 05450**
**(802) 933-2518**

David Stromeyer brings twenty years' experience to his environmental sculpture. Large selection of unique works for indoors and out available immediately. Site specific commissions accepted. Artist handles all aspects of design, fabrication, transport, and installation.

Price range: $18,000–$100,000.

"Yellow Stars in the Magenta Skies" 8′×10′×8′ painted steel.

"Turn for the Better" MA Percent for Arts Comm. for Worcester County Jail 19′×28′×37′ painted steel.

436

# Alice Van Leunen
# Nexus

P.O. Box 408
Lake Oswego, OR 97034
(503)636-0787

Van Leunen specializes in two areas: paper relief sculpture (as Nexus) and site-specific installation using revolutionary techniques with new durable industrial materials requiring minimum maintenance. The works range in size from small intimate pieces up to installations of architectural scale, including suspended constructions for atria.

Surface treatments include watercolor, airbrush and other paint media, pastel, collage and reflective foil. Works are represented in numerous private, corporate and public collections. Commissions, including collaborations, are welcomed, and the artist is available to supervise installations of major works. Prices, slides, and further information furnished on request.

(Top right & top & bottom left) "Haiku: Iris Ascendant", Four-story aerial sculpture of painted plastic with metallic foil - commissioned by The Hillman Corporation for Kruse Woods I, Lake Oswego, OR
(Bottom right) "Shibumi", painted plastic with iridescent metallic foil, 7' × 6½' × 3"

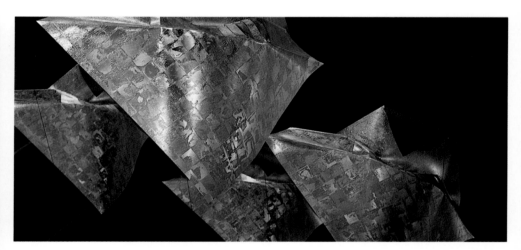

# David Wilson

**RD2, Box 121A**
**South New Berlin, NY 13843**
**(607) 334-3015**

David Wilson Design offers consultation, design, fabrication, and installation for projects that integrate art with architecture. Collaboration with client and architect is considered a part of the site specific design process.

Main Reading Room, St. George Public Library, Staten Island, New York. David Paul Helpern—Architect.

A percent for art project through the Department of Cultural Affairs, City of New York.

Award for excellence in design from the Art Commission of the City of New York.

(Under bottom photo only) Photo by Leland A. Cook

# Galleries and Representatives

# Campanile Capponi

1252 North State Parkway
Chicago, IL 60610
(312) 642-3869
(312) 663-3856 (Fax)

John Bucci-Designer — Blending the synthetic properties of acrylic resin with crossections of natural wood, he achieves a subtle mix of colors and textures within each signed and unique table.

robert Gadomski-Painter — Vibrant and intensely detailed interpretations of his early Chicago environs quiver with reverence and pungent wit. His Bucolic landscapes revail the artists closeness with nature and her ever changing moods.

Renee Zelenka-Sculptor — These unique sculptoral works reflect an inate sense for natural and organic forms. Primarily paper mache, the sculpture is totally constructed of natural and organic materials.

(Left) John Bucci-acrylic resin, natural wood-36″×36″×4″ $5000 and up
(Center) Robert Gadomski-acrylic on canvas-48″×72″ $6000 and up
(Right) Renee Zelenka-paper mache, reed-48″×48″×9″ $4000 and up

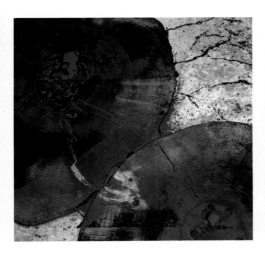

# Brown/Grotta Gallery

**39 Grumman Hill Road**
**Wilton, CT 06897**
**(203) 834-0623**
By appointment only.

The Brown/Grotta Gallery provides a unique opportunity to view the work of acclaimed artists in an informal, at-home environment.

Among the artists whose work is available for sale or on commission for residential or commercial installation: Bill Accorsi-wood sculpture, Ken Goldstrum-ceramic tile, Tom Grotta-photography, Brigitte Keller-paintings on paper and canvas, Rebecca Medel-fiber, Richard Meier-collage, Thom Maltbie-ceramic, Cynthia Pannucci-quilts, mixed media, Dana Romeis-fiber, Claude Vermette-paintings on paper and canvas, ceramic and sculpture, Mariette Rousseau-Vermette-fiber.

(Top) Ken Goldstrum: table tiles. (Bottom) Thom Maltbie: ceramic plate with wood frame; Brigitte Keller: series—pastel, pencil on paper.

442

(Top left) Bill Accorsi: wood sculpture;
Claude Vermette: painting.
(Top right) Mariette Rousseau-Vermette: fiber;
Claude Vermette: tables tiles.
(Bottom) Claude Vermette: paintings.

# Brown/Grotta Gallery

**39 Grumman Hill Road**
**Wilton, CT 06897**
**(203) 834-0623**
By appointment only.

# Illinois Artisans Shop

**State of Illinois Center**
**100 W. Randolph Street**
**Chicago, IL 60601**
**(312) 917-5321**

The first shop of its kind in Illinois, the Illinois Artisans Shop houses a superb collection of the finest crafted artwork made in the state. Functioning as a showcase and sales gallery, it provides an opportunity to view and purchase works from more than 450 Illinois craft artists.

The traditional, contemporary, folk and ethnic art forms reflect the richness and diversity of the cultural history of different regions of the state. Among the many crafts on display are examples of ceramics, glass, prints, fiber arts, wood, basketry, forge work, paper and sculpture.

Prices range up to $5,000, according to media, size and complexity. Corporate and residential commissions are welcome.

The Illinois Artisans Shop is a not-for-profit enterprise of the Illinois State Museum Society.

(Top left) Hand forged "Courting" candle holders, Gary Jameson
(Top right) Coiled basket, waxed linen on fiber rush, Char Wiss
(Bottom) Wool gobelin tapestry, 5 ft by 7 ft Ulla-May Berggren

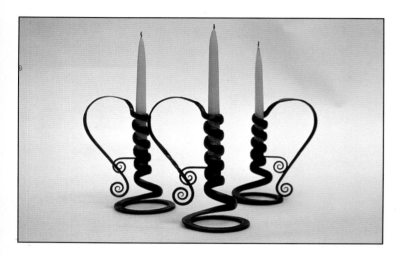

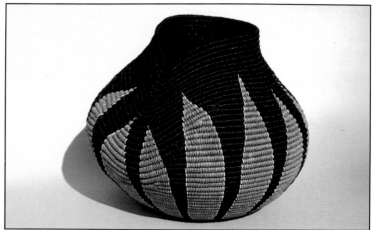

Mary A. Root

Printed in Japan ©1990 The Guild: A Sourcebook of American Craft Artists

# The ODC Gallery

**2164 Riverside Drive**
**Columbus, OH 43221**
**(614) 486-7119**

The Ohio Designer Craftsmen Gallery features significant contemporary work by Ohio artists in ceramics, glass, fiber, metal and other selected media. The current exhibition schedule includes: "Good As Gold" unique concepts in personal adornment created from materials other than gold; "Pacesetter VII", featuring porcelain by Curtis and Suzan Benzle; and "Fired with Enthusiasm", ceramics by university faculty in Ohio. Previous Pacesetter exhibition artists include Jon Wahling, Michael Chipperfield, Jack Smith, David Williamson, Roberta Williamson, Doug Anderson, Deborah Banyas and Nancy Crow.

Since 1980, the ODC Gallery has maintained a slide reference file with works by 200 artists. It offers special consulting services for private and corporate collections.

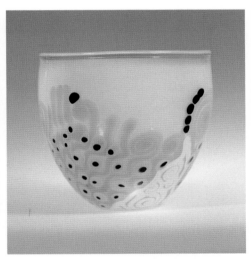

Meredith Wenzel, blown glass, 7½"w. × 8"h. × 7½"d.

Tim Mather, stoneware, 6"w. × 12"h. × 6"d.

# Judith Litvich

**CONTEMPORARY FINE ARTS**
2 Henry Adams Street M-69
San Francisco, CA 94103
(415) 863-3329

**By appointment.**

Lobbies, hallways, conference rooms, private offices. Hotels, business complexes, hospitals, department stores. Public spaces, private residences. All are served by distinguished artists represented by Judith Litvich.

Artworks include handpainted corded silk wall pieces, dimensional weavings, mixed media screens, painted metal reliefs, kinetic sculpture, metal/wood/paper sculpture, ceramic vessels, mixed media collage.

Other works of special interest are handmade paper, monotypes, prints—etchings, lithographs, screenprints—and paintings on paper.

The artists are from the Bay Area as well as from places around the country. All have a professional and personal commitment to art. Their works have been exhibited and are in the permanent collections of museums and corporations. They have won distinguished awards in both national and international competitions.

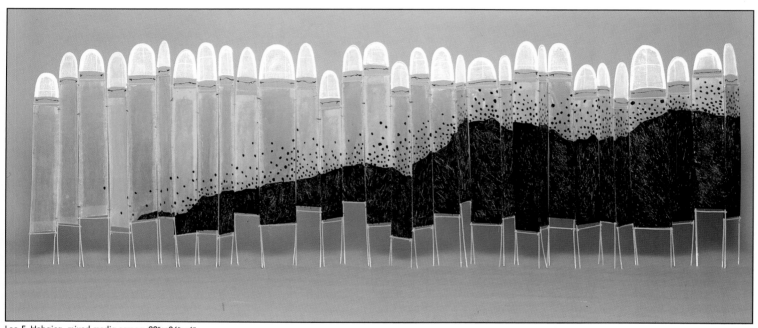

Leo F. Hobaica, mixed media screen, 22″ × 96″ × 6″

Susan Bland, mixed media collage, 9″ × 12″ × ½″

Mary Boone Wellington, pastels/oil stick/pigments 24″ × 24″

Daniel Joshua Goldstein, painted expanded aluminum, 6′ × 6′ × 2′6″

446

Judith Litvich

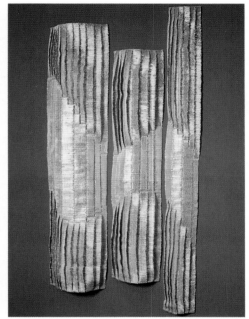

Joan Russell, weaving, 5' × 3' × 4"

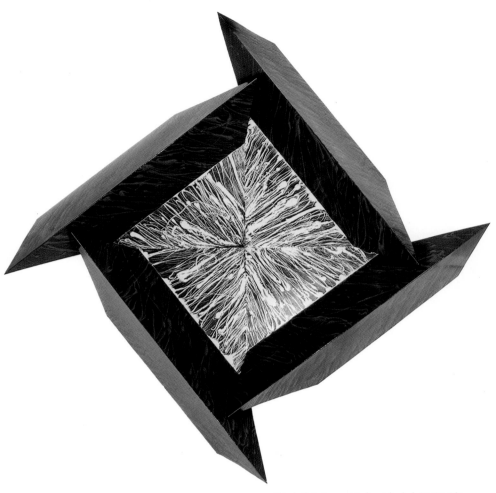

Elizabeth Saltos, painted metal relief, 8' × 8' × 10"

Susan Gilmour, handpainted corded silk, 5'3" × 12'

Printed in Japan   © 1990 The Guild: A Sourcebook of American Craft Artists

# Spectrum Contemporary Fine Art

**Valerie Miller & Associates**
**72-785 Highway 111**
**Palm Desert, CA 92260**
**(619) 773-9281**
**(213) 467-1511**

Spectrum Contemporary Fine Art and Valerie Miller & Associates represent established painters and sculptors as well as artists creating distinctive works in fiber, ceramics, glass, photography, mixed media and printmaking.

Professional services range from art consultation and selection to installation. A comprehensive slide reference file representing over 1000 artists is maintained.

Among the artists whose work is available for commission for private or commercial installation: Melissa Greene, pottery vessels; Michelle Lester, tapestry; Arthur Stern, architectural glass; Vasa, luminous constructions.

James Erickson (top left), "Vitreous Humor," glass on wood, 30"h. × 66"w.
Ray Howlett (bottom left), "Inner Pyramid Stripe," coated Glass & light.
Dora De Larios (top right), "Woman in Red," wood/acrylic, 66"h. × 74"w.
Kate Petley (bottom right), "Exploding Vertical, Ceramics—oil on canvas. 70"h × 60"w.

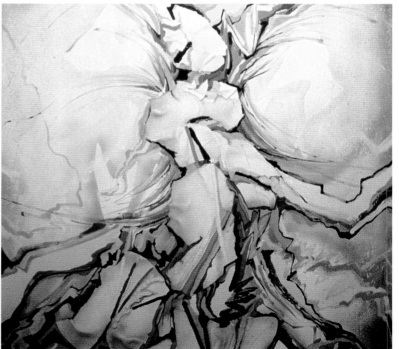

Printed in Japan © 1990 The Guild: A Sourcebook of American Craft Artists

# The following pages consist of:

# THE GUILD

# 3rd American Crafts Awards

In 1987, Kraus Sikes Inc. established a major national competition to recognize the exciting new products being created for the home furnishings market. THE GUILD American Crafts Awards honor the best of artists, new designers and fine craftsmanship in seven categories: Furniture, Textiles and Fabrics, For the Wall, For the Table, Functional Decorative Objects, Non-Functional Decorative Objects, and Installed Architectural Elements.

Winners of the third annual competition were announced in the Spring of 1990. From over 1,300 entries, 58 were singled out be the two juries as outstanding in design and execution. Seven of these won Grand Prices — extraordinary work that the juries chose unanimously.

The 58 selections reflect the excitement and enormous diversity of today's craft field. Winning products range from an elegantly crafted rocking chair to a whimsically fabricated coffee pot.

Work that is made of traditional materials using traditional techniques is honored along with pieces made in unexpected ways with innovative materials.

The winning artists are diverse, coming from all over the country. The group includes acknowledged leaders in their media, artists in mid-career who are just beginning to receive prominence, and some artists relatively new on the scene. All are producing unique, hand-made work for the contemporary home.

Kraus Sikes Inc. owes a great debt to these artists for setting the tone of what will certainly become a tradition of excellence for THE GUILD American Crafts Awards. In addition, the jurors deserve their own award because they worked tirelessly and enthusiastically through a long, arduous process. Finally, recognition should go to Cynthia Snook, project coordinator, whose efforts and unequalled attention to detail pulled this competition off in grand style.

---

## JURIES

**For Furniture, Textiles and Fabrics, For the Wall, and For the Table:**
Michael W. Monroe, Curator, Renwick Gallery, Smithsonian Institution
Kevin Walz, President, Walz Design
Donna Warner, Editor, Food and Design, Metropolitan Home

**For Functional Decorative Objects, Non-Functional Decorative Objects, and Installed Architectural Elements:**
Mildred F. Smertz, Editor-in-Chief, Architectural Record
Kenneth F. vonRoenn, Jr. architect/glass designer —
Grand Prize Winner of First American Crafts Awards
James Wines, President, SITE

# Merit Awards

| | | |
|---|---|---|
| **FURNITURE** | Beth Forer | New York, NY |
| | Bonnie Meltzer | Portland, OR |
| | Colin Reid (2 Merits) | Oakland, CA |
| | Grady Mathews | Brier, WA |
| | Kevin Earley | Madison, WI |
| | Ronald C. Puckett | Richmond, VA |
| | Wm. B. Sayre | Easthampton, MA |
| **FOR THE TABLE** | Debra Stark | Layton, NJ |
| | Ginger Kelly/Michael Jaross | Seattle, WA |
| | Jan Schachter | Palo Alto, CA |
| | Marek Cacula | New York, NY |
| | Randy Long | Bloomington, IN |
| | Susan R. Ewing | Oxford, OH |
| **FOR THE WALL** | Ann M. Adams | San Antonio, TX |
| | Ann Trusty | Garrison, NY |
| | Mary Jane Moross | New York, NY |
| | Siglinda Scarpa/Margarita Tricarico | Peekskill, NY |
| | Susan Ferrari Rowley | Churchville, NY |
| | Susan Kristoferson | Corvallis, OR |
| **TEXTILES AND FABRICS** | Francoise Barnes | Colorado Springs, CO |
| | Hilary Law | Cambridge, MA |
| | John Dunnigan/Wendy Wahl | Saunderstown, RI |
| | Laurie Ann Kovack | Seattle, WA |
| | Maleesa Davis | Denver, CO |
| | Solveig Nielsen | Mineral Point, WI |
| | Susan Winfrey | Atlanta, GA |
| **INSTALLED ARCHITECTURAL ELEMENTS** | Charles Totten/Cherie Harnden | Seattle, WA |
| | Cliff Garten | St. Paul, MN |
| | Elizabeth McDonald | Bridgewater, CT |
| | Keith Jellum | Sherwood, OR |
| | Nol Putnam | The Plains, VA |
| | Tim O'Neill | Troutdale, OR |
| **FUNCTIONAL DECORATIVE OBJECTS** | Gary A. Hyman | Los Angeles, CA |
| | Karl E. Derrah | Phoenix, AZ |
| | Mara Superior | Williamsburg, MA |
| | Pam Castano | Phoenix, AZ |
| | Penelope Fleming | Elkins Park, PA |
| | Sarah Pringle | Easthampton, MA |
| | Sidney R. Hutter | Jamaica Plain, MA |
| | Stephan Cox River | Falls, WI |
| | Tom Barron | Crete, IL |
| | Meryl Waitz | New York, NY |
| **NON-FUNCTIONAL DECORATIVE OBJECTS** | Bea Wax | Palo Alto, CA |
| | Carolyn M. Springer | San Diego, CA |
| | Carolyn Y. Raps | San Diego, CA |
| | Catherine M. Daters | Omaha, NE |
| | Charles Golden | New York, NY |
| | Chris & Pat Shatsby | Lewisburgs, OH |
| | Kathleen Dinan | New Rochelle, NY |
| | Raymond D. Tomasso | Englewood, CO |
| | Robin Renner | Farmington, NM |

# Grand Prize Winners

**MICHAEL HURWITZ,
GRAND PRIZE WINNER**
**in Furniture category**
Chaise Lounge on Rockers,
7½' × 3' × 2'
Milk Paint over Mahogany.
Photo supplied by Pritam & Eames Gallery,
Easthampton, L.I.

**FOR THE TABLE**

**Tom Muir**
Harper Woods, MI
"Cycladic Figure Impregnated"
Coffee Server, sterling silver, 18 karat gold,
anodized aluminum, oxidized copper,
11" × 3" × 4"

**FOR THE WALL**

**Gloria Kosco**
Silverdale, PA
Wall piece, ceramic and masonry,
62" × 40" × 4"

**TEXTILES AND FABRICS**

**Sonja Flavin**
Rochester, NY
"for the Bibendum chair"
Handwoven rug in wool and linen, flat
tapestry weave, 40" × 60"

**INSTALLED ARCHITECTURAL ELEMENTS**

**Ted Galeza**
New York, NY
Custom-made utility wall with mounting
hardware, glass and chrome-plated brass,
3' × 7'
Sink stand, aluminum chrome-plated, steel
tubing and cable,
40"h × 24" diameter

**FUNCTIONAL DECORATIVE OBJECTS**

**Bliss Kolb**
San Francisco, CA
Lamp, flex conduit, electrical parts, steel,
fabric, paint, 60"h × 16" base,
11" shade

**NON-FUNCTIONAL DECORATIVE
OBJECTS**

**Ann Troutner**
Seattle, WA
"Electric Tripeds," blown glass, 3'w × 1½'h

# Resources

**A listing of Galleries,
Art Consultants and
Artist Representatives**

## ALABAMA

Maralyn Wilson Gallery
2010 Cahaba Road
Birmingham, AL 35223
(205) 879-0582

New Directions Gallery
102 2nd Street S.E.
Cullman, AL 35055
Diana Douglass Jones
(205) 737-9933

## ARIZONA

Art Concepts
5711 Echo Canyon Circle
Phoenix, AZ 85018
Arlene Scult
(602) 952-8866

**ArtEsprit
4236 North 12th Street, Studio A
Phoenix, AZ 85014
Pat Harper
(602) 274-8589**

Gifted Hands Gallery
P.O. Box 1388, Tlaquepaque Village
Sedona, AZ 86336
Deanne or Byron McKeown
(602) 282-4822

Mind's Eye Craft Gallery
4200 North Marshall Way
Scottsdale, AZ 85251
Jane Welsh
(602) 941-2494

Obsidian Gallery
4340 North Campbell, #90
Tucson, AZ 85718
Elouise Evans
(602) 577-3598

Raku Gallery
P.O. Box 965
Jerome, AZ 86331
Tracy Weisel
(602) 634-2876

Sky Fire
39 Main Street
Jerome, AZ 86331
Carol Wittner
(602) 634-8081

The Hand and the Spirit Gallery
4222 North Marshall Way
Scottsdale, AZ 85253
Joanne Rapp
(602) 949-1262

## CALIFORNIA

**Anne Goodman Art Consulting
4337 Marina City Drive, #739
Marina del Rey, CA 90292
Hope Jones, Manager
(213) 821-8585**

Appalachia
14440 Big Basin Way
Saratoga, CA 95070
Wendy & Owen Nagler
(408) 741-0999

**Art Options
1635 Divisadero
San Francisco, CA 94131
Reva Broder
Joan Shain
(415) 567-8535**

Art Options
2507 Main Street
Santa Monica, CA 90405
Fran Cey
Marlene Riceberg
(213) 392-9099

Art Source L.A., Inc.
671 North La Cienega Boulevard
Los Angeles, CA 90278
Francine Ellman
(213) 652-9285

Artifacts
3024 Fillmore Street
San Francisco, CA 94123
Patricia Blume
(415) 922-8465

Artrep
1200 Taylor #30
San Francisco, CA 94108
Brigid Guinan
(415) 771-5440

Banaker Gallery
1373 Locust Street
Walnut Creek, CA 94596
(415) 930-0700

Brendan Walter Gallery
1001 Colorado Avenue
Santa Monica, CA 90401
(213) 395-1155

Claudia Chapline Gallery
3445 Shoreline Highway
Stinson Beach, CA 94970
Maudi Wallace
(415) 868-2308

**Cobweb Collection
79-83 Main Street
Sutter Creek, CA 95685
John & Betty Lopez
(209) 267-0690**

Compositions Gallery
2801 Leavenworth (The Cannery)
San Francisco, CA 94133
Siegfried Ehrmann
(415) 441-0629

Couturier Gallery
166 North La Brea Avenue
Los Angeles, CA 90036
Darrel Couturier
(213) 933-5557

Crock-R-Box
73425 El Paseo
Palm Desert, CA 92260
John Wenzell
Joann Becker
(619) 568-6688

del Mano Gallery
33 East Colorado Boulevard
Pasadena, CA 91105
Jan Peters
Ray Leier
(818) 793-6648

del Mano Gallery
11981 San Vicente Boulevard
Los Angeles, CA 90049
Ray Leier
Jan Peters
(213) 476-8508

Discoveries: Art-To-Wear
17350 17th Street, Suite E
Tustin, CA 92680
Tena Broderhausen
(714) 544-6206

Don Ulrich/Creative Arts
P.O. Box 684
Ventura, CA 93002
Lamia & Don Ulrich
(805) 643-4160

Dorothy Weiss Gallery
256 Sutter Street
San Francisco, CA 94108
(415) 397-3611

Elizabeth Fortner Gallery
1114 State Street, #9
Santa Barbara, CA 93101
Theil Morgan
(805) 966-2613

Faith Nightingale Galery
535 Fourth Avenue
San Diego, CA 92101
(619) 236-1028

Fresno Art Museum Shop
2233 North First Street
Fresno, CA 93703
Jerrie Peters
(209) 485-4810

**Gallery Eight**
**7464 Girard Avenue**
**La Jella, CA 92037**
**Ruth Newmark**
**(619) 454-9781**

Gallery Fair
Box 263
Mendocino, CA 95460
Bill Zimmer
(707) 937-5121

Garth Clark Gallery
170 South La Brea
Los Angeles, CA 90036
Wayne Kuwada
(213) 939-2189

Hank Baum Gallery
P.O. Box 26689
San Francisco, CA 94126
(415) 752-4336

Henley's Gallery On The Sea Ranch
1000 Annapolis Road
The Sea Ranch, CA 95497
Marion H. Gates
(707) 785-2951

Images Of The North
1782 Union Street
San Francisco, CA 94123
Lesley Leonhardt
(415) 673-1273

International Gallery
643 G Street
San Diego, CA 92101
Stephen Ross
(619) 235-8255

**James Lodge & Associates**
**18023 Skypark Circle F.1**
**Irvine, CA 92714**
**James Lodge**
**(714) 261-2262**

Japonesque Inc.
50 Post Street
San Francisco, CA 94114
Koichi Hara
(415) 398-8577

Judith Kindler
550 15th St., Showplace Square West
San Francisco, CA 94103
(415) 621-3666

Kurland/Summers Gallery
8742A Melrose Avenue
Los Angeles, CA 90069
Ruth Summers
(213) 659-7098

**Litvich Contemporary Fine Arts**
**2 Henry Adams Street M-69**
**San Francisco, CA 94103**
**Judith Litvich**
**(415) 863-3329**

M.O.A. Art Gallery
8554 Melrose Avenue
West Hollywood, CA 90069
Jose Luis Rienzi
(213) 657-7202

Marquardt Fine Art
1260 North Dutton Avenue
Santa Rosa, CA 95401
Trudy Marquardt
(707) 579-9908

Michael Himovitz Gallery
1020 Tenth Street
Sacramento, CA 95814
(916) 448-8723

Modern Life Designs
682 Post Street
San Francisco, CA 94109
Douglas Brett
(415) 441-7118

New Stone Age
8407 West 3rd Street
Los Angeles, CA 90048
Susan Skinner
Fran Ayres
(213) 658-5969

Olive Hyde Art Gallery
123 Washington Blvd., P.O. Box 5006
Fremont, CA 94537
Cynthia Raap
(415) 791-4357

Orr's Gallery
2222 Fourth Avenue
San Diego, CA 92101
Dan Jacobs, Owner
Merika Adams
(619) 234-4765

Palumbo
Box 5727, Dolores and Sixth
Carmel, CA 93921
Gail Palumbo
(408) 625-5727

Paul-Luster Gallery
336 Hayes Street
San Francisco, CA 94102
Barbara Paul
Elizabeth Luster
(415) 431-8511

Plums Contemporary Art
2405 Capitol Street
Fresno, CA 93721
Polly Brewer
(209) 237-1822

Pottery Plus
189 South Washington Street
Sonora, CA 95370
Virginia Seibert
(209) 533-1309

Rookie-To Gallery
P.O. Box 606, 14300 Hwy. 128
Boonville, CA 95415
Bob Altaras
(707) 895-2204

Running Ridge Gallery
310 East Ojai Avenue
Ojai, CA 93023
David Willis
(805) 646-1525

Sculpture To Wear
8441 Melrose Avenue
Los Angeles, CA 90069
Jan Ehrenworth
(213) 651-2205

Seekers
P.O. Box 521, 4090 Burton Drive
Cambria, CA 93428
Lynda Adelson
(805) 927-8626

**Spectrum Contemporary Fine Art**
**72-785 Highway 111**
**Palm Desert, CA 92260**
**Valerie Miller**
**Glenda Wormington**
**(619) 773-9281**

Susan Cummins Gallery
32 Miller Avenue
Mill Valley, CA 94941
(415) 383-1512

T. Marquardt Fine Art
1260 North Dutton Avenue
Santa Rosa, CA 95401
Trudy Marquardt
(707) 579-9908

Tarbox Gallery
1202 Kettner Boulevard
San Diego, CA 92101
Ruth Tarbox
(619) 234-5020

The Aesthetics Collection, Inc.
1060 17th Street
San Diego, CA 92101
Annette Ridenour
(619) 238-1860

The Allrich Gallery
251 Post Street, 4th floor
San Francisco, CA 94108
Michelle Bello
(415) 398-8896

The Bayside Gallery
1201 First Street, Suite 207
Coronado, CA 92118
Robert Hesse
(619) 437-4696

**The Casey Collection**
**64-40 Lusk Boulevard, Suite D10**
**San Diego, CA 92121**
**Melanie Scott**
**(619) 552-1020**

**The Casey Collection**
**Atrium Design Ctr., 69-930 Hwy 111**
**Rancho Mirage, CA 92270**
**Richard Casey**
**(619) 322-4473**

Tops
23410 Civic Center Way
Malibu, CA 90265
Judy & Robert Walker
(213) 456-8677

Valerie Miller & Associates
419 Larchmont
Los Angeles, CA 90004
Valerie Miller
Barbara Owens
(213) 467-1511

Viewpoint Gallery
224 Crossroads Boulevard
Carmel, CA 93923
Chistopher Winfield
(408) 624-3369

Virginia Breier Gallery
3091 Sacramento Street
San Francisco, CA 94115
(415) 929-7173

Walter White Fine Arts
107 Capitola Avenue
Capitola, CA 95010
Melissa Smith
(408) 476-7001

Walter White Fine Arts
7th & San Carlos
Carmel, CA 93921
Amy Essick
(408) 624-4957

Wild Blue
7220 Melrose Avenue
Los Angeles, CA 90046
Sherry Kaine
Vesna Breznikar
(213) 939-8434

**Wilder Place**
**7975 ½ Melrose Avenue**
**Los Angeles, CA 90046**
**Jo Wilder**
**(213) 655-9072**

Zola Fine Art
8730 West Third Street
Los Angles, CA 90048
Carla Troeger
(213) 273-8502

Zosaku Fine Crafts
2110 Vine Street
Berkeley, CA 94709
Nelda Barchers
(415) 549-3373

## COLORADO

Applause
2820 East 3rd Street
Denver, CO 80206
Jody Hunker
Pauline Olson
(303) 442-7729

Caviano Contemporary Craft Gallery
5910 South University
Littleton, CO 80121
Rae Ann McMurtry
(303) 798-6696

**Commonwheel Artist Co-Op
102 Canon Avenue
Manitou Springs, CO 80829
Ann Wardlow Rodgers
(719) 685-1008**

Hibberd McGrath Gallery
101 North Main Street/P.O. Box 7638
Breckenridge, CO 80424
Terry McGrath
Martha Hibberd
(303) 453-6391

Joan Robey Gallery
939 Broadway
Denver, CO 80203
Joan Robey
(303) 892-9600

Panache Craft Gallery
315 Columbine
Denver, CO 80206
Judy Kerr
(303) 321-8069

Rachel Collection
201 South Galena
Aspen, CO 81611
Lindsay Frank
Charlie Knight
(303) 920-1313

Roach Galleries
1142 13th Street
Boulder, CO 80302
Sandi
(303) 444-4968

The Unique
21 ½ East Bijou Street
Colorado Springs, CO 80903
Evagerd Asher
(719) 473-9406

## CONNECTICUT

Artsource
10 Bay Street, Suite 58
Westport, CT 06880
Ellen Schiffman
(203) 222-9264

Artworks And Company
15 Potter Drive
Old Greenwich, CT 06870
Wendy T. Kelley
(203) 637-5562

Atelier Studio/Gallery
27 East Street
New Milford, CT 06776
Beth Collings
(203) 354-7792

Brookfield Craft Center
P.O. Box 122, Route 25
Brookfield, CT 06804
(203) 775-4526

Brookfield Craft Center
127 Washington Street
South Norwalk, CT 06854
(203) 853-6155

**Brown/Grotta Gallery
39 Grumman Hill Road
Wilton, CT 06897
Tom Grotta
(203) 834-0623**

Contemporary Crafts Gallery
P.O. Box 246, Route 20
Riverton, CT 06065
Grace Butland
(203) 379-2964

Endleman Gallery
1014 Chapel Street
New Haven, CT 06510
Sally-Ann Endleman
(203) 776-2517

Evergreen Gallery
23B Water Street
Guilford, CT 06437
Sharon Silvestrini
(203) 453-4324

Fisher Gallery Shop
25 Bunker Lane
Avon, CT 06001
Linda Ronis-Kass
(203) 678-1867

Gallery/Shop At Wesleyan Potters
350 South Main Street
Middletown, CT 06457
Maureen LoPresti, Director
(203) 344-0039

Mendelson Gallery
Titus Square
Washington Depot, CT 06794
Carol Mendelson
(203) 868-0307

Silvermine Guild Arts Center
1037 Silvermine Road
New Canaan, CT 06840
Beth Northrop, Manager
(203) 966-5617

Susan Daniel Associates
607 Chapel Street
New Haven, CT 06511
(203) 777-8865

The American Hand
125 Post Road East
Westport, CT 06880
Susan Hirsch
(203) 226-8883

The Company Of Craftsmen
43 West Main Street
Mystic, CT 06355
Jack Steel
(203) 536-4189

The Elements
14 Liberty Way
Greenwich, CT 06830
Lisa Hampton
(203) 661-0014

Wayside Furniture of Milford
1650 Boston Post Road
Milford, CT 06460
Carole R. Greenbaum
(203) 878-1781

## DELAWARE

Corporate Art-Thornapple Ltd.
1409 Silverside Road
Wilmington, DE 19810
Ruth J. Kaplan
(302) 475-5096

The Blue Streak
1723 Delaware Avenue
Wilmington, DE 19806
(302) 429-0506

## DISTRICT OF COLUMBIA

Anne O'Brien Gallery
2114 R Street, N.W.
Washington, DC 20008
(202) 328-8222

Franklin Parrasch Gallery
2114 R Street N.W.
Washington, DC 20008
(202) 328-8222

Maurine Littleton Gallery
3222 N Street, N.W.
Washington, DC 20007
(202) 333-9307

Sansar
4200 Wisconsin Avenue N.W.
Washington, DC 20016
Veena Singh
(202) 244-4448

Shelly Guggenheim
1000-16th Street N.W., Suite 400
Washington, DC 20036
(202) 429-6818

## FLORIDA

Albertson-Peterson Gallery
329 Park Avenue South
Winter Park, FL 32789
Louise Peterson
(407) 647-6500

American Details
3107 Grand Avenue
Coconut Grove, FL 33133
Sharon LePak, Manager
(305) 448-6163

Art Sources, Inc.
1253 Southshore Drive
Orange Park, FL 32073
Jacqueline Holmes
(904) 269-2014

Artcetera
3200 S. Congress Avenue, Suite 201
Boynton Beach, FL 33426
Gloria Waldman
(407) 737-6953

**Christy Taylor Gallery Inc.**
**5050 Town Center Circle, Suite 243**
**Boca Raton, FL 33486**
**Jack Nicks, Owner**
**Carrie Frifeldt, Director**
**(407) 394-6387**

Claudia Sabin Associates
710 S.W. 27th Street
Gainsville, FL 32607
(904) 378-4240

**Dakota Gallery**
**5250 Town Center Circle, Suite 141**
**Boca Raton, FL 33486**
**Wrendi Faulkner, Director**
**(407) 394-9134**

Florida Craftsmen Gallery
235 Third Street South
St. Petersburg, FL 33701
Michele Tuegel, Executive Director
(813) 821-7391

Gallery Five
363 Tequesta Drive
Tequesta, FL 33469
Paula Coben
(407) 747-5555

Habatat Galleries
608 Banyan Trail
Boca Raton, FL 33431
Thomas Boone
(407) 241-4544

Hoffman Gallery
2000 East Sunrise Blvd., Level 2
Fort Lauderdale, FL 33304
William S. Hoffman
(305) 763-5371

Image Gallery
500 North Tamiami Trail
Sarasota, FL 34236
Ruth Katzman
(813) 366-5097

Tequesta Galleries, Inc.
361 Tequesta Drive
Tequesta, FL 33469
Carol A. Saunders
(407) 744-2534

**The Casey Collection**
**531 Harbour Road**
**Long Boat Key, FL 34228**
**Cherie Sullivan**
**(813) 383-3607**

The Cooper Gallery
205 South Ocean Boulevard
Manalapan, FL 33462
Ilyne Cooper
(407) 585-2830

The Suwannee Triangle Gallery
P.O. Box 341
Cedar Key, FL 32625
Clair Teetor, Manager
(904) 543-5744

## GEORGIA

Avery Gallery
145 Chruch Street
Marietta, GA 30060
Kip Knauth
(404) 427-2459

Barkin-Leeds Ltd.
2880 Vinings Way
Atlanta, GA 30339
Temme Barkin-Leeds, President
(404) 351-2880

Davis-Moye & Associates
P.O. Box 76220
Atlanta, GA 30358
Dorothy Davis Moye
(404) 255-5366

Eve Mannes Gallery
116 Bennett Street, Suite A
Atlanta, GA 30309
(404) 351-6651

Gini L. Pettus Associates, Inc.
P.O. Box 52066
Atlanta, GA 30355
Gini L. Petutus, President
(404) 876-6880

**Great American Gallery**
**1925 Peachtree Road**
**Atlanta, GA 30309**
**Martha & Pat Connell, Directors**
**(404) 351-8210**

Indigo Moon Gallery
1751 Marietta Highway
Canton, GA 30114
Madeleine Cox
(404) 479-1311

Out Of The Woods Gift Gallery
1311 Johnson Ferry Road N.E.
Marietta, GA 30068
Deb Douglas
(404) 977-1323

Riverworks Craft Gallery
103 East River Street
Savannah, GA 31401
Linda M. Jeanne
(912) 236-2012

Vespermann Glass Gallery
2140 Peachtree Road, N.W.
Atlanta, GA 30309
(404) 350-9698

**IDAHO**

Anne Reed Gallery
620 Sun Valley Road, Box 597
Ketchum, ID 83340
(208) 726-3036

Gail Severn Gallery
Box 1679, 620 Sun Valley Road
Ketchum, ID 83340
(208) 726-5079

**ILLINOIS**

Betsy Rosenfield Gallery
212 West Superior
Chicago, IL 60610
(312) 787-8020

**Campanile & Capponi**
**1252 North State Parkway**
**Chicago, IL 60610**
**Howard B. Capponi**
**(312) 642-3869**

**Cyrna International**
**12-101 Merchandise Mart**
**Chicago, IL 60654**
**Cyrna S. Field**
**(312) 329-0906**

Esther Saks Gallery
311 West Superior
Chicago, IL 60610
Esther Saks
Ingrid Fassbender
(312) 751-0911

Fumie Gallery
19 South La Salle
Chicago, IL 60603
Richard M. Hartnett
(312) 726-0080

Galesburg Civic Art Center
114 East Main Street
Galesburg, IL 61401
Steve Seager, Director
(309) 342-7415

Gimcracks
1513 Sherman Avenue
Evanston, IL 60201
Lucile Krasnow
(312) 475-0900

Graphic Resources Corp. Art Service
465 Lakeside Place
Highland Park, IL 60035
Alyson Breuer
(312) 433-3688

**Illinois Artisans Gallery**
**100 W. Randolph St.**
**Chicago, IL 60601**
**Ellen Gantner**
**(312) 917-5321**

Lill Street
1021 West Lill
Chicago, IL 60614
Paula Bass, Director
(312) 477-6185

Martha Schneider Gallery, Inc.
2055 Green Bay Road
Highland Park, IL 60035
Elsie Loeb
(312) 433-4420

Mindscape Gallery
1521 Sherman Avenue
Evanston, IL 60201
Ron Isaacson
(708) 864-2260

Nina Owen, Ltd.
212 West Superior Street
Chicago, IL 60610
(312) 664-0474

Objects Gallery
134 Merchandise Mart
Chicago, IL 60654
Ann Nathan
(312) 664-6622

Perimeter Gallery, Inc.
750 North Orleans
Chicago, IL 60610
Frank Paluch, Director
(312) 266-9473

**Pieces**
**644 Central**
**Highland Park, IL 60015**
**Lynn, Lori, or Louise**
**(312) 432-2131**

Rezac Gallery
301 West Superior Street, 2nd floor
Chicago, IL 60610
Suzan Rezac
(312) 751-0481

Ruth Volid Gallery Ltd.
225 West Illinois Street
Chicago, IL 60610
Susan Meneley, Director
(312) 644-3180

Sorenson Contemporary Art
1152 Spring Garden Circle
Naperville, IL 60563
Ellen C. Sorenson
(312) 898-6403

The Artisan Shop & Gallery
1515 Sheridan Road, Plaza del Lago
Wilmette, IL 60091
Lynn Hansen
(312) 251-3775

**The Casey Collection**
**40 South Dunton**
**Arlington Heights, IL 60005**
**Peggy Ratigan**
**(312) 818-0100**

The Masters Portfolio
2049 North Fremont, Suite A
Chicago, IL 60614
Dr. Scott B. Johnson
(312) 248-8074

## INDIANA

Centre Gallery
170 East Carmel Drive
Carmel, IN 46032
Susan Musleh
(317) 844-6421

The Art Source
8060 Knue Road, Suite 140
Indianapolis, IN 46250
Kathy Huston
(317) 848-3139

## IOWA

The Pot Shop
U.S. 169 South
Humboldt, IA 50548
Niram Shouse
(515) 332-4210

## KANSAS

Silver Works & More
715 Massachusetts Street
Lawrence, KS 66044
Jim & Cara Connelly
(913) 842-1460

## KENTUCKY

Artique
410 West Vine, Civic Center Shop
Lexington, KY 40507
Michael Stutland
(606) 235-1774

The Promenade Gallery
204 Center Street
Berea, KY 40403
Kathy West
(606) 986-1609

## LOUISIANA

Interiors & Extras
324 Metairie Road
Metairie, LA 70005
Nancy Lassen
(504) 835-9902

Stoner Arts Center
516 Stoner Avenue
Shreveport, LA 71101
Linda T. Snider
(318) 222-1780

## MAINE

**Frick Gallery**
**139 High Street**
**Belfast, ME 04915**
**Rose Marie Frick**
**(207) 338-3671**

Nancy Margolis Gallery
367 Fore Street
Portland, ME 04101
(207) 775-3822

The Stein Gallery
20 Milk Street
Portland, ME 04101
Philip Stein
(207) 772-9072

**Victorian Stable Gallery**
**Water Street, P.O. Box 728**
**Damariscotta, ME 04543**
**Barbara P. Briggs**
**(207) 563-1991**

## MARYLAND

Art Connections
4812 Auburn Avenue
Bethesda, MD 20814
Gayley Knight
Candace Forsyth
(301) 951-1026

Art Institute & Gallery
Route 50 & Lemmon Hill Lane
Salisbury, MD 21801
Diana Phillips
(301) 546-4748

Artists Circle Ltd.
11544 Spring Ridge Road
Potomac, MD 20854
Sharon Buchanan
(301) 921-0572

Discoveries
8055 Main Street
Ellicott City, MD 21043
(301) 461-9600

Glass Gallery
4720 Hampden Lane
Bethesda, MD 20814
Sarah Hansen
(301) 657-3478

Partners Gallery, Ltd.
4724 Hampden Lane
Bethesda, MD 20814
Susan Turner
(301) 657-2781

Pieces Of Olde
716 West 36th Street
Baltimore, MD 21211
Nancy Wertheimer
(301) 366-4949

Tomlinson Craft Collection
516 North Charles Street
Baltimore, MD 21201
(301) 539-6585

**MASSACHUSETTS**

**Alianza**
**154 Newbury Street**
**Boston, MA 02116**
**Karen Rotenberg**
**(617) 262-2385**

Baracca Gallery
P.O. Box 85
N. Hatfield, MA 01066
B. Minisci
(413) 247-5262

Bhadon Gift Gallery
18 Sunnyhill Drive
Worcester, MA 01602
Jackie Ford
(508) 798-0432

Clark Gallery
P.O. Box 339, Lincoln Station
Lincoln, MA 01773
Pamela Clark Cochrane
(617) 259-8303

Divinity's Splendour-Glow
8 Medford Street
Arlington, MA 02174
Renuka O'Connell
(617) 648-7100

Ferrin Gallery/Pinch Pottery
179 Main Street
Northhampton, MA 01060
Mara Superior
Leslie Ferrin
(413) 586-4509

Fiber Designs
Main Street, P.O. Box 614
Wellfleet, MA 02667
Rebecca Smith
(508) 349-7434

Fire Opal
7 Pond Street
Jamaica Plain, MA 02130
Susannah Gordon
(617) 524-0262

Fuller Museum Of Art (Museum Shop)
455 Oak Street
Brockton, MA 02401
Phyllis Honflig
(508) 588-6000

G/M Galleries
Main Street
West Stockbridge, MA 01266
Marie J. Bonamici-Woodcock
(413) 232-8519

Half Moon Harry
19 South Bearskin Neck
Rockport, MA 01966
Tim Giarrosso
(508) 546-6601

Limited Editions, Inc.
1176 Walnut Street
Newton Highlands, MA 02161
Jo-Ann Isaacson
(617) 965-5474

Norton-Shanel Art Consultants, Inc.
20 Shepard Street
Cambridge, MA 02138
Madlyn Shanel
(617) 492-2385

Salmon Falls Artisans Showroom
P.O. Box 176, Ashfield Street
Shelburne Falls, MA 01370
Nancy Dean
(413) 625-9833

Signature
Dock Square, North Street
Boston, MA 02109
Karen Garland
(617) 227-4885

Skera
221 Main Street
Northampton, MA 01060
Harriet Rogers
(413) 586-4563

**Ten Arrow Gallery**
**10 Arrow Street**
**Cambridge, MA 02138**
**Elizabeth R. Tinlot**
**(617) 876-1117**

The Balcony
P.O. Box 489
Vineyard Haven, MA 02568
Suzanne Warren
(508) 693-5127

**The Hand of Man Craft Gallery**
**29 Wendell Avenue**
**Pittsfield, MA 01201**
**Marilyn & Stephen Barry, A.I.A.**
**(413) 443-6033**

The Hand of Man Craft Gallery
The Curtis Shops, Walker Street
Lenox, MA 01240
Stephen D. Barry, President
(413) 637-0632

The Society Of Arts And Crafts
175 Newbury Street
Boston, MA 02116
Pamela Shaffer
(617) 266-1810

**MICHIGAN**

Ann Arbor Art Association
117 West Liberty
Ann Arbor, MI 48104
Beth Baloah, Gallery Director
(313) 994-8004

Carol/James Gallery
301 South Main Street
Royal Oak, MI 48067
Carol Ann Foster
(313) 541-6216

Deco Art
815 First Street
Menominee, MI 49858
Lori Schappe
(906) 863-3300

Habatat Galleries
32255 Northwestern Highway
Farmington Hills, MI 48018
John Lawson
(313) 851-9090

Ilona and Gallery
31045 Orchard Lake Road
Farmington Hills, MI 48018
Hirschel Levine
(313) 855-4488

Pine Tree Gallery
824 East Cloverland, U.S.-2
Ironwood, MI 49938
Philip J. Kucera
(906) 932-5120

Selo/Shevel Gallery
329 South Main Street
Ann Arbor, MI 48104
Elaine Selo
(313) 761-6263

Touch Of Light
23426 Woodward Avenue
Ferndale, MI 48220
John Fitzpatrick
(313) 543-1868

**MINNESOTA**

Bois Fort Gallery
130 East Sheridan Street
Ely, MN 55731
Judy Danzl
(218) 365-5066

Carol Simonson Portfolio
2320 Newton Avenue South
Minneapolis, MN 55405
(612) 374-5704

Forum Gallery
119 North Fourth Street, Suite 101
Minneapolis, MN 55401
Margo Sanioa
(612) 333-1825

Made In The Shade
600 East Superior Street
Duluth, MN 55802
Ruth Ann Eaton
(218) 722-1929

Raymond Avenue Gallery
761 Raymond Avenue
St. Paul, MN 55114
Joeseph Brown
(612) 644-9200

Three Rooms Up
3515 West 69th Street/Galleria
Edina, MN 55435
Patricia Byrrets
(612) 926-1774

**MISSISSIPPI**

Chimneyville Crafts
1150 Lakeland Drive
Jackson, MS 39216
(601) 981-0019

Mississippi Crafts Center
P.O. Box 69
Ridgeland, MS 39158
Majorie Bates
(601) 981-0019

Old Trace Gallery, Ltd.
120 East Jefferson, P.O. Box 307
Kosciusko, MS 39090
Polly Brown
(601) 289-9170

**MISSOURI**

Barbara Okun Fine Arts
13 Westwood C.C. Grounds
St. Louis, MO 63131
(314) 432-4021

By Design
2420 East Linwood Blvd., South 300
Kansas City, MO 64109
Soheil Anderson
(816) 861-8330

Craft Place
506 South Main Street
St Charles, MO 63301
Christine Raecke
(314) 723-9398

Kansas City Contemporary Art Center
P.O. Box 5948
Kansas City, MO 64111
Della A. Millin
(816) 221-1036

Leedy-Voulkos Gallery
1919 Wyandotte
Kansas City, MO 64108
(816) 474-1919

Objects: St Louis
5595 Pershing Avenue
St. Louis, MO 63112
Marcy Rosenthal
(314) 361-6670

Randall Gallery
999 North 13th Street
St. Louis, MO 63106
William Shearburn
(314) 231-4808

Schuetz Architects
5729 Cherry
Kansas City, MO 64110
Michael Schuetz
(816) 363-2631

The Kansas City Cont. Art Center
P.O. Box 5948
Kansas City, MO 64111
Della A. Millin
(816) 221-1036

The Source Fine Arts
208 Delaware
Kansas City, MO 64105
Denyse Johnson
(816) 842-6466

**MONTANA**

Artistic Touch
209 Central Avenue
Whitefish, MT 59937
Mary Kay Huff
(406) 862-4813

**NEBRASKA**

Lewis Art Gallery
8025 West Dodge Road
Omaha, NE 68114
Carolyn Lewis
(402) 391-7733

**NEW HAMPSHIRE**

Gallery 33
111 Market Street
Portsmouth, NH 03801
Priscilla Glastra Van Loon
(603) 431-7403

Golden Toad Gallery
65 Elm Street
Milford, NH 03055
Sandy Hammond
(603) 673-6596

McGowan Fine Art Inc.
10 Hills Avenue
Concord, NH 03301
Mary Strayer McGowan
(603) 225-2515

**NEW JERSEY**

America House Gallery
24 Washington Avenue
Tenafly, NJ 07670
Betty Turino
(201) 569-2526

**Art Underfoot, Inc.**
**12 Godfrey Road**
**Upper Montclair, NJ 07043**
**Cathy Comins**
**(201) 744-4171**

By Hand Fine Craft Gallery
142 Kings Highway East
Haddonfield, NJ 08033
Marjorie Harris
(609) 429-2550

Contrasts
49 Broad Street
Red Bank, NJ 07701
Rosalie Rosin
(201) 741-9177

Creative Glass Center Of America
P.O. Box 646
Millville, NJ 08332
Susan Whitehouse, Managing Director
(609) 825-6800

E.M.R. Gift Gallery
5206 Atlantic Avenue
Ventnor, NJ 08406
Steven A. Rossman
(609) 823-2404

Galman Lepow Associates, Inc.
1879 Old Cuthbert Road, #12
Cherry Hill, NJ 08034
Elaine Galman
Judith Lepow
(609) 354-0771

Lee Sclar Gallery
14 South Street
Morristown, NJ 07960
(201) 538-0711

Limited Editions
2200 Long Beach Boulevard
Surf City, NJ 08008
Frank & Lorraine Cilluffo
(609) 494-0527

N.K. Thaine Gallery Corp.
150 Kings Highway East
Haddonfield, NJ 08033
Elaine & Garry Thaine
(609) 428-6961

Sheila Nussbaum Galleries
Princeton Shop Ctr./N. Harrison St.
Princeton, NJ 08542
Sheila Nussbaum
(609) 683-7474

Sheila Nussbaum Galleries
358 Millburn Avenue
Millburn, NJ 07041
Sheila Nussbaum
(201) 467-1720

The Elvid Gallery
41 East Palisade Avenue
Englewood, NJ 07631
(201) 871-8747

**NEW MEXICO**

Clay and Fiber Gallery
Box ZZ, 135 Paseo Pueblo Del Norte
Taos, NM 87571
John E. Wilson
Kaaren Hardenbrook, Director
(505) 758-8093

Handcrafters Gallery
227 Galisteo Street
Santa Fe, NM 87501
Eden Spencer
(505) 982-4880

Katie Gingrass Gallery
225 Canyon Road
Santa Fe, NM 87501
Patricia Smith
Pat Brophy
(505) 982-5501

Mariposa Gallery
113 Romero Northwest
Albuquerque, NM 87104
Fay Abrams
(505) 842-9097

Running Ridge Gallery
640 Canyon Road
Santa Fe, NM 87501
Patt Abbott
(505) 988-2515

Weaving Southwest
216 B Paseo Del Pueblo Norte
Taos, NM 87571
Rachel Brown
(505) 758-0433

**NEW YORK**

A Show of Hands
531 Amsterdam Avenue
New York, NY 10024
Christine H. MacKellar
(212) 787-0924

Aaron Faber Gallery
666 Fifth Avenue
New York, NY 10019
Patricia Kiley Faber
(212) 586-8411

Accents and Images
1020 2nd Avenue
New York, NY 10022
Christopher McCall
(212) 838-3431

Alexander F. Milliken, Inc.
98 Prince Street
New York, NY 10012
Carol Craven, Manager
(212) 966-7800

ARC International
91 Fifth Avenue
New York, NY 10003
Carole Lavin
(212) 727-3340

**Art Dynamics (ADI)**
**440 Park Avenue South, 16th Floor**
**New York, NY 10016**
**Harriet Jaffie, MFA ASID**
**(212) 679-1000**

Art et Industrie
106 Spring Street
New York, NY 10012
Rick Kaufmann
Kim Kuzmenko
(212) 431-1661

**Art Options Inc.**
**3 East 76th Street**
**New York, NY 10021**
**Sarina Tang**
**Suzanne Gaba**
**(212) 517-7401**

Austin Harvard Gallery
50 State Street
Pittsford, NY 14534
Adele Elmer, Director
(716) 383-1472

Authentique
1499 Old Northern Boulevard
Roslyn, NY 11576
Neshe Karakaplan
(516) 484-7238

**Bellwido Ltd.**
**100 Christopher Street**
**New York, NY 10014**
**Paul Bellwido**
**(212) 675-2668**

Contemporary Porcelain
105 Sullivan Street
New York, NY 10012
Lanie Cecula
(212) 219-2172

Corporate Art Associates, Ltd.
270 Lafayette Street, Suite 402
New York, NY 10012
Charles Rosoff
James Cavello
(212) 941-9685

Craft Company No. 6.
785 University Avenue
Rochester, NY 14607
Susan O'Toole, Manager
(716) 473-3413

Cross Harris Fine Crafts
979 Third Avenue, 3rd Floor
New York, NY 10022
Fredda Harris
Rise Cross
(212) 888-7878

Dawson Gallery
349 East Avenue
Rochester, NY 14604
Beverly McInerny
Shirley Dawson
(716) 454-6966

**Dexterity Limited**
**26 Chruch Street**
**Montclair, NY 07042**
**Shirley Zafirair**
**(201) 746-5370**

Eddy/Beasley Associates
P.O. Box 6674
New York, NY 10150
Kay Eddy
Betsy Beasley
(212) 688-5037

Gallery 10
7 Greenwich Avenue
New York, NY 10014
Marcia Lee Smith
(212) 206-1058

Garth Clark Gallery
24 West 57th Street
New York, NY 10019
Mark Del Vecchio
(212) 246-2205

Gayle Willson Gallery
16 Jobs Lane
Southampton, NY 11968
Gayle Willson
(516) 283-7430

Helen Drutt Gallery
724 Fith Avenue, 9th Floor
New York, NY 10019
(212) 974-7700

Heller Gallery
71 Greene Street
New York, NY 10012
Douglas Heller
(212) 966-5948

**HoltHaus Fiber Art Gallery**
**7 Irma Avenue**
**Port Washington, NY 11050**
**Mary Ann Holthaus**
**(516) 883-8620**

**Hudson River Gallery**
**217 Main Street**
**Ossining, NY 10562**
**Pat Lawrence, Director**
**(914) 762-5300**

Hummingbird Designs
29 Third Street
Troy, NY 12180
Kathy & John Bloom
(518) 272-1807

Incorporated Gallery
1200 Madison Avenue
New York, NY 10128
Riis Layman
(212) 831-4466

Joel Schwalb Gallery
12 South Broadway
Nyack, NY 10960
(914) 358-1701

John Christopher Gallery
131 Main Street
Stony Brook, NY 11790
Christopher DeVeau
(516) 689-1601

John Christopher Gallery
43 Main Street
Cold Spring Harbor, NY 11724
John Chandler
(516) 367-3978

Landing Gallery
7956 Jericho Turnpike
Woodbury, NY 11797
Bruce Busko
(516) 364-2787

Leo Kaplan Ltd.
967 Madison Avenue
New York, NY 10021
Scott Jacobson
(212) 249-6766

Mari Galleries Of Westchester, Ltd.
133 East Prospect Avenue
Mamaroneck, NY 10543
Carla Reuben
(914) 698-0008

Michael Ingbar Gallery
578 Broadway
New York, NY 10012
M. Ingbar
(212) 334-1100

One Of A Kind Ltd.
978 Broadway
Thornwood, NY 10594
Andrea Kleuman
Elyse Garis
(914) 769-5777

**Opus II**
**979 Third Avenue**
**New York, NY 10022**
**Irv Frank**
**(212) 980-1990**

P. Pullman
310 East 65th Street
New York, NY 10021
(212) 517-7657

Pritam & Eames
29 Race Lane
East Hampton, NY 11937
Bebe Johnson
Warren Johnson
(516) 324-7111

Rosanne Raab Associates
167 East 61st Street
New York, NY 10021
(212) 371-6644

**Showcase Gallery**
**169 Main Street**
**Cold Spring Harbor, NY 11724**
**Cornelia P. Reina**
**(516) 367-3037**

Studio Connection
65 Main Street
Southampton, NY 11968
Kerry Sharkey-Miller
(516) 283-9649

Sweet Nellie
1262 Madison Avenue
New York, NY 10128
Pat Ross
(212) 876-5775

**The Artisans Gallery Ltd.**
**6 Bond Street**
**Great Neck, NY 11021**
**Selma Phillips**
**Judi Marcus**
**(516) 829-6747**

The Artists' Rep
P.O. Box 81
North Creek, NY 12853
Sally K. Heidrich
(518) 251-2733

The Center For Tapestry Arts
167 Spring Street, 2nd Floor
New York, NY 10012
Jean West, Director
(212) 431-7500

The Clay Pot
162 Seventh Avenue
Brooklyn, NY 11215
Robert Silberberg
Celia Ihne
(718) 788-6564

The Craftsman's Gallery, Ltd.
16 Chase Road
Scarsdale, NY 10583
Sybil Robins, Director
(914) 725-4644

The Gallery at 15 Steps
Clinton Hall, 112 N. Cayuga Street
Ithaca, NY 14850
Ken Jupiter
Bettsie Park
(607) 272-4902

The Grateful Gift
42 West Park Avenue
Long Beach, NY 11561
Nancy & Don Terry
(516) 431-9159

Treadles, N.Y.
351 Bleecker Street
New York, NY 10014
Lisa Wagner
(212) 633-0072

Winston & Company
97-A Seventh Avenue
Brooklyn, NY 11215
Ann Winston
(718) 638-7942


**NORTH CAROLINA**

Continuity, Inc.
P.O. Box 999, U.S. Hwy. 19
Maggie Valley, NC 28751
Elizabeth Lurie
(704) 926-0333

Hodges Taylor Gallery
227 North Tryon Street
Charlotte, NC 28202
Christie Taylor
(704) 334-3799

Horizon Gallery
905 West Main Street
Durham, NC 27701
Sandi Norton
(919) 688-0313

Laurance Triplette, Inc.
P.O. Box 60
Winston-Salem, NC 27102
(919) 721-0799

Morning Star Gallery
Rt. One, P.O. Box 454
Banner Elk, NC 28604
Maggie Wilson
(704) 963-6902

New Elements Gallery
216 North Front Street
Wilmington, NC 28401
Merrimon Long
(919) 343-8997

Skillbeck Grosse Gallery
119 East 7th Street
Charlotte, NC 28202
Cher Skillbeck
Susan Grosse
(704) 332-6767

Tar Heel Trading Co.
P.O. Box 1036, Sea Holly Square
Kill Devil Hills, NC 27948
Mary Ames
(919) 441-6235

The Mountain Pottery
Church Street
Dillsboro, NC 28725
Rick Urban
(704) 293-9406

Urban Artifacts
Forum IV, 3200 Northline Avenue
Greensboro, NC 27408
Jan Detter
JoAnne Vernon
(919) 855-0557

**OHIO**

American Crafts Gallery
13010 Larchmere
Cleveland, OH 44120
Sylvia Ullmann
Marilyn Bialosky
(216) 231-2008

Brenda Kroos Gallery
63 Parsons Avenue
Columbus, OH 43215
Kate Garvin
(614) 221-3636

Don Drumm Studios & Gallery
437 Crouse Street
Akron, OH 44311
Lisa & Don Drumm
(216) 253-6268

Gallery '400'
4659 Dressler Road N.W.
Canton, OH 44718
Jimmie Ivan
Barbara Levy
(216) 492-2600

Kaufman Gallery
P.O. Box 185
Berlin, OH 44610
Stanley A. Kaufman
(216) 893-2842

L'Idee Corporate Art Concepts
945 Hatch Street
Cincinnati, OH 45202
B. Alden Olson
MaryLee Olson
(513) 241-3769

**ODC**
**2164 Riverside Drive**
**Columbus, OH 43221**
**Harold Steven**
**(614) 486-7119**

Omni Gallery
46 The Arcade, 401 Euclid Avenue
Cleveland, OH 44114
Stuart & Patricia Zolten
(216) 781-3444

Riley Hawk Glass Gallery
2026 Murray Hill Road, Room 103
Cleveland, OH 44106
Tom Riley
(216) 421-1445

Riley Hawk Glass Gallery
642 North High Street
Columbus, OH 43215
Sherrie Hawk
(614) 228-6554

The Murray Hill Market
2181 Murray Hill Road
Cleveland, OH 44106
Thomas Houser
(216) 791-9679

The Private Collection
21 East 5th Street
Cincinnati, OH 45202
Jennifer Beedon
(513) 381-1667

**OKLAHOMA**

Crain/Wolov Gallery
8146-D South Lewis
Tulsa, OK 74137
Nancy Wolov
(918) 299-2299

**OREGON**

American Tapestry Alliance
HC 63, Box 570D
Chiloquin, OR 97624
Jim Brown
(503) 783-2507

Contemporary Crafts Gallery
3934 S.W. Corbett Avenue
Portland, OR 97201
Marlene Gabel
(503) 223-2659

Maveety Gallery
842 S.W. First Avenue
Portland, OR 97204
Billye Turner, Selby Key
(503) 224-9442

The Real Mother Goose Gallery
901 S.W. Yamhill
Portland, OR 97205
Stan F. Gillis
(503) 223-9510

## PENNSYLVANIA

**Art Dynamics (ADI)**
**P.O. Box 1624**
**Allentown, PA 18105**
**Harriet Jaffie, MFA ASID**
**(215) 434-3841**

**Art South, Inc.**
**4401 Cresson Street**
**Philadelphia, PA 19127**
**Sue Wiggins Strite**
**(215) 482-4500**

Artisans Three
The Village Center
Spring House, PA 19477
Helen Highley
(215) 643-4504

Corporate Interiors
100 North 20th Street
Philadelphia, PA 19103
Clara Hollander
(215) 972-8090

Craftsmen's Gallery
Star Route 2, Box 16E
Hawley, PA 18428
Rose-Marie Chapman, Partner
(717) 226-4111

Dina Porter Gallery
3900 Hamilton Boulevard
Allentown, PA 18103
Susan H. Coker
(215) 434-7363

**Gallery 500**
**Church & Old York Roads**
**Elkins Park, PA 19117**
**Rita Greenfield**
**Harriet Friedberg**
**(215) 572-1203**

Gallery Riggione
Mallard Cr. Vil./130 Almshouse Road
Richboro, PA 18954
Joseph Riggione
Adelina Riggione
(215) 322-5035

Glass Growers Gallery
701 Holland Street
Erie, PA 16501
Deborah G. Vahanian
(814) 453-3758

Image Gallery & Gifts
3330 West 26 Street/Village West #1
Erie, PA 16506
Gene & Nancy Ware
(814) 838-8077

Latitudes Gallery
4325 Main Street
Philadelphia, PA 19127
Joan Castronuovo
(215) 482-0417

Snyderman Gallery
317 South Street
Philadelphia, PA 19147
Kristin Peterson
Richard Snyderman
(215) 238-9576

Strawberry & Co.
7-9 West King Street
Lancaster, PA 17603
Wayne Lucas
(717) 392-5345

The Blue Sky Gallery Inc.
6022 Penn Circle South
Pittsburgh, PA 15206
Mimsie Stuhldreher
(412) 661-3600

The Clay Place
5416 Walnut Street
Pittsburgh, PA 15232
Elvira Peake
(412) 682-3737

The Country Studio
Rd #1, Box 1124
Hadley, PA 16130
Lynn Linton
(412) 253-2493

The Otter Creek Store
106 South Diamond Street
Mercer, PA 16137
Nancy Myal Griffin
(412) 662-2830

The Studio In Swarthmore
14 Park Avenue
Swarthmore, PA 19081
Lee Gilbert
(215) 543-5779

The Works Gallery
319 South Street
Philadelphia, PA 19147
Bruce Hoffman
(215) 922-7775

Views
4404 Main Street
Philadelphia, PA 19127
Diana Hollander
(215) 487-1377


## SOUTH CAROLINA

Bohemian
2736 Devine Street
Columbia, SC 29205
Bruce Schultze
(803) 256-0629

Carol Saunders Gallery
927 Gervais Street
Columbia, SC 29201
(803) 256-3046

Nina Liu & Friends
24 State Street
Charleston, SC 29401
(803) 722-2724

Southern Galleries
402 S.E. Main Street
Simpsonville, SC 29681
Ben Holder
(803) 963-4893

The Craftseller
216 West Street
Beaufort, SC 29902
Sandra Williams
(803) 525-6104

The Duke Street Gallery
109 Duke Street
Pendleton, SC 29670
Peggy D. Acorn
(803) 646-3469

## TENNESSEE

Boones Creek Pottery
Route 13, Box 9
Johnson City, TN 37615
Betty Muse
(615) 282-2801

Metalwerks Gallery
97 South Second Street
Memphis, TN 38103
Pamela Petterson
(901) 521-9440

Norman Worrell Associates, Inc.
315 Tenth Avenue, Suite 102
Nashville, TN 37215
(615) 255-8844

The Browsery
2794 Wilma Rudolph Boulevard
Clarksville, TN 37040
Lou Ann Brown
(615) 552-2733

## TEXAS

Artscape
6360 LBJ Freeway, Suite #100
Dallas, TX 75240
Laura Schneider
(214) 960-8672

Carey Ellis Company
1414 Sul Ross
Houston, TX 77006
Laura Ellis, President
(713) 523-8753

Creative Arts Gallery
836 North Star Mall
San Antonio, TX 78216
Luann Cohen
(512) 342-8659

Culler Concepts Inc.
109 Mandalay Canal
Irving, TX 75039
Donna Hurd
(214) 869-1937

E.M. Amend and Associates
13616 Gamma, #101
Dallas, TX 75244
Nancy Bohlander
(214) 458-7785

Eclections
3408-B Camp Bowie Boulevard
Fort Worth, TX 76107
Barbara Mabli
(817) 332-4407

Fossil Rim Wildlife Center Gallery
Route 1, P.O. Box 210
Glen Rose, TX 76043
Judy Shelton
(817) 897-2960

Heartland Gallery
4006 South Lamar, Suite #950
Austin, TX 78704
Holly Plotner
(512) 447-1171

**Judy Youens Gallery**
**2631 Colquitt Street**
**Houston, TX 77098**
**(713) 527-0303**

Michael Atkinson Fine Art Prints
102-Concho-Market Square
San Antonio, TX 78207
Jeanne Smith
(800) 433-0187

Omni Art, Inc.
13616 Gamma, #101
Dallas, TX 75244
Nancy Bohlander
(214) 458-9591

R.S. Levy Gallery
3 Republic Plaza, 333 Guadalupe
Austin, TX 78701
Rebecca Levy
Alise Mullins
(512) 473-8926

Richard Wierzbowski, Art Advisor
1114 Barkdull
Houston, TX 77006
(713) 523-1714

Rock House Gallery
1311 West Abram
Arlington, TX 76013
Jo Ann Bushart
(817) 265-5874

Spicewood Gallery
1206 West 38th Street
Austin, TX 78705
Jackie Depew
(512) 458-6575

Ursuline Gallery
300 Augusta Avenue
San Antonio, TX 78205
Nancy Billups
(512) 224-1848

William Campbell Contemporary Art
4935 Byers Avenue
Ft. Worth, TX 76107
Pam Campbell
Bill Campbell
(817) 737-9566

## VIRGINIA

Cave House Craft Shop
279 East Main Street
Abingdon, VA 24210
William Gable, Director
(703) 628-7721

Country Heritage
Main Street, P.O. Box 148
Washington, VA 22747
Nancy Thomasson
(703) 675-3738

Cudahy's Gallery
1314 East Cary Street
Richmond, VA 23219
Helen Levinson, Director
(804) 782-1776

Electric Glass Gallery
823 West Pembroke Avenue
Hampton, VA 23669
Bobo Vines
(804) 722-6300

Elizabeth Michaels Associates
6414 Lakeview Drive
Falls Church, VA 22041
(703) 256-6395

**Fiber Designs**
**823 King Street**
**Alexandria, VA 22314**
**Rebecca Smith**
**(703) 548-1461**

**Gallery 3**
**213 Market Street**
**Roanoke, VA 24011**
**Andy Williams**
**(703) 343-9698**

On The Hill Creative Arts Center
121 Alexander Hamilton, P.O.Box 222
Yorktown, VA 23690
Carol Conway, Manager
(804) 898-3076

Paula Lewis - Court Square
216 4th Street N.E.
Charlottesville, VA 22901
(804) 295-6244

Signet Gallery
212 Fifth Street N.E.
Charlottesville, VA 22901
Priscilla F. Bosworth
(804) 296-6463

Susan E. Conway
813 Green Street
Alexandria, VA 22314
(703) 739-0293

Tactile
105 North Union Street
Alexandria, VA 22314
Jean Thompson
(703) 549-8490

The Shop In The Cultural Center
Capitol Complex
Charleston, VA 25305
Rebecca E. Stelling
(304) 348-0240

Vista Fine Crafts
8 North Madison Street/P.O.Box 2034
Middleburg, VA 22117
Sherrie Posternak
(703) 687-3317

Whistle Walk Crafts Gallery
7 South King Street
Leesburg, VA 22075
Velda A. Warner
(703) 777-4017

## VERMONT

Designer's Circle
21 Church Street
Burlington, VT 05401
Dennis Bosch
(802) 864-4238

Handworks On The Green
P.O. Box 1867, On The Green
Manchester Center, VT 05255
Barbara Nashner
(802) 362-5033

Stowe Pottery & Craft Gallery
P.O. Box 262
Stowe, VT 05672
Mr. Patnode
(802) 253-4693

The Vermont State Craft Center
Frog Hollow
Middlebury, VT 05753
Pamela Siers, Executive Director
(802) 388-3177

Woodstock Gallery Of Art
Gallery Place, Route 4 East
Woodstock, VT 05091
Lisa Wharton
(802) 457-1900

## WASHINGTON

Art Link
7025 North Mercer Way
Mercer Island, WA 98040
Susan Nixon
(206) 236-2713

Bela Bellena Ltd.
8825 North Harborview Drive
Gig Harbor, WA 98335
Pat Semon
(206) 858-7434

Carnegie Center, Inc.
109 South Palouse
Walla Walla, WA 99362
Christine Bishop, Director
(509) 525-4270

Corporate Art West, Inc.
1600 124th Avenue N.E.
Bellevue, WA 98005
Carol A. Young
(206) 454-2595

Crackerjack Contemporary Crafts
1815 North 45th Street, #212
Seattle, WA 98133
Kathleen D. Koch
(206) 547-4983

Earthenworks
713 First Street, P.O. Box 702
La Conner, WA 98257
Cynthia Hoskins
(206) 466-4422

Earthenworks
1002 Water Street
Port Townsend, WA 98368
Donald Hoskins
(206) 385-0328

Elements Gallery
113 Seafirst Bldg./10500 NE 8th St.
Bellevue, WA 98004
Kelly Knapp
(206) 454-8242

Ellenburg Community Art Gallery
408 ½ North Pearl Street
Ellensburg, WA 98926
Eveleth Green, Director
(509) 925-2670

FireWorks Galleries
400 Pine Street
Seattle, WA 98101
Michele Manasse
(206) 682-8707

FireWorks Galleries
210 1st Avenue South
Seattle, WA 98104
Michele Manasse
(206) 682-8707

Flying Shuttle
607 First Avenue
Seattle, WA 98104
Vicki Leslie
(206) 343-9762

Foster/White Gallery
311 ½ Occidental Avenue South
Seattle, WA 98104
Donald Foster, Owner
(206) 622-2833

Foster/White Gallery
5th & Pine, Frederick & Nelson
Seattle, WA 98111
Cale Kinne
(206) 382-8538

Northwest Discovery
142 Bellevue Square
Bellevue, WA 98004
(206) 454-1676

Panaca Gallery
133 Bellevue Square
Bellevue, WA 98004
(206) 454-0234

**The Casey Collection**
**5701 6th Avenue South, Suite #222**
**Seattle, WA 98108**
**Deborah Briggs**
**(206) 762-4649**

William Traver Gallery
2219 Fourth Avenue
Seattle, WA 98121
William Traver
(206) 448-4234

Wood Merchant
707 South 1st Street
La Conner, WA 98257
Stuart & Laurie Hutt
(206) 466-4741

**WEST VIRGINIA**

Sanguine Gryphon
P.O. Box 3120
Shepherdstown, WV 25443
Richard C. Jentsch
(304) 876-6569

**WISCONSIN**

Bridge Road Gallery
N70 W6340 Bridge Road
Ceddarburg, WI 53012
Pat & David Eitel
(414) 375-1226

Caryl Robers & Associates, Inc.
P.O. Box 11755
Milwaukee, WI 53211
(414) 332-6622

D. Erlien Fine Art, Ltd.
306 North Milwaukee Street
Milwaukee, WI 53202
Gloria Dee Erlien
(414) 224-1773

Fanny Garver Gallery
230 State Street
Madison, WI 53703
Fanny Garver
Reena Tyler, Manager
(608) 256-6755

Katie Gingrass Gallery
714 North Milwaukee Street
Milwaukee, WI 53202
Pat Brophy
Patricia Smith
(414) 289-0855

Posner Gallery
207 North Milwaukee Street
Milwaukee, WI 53202
Judith Posner
(414) 273-3097

Tory Folliard Gallery
6862 North Santa Monica
Milwaukee, WI 53217
(414) 351-2405

**WYOMING**

Art West Gallery
P.O. Box 1248
Jackson, WY 83001
Susan Thulin
(307) 733-6379

# Craft Artists
# and Companies

# Craft Artists by State

# Photo Credits